# Dao and Rafter:

*The Chronicle of Those Who Fled to Hong Kong for Freedom*

Edited by Wong Zichang

Remembering Publishing. USA

Copyright © 2025 by Remembering Publishing, LLC. USA

Dao and Rafter:

*The Chronicle of Those Who Fled to Hong Kong for Freedom*

Edited by Wong Zichang

ISBN:   978-1-68560-176-8  (Print)
        978-1-68560-177-5  (eBook)
LCCN:   2025 910620

June 2025, First Edition, First Printing

Remembering Publishing, LLC
RememPub@gmail.com

---

All Rights Reserved.

No part of this book may be reproduced in any form or by any electronic or mechanical means including information storage and retrieval systems, without permission in writing from the publisher. The only exception is by a reviewer, who may quote short excerpts in review.

# PREFACE

# Seeking Refuge in an Angry Sea

*By Wong Zichang*

*Give me liberty or give me death!* — *Patrick Henry*

The famous historian Yu Yingshi said that we of this era (1949-1979) are those of the "Great Banishment" of the Intelligentsia, from the *laogai* labor camps to the *xiafang* demotions to the Back to the Countryside Movement.

Since the ancient times, China's intellectuals and bureaucrats have, by political disagreement or by words, been found guilty and exiled by the imperial court to the administration of border regions. However, in the social order of modern China, the extent of exile has been unprecedented. With regards to both population and scale, the era was record-breaking among all times and places. The most ordinary middle schoolers were implicated, yet the number of people involved is staggering (according to the statistics, between 1967 and 1977, it totaled 80 million people); practically every family in every city in China was ensnared. In terms of severity, ordinary junior and senior high school students were considered intellectuals; in the Cultural Revolution alone, these students' schooling was cut short, and they were drawn into political fights; ignorant students were made chess pieces, gunmen of the political debates with blind adoration of the party's leaders.

At the encouragement of the political party Leaders, the high school Red Guards wantonly destroyed outstanding cultural artifacts and valuable historical relics from China's thousands of years history, humiliated and persecuted, and slaughtered teachers, scholars .., and wrought an unprecedented level of catastrophic destruction on Chinese culture, tangible and intangible. When it was all over, the same students were exiled (to be precise, they were "driven out and sent to") by executive order to the countryside and the remote wilderness. This was a bitter style completely unlike the historical banishment of intellectuals. Its result was to bring about immeasurable societal conflict and human tragedy, to universally make the students of this era feel deeply cheated, manipulated: they were not only deprived of the right of continuing their education and the ability to freely choose their work, let alone where they could live, but they were, like slaves, compelled by overseers to participate in the harsh work of the countryside, confronted with high-level politics, and manipulated and left without prospects for the future. It was in this context that the current period of large scale of the "Zhi Qing (知青, student) fleeing from China's border regions was brought about.

Confucius says: "If the Way fails us, we will float out to sea on the rafters."

It was in these circumstances that these young students put into practice Confucius's prophecy. In the South of China, they braved the shark-infested violent surf of Daya and Shenzhen Bays swimming to Hong Kong; they hid from the ignorant and armed cruel border guards with their well-trained K-9s, and the wolves and wild dogs of Zhuhai and Zhongshan to sneak into Macau; they drove little wooden boats, dodging the hunt of soldiers and the para-militias, braving forests of guns and hail of bullets and terrifying waves down the Pearl River Delta to Hong Kong. In the hardships of the long and difficult and dangerous trek, unknown multitudes died of illness or starved, fell off cliffs to their deaths, were mercilessly ripped apart by sharks, were ruthlessly shot dead by soldiers and para-militias and policemen, drowned on a sinking boat, in a storm on the angry sea…

You could say that the border and coastal waters between Guangdong province and Hong Kong was the East's "Berlin Wall"; the exodus of China's youth would be comparable to the magnificent feats of freedom-seeking East Germans who risked death to cross the Wall into West Germany; in its extent, solemnity, and investment of human life, it's no less in magnitude.

Forty years later, the Berlin Wall has fallen, and the Iron Curtain that once cut off mainland China from the world no longer exists; the governing hierarchy that has now taken the stage has spurned the extreme ways of the old days and adopted a relatively relaxed policy and replaced the economy of the Great Leap Forward; these sudden reversals, alike that of the overnight collapse of the Eastern European socialist alliance, the causes to which had no doubt been played in part by the feats of these hot-blooded youth who risked their lives escaping to Hong Kong, fled to freedom.

China's history would not be long enough to let the events of these pages fall ignored.

In this book, the real-life stories were each written by authors who risked their lives fleeing to Hong Kong for freedom successfully during the sixties and seventies of the late twentieth century.

# Table of Contents

PREFACE  *Seeking Refuge in an Angry Sea*      I
  *By Wong Zichang*

Nine One Six      1
  *By Tu Bin*

Escape: The Cost of a Life      37
  *By Zhi You*

Life is Limited, and Freedom is Priceless      57
  *By Ocean*

I am Just a Little Bird      74
  *By Xi Man*

Indomitable, Swim to Freedom      89
  *By Old Guy, Pan*

The Braves Have No Fears      130
  *By Wong Zichang*

My Path is Not Walked Alone  Part I      145
  *By Wong Zichang*

My Path is Not Walked Alone  Part II      162
  *By Wong Zichang*

Old Soldiers Never Die                                168
   *By A Ho*

The Fiery Dragon on the Road to Freedom              193
   *A Qiang (narrator), Zhao Jineng*

POSTSCRIPT                                           234

# Nine One Six

*By Tu Bin*

From the time of Mao Zedong's "Supreme Directive" that "it is essential that the educated youths be sent to the countryside to accept the re-education of poor peasants," "delegated" us to the Aowei Production Team, Xiani Production Brigade in the Commune of Lingshan Township, Panyu County, Guangdong Province, to the beginning of 1971, three years had passed.

In those three years, we, the supposed intellectual youth with only middle- and high school-level history, were "driven out" to the countryside by the millions. We arrived in the countryside and worked as ordinary farmers, tilling the soil, raising animals, and fishing. Working at sunup, resting at sundown, we endured our hardships.

(I use the words "driven out," and some may disagree, but remember the scenes of parents of that year in train stations and on docks "seeing off their revolutionary children as they rushed to the countryside," every one of them crying his heart out, and not one was willing to let them go. Even if any individual student disobeyed and didn't sign up to participate in the ranks, their working parents could be "reasoned with," for if their children did not accept "the necessity of revolution," they could be implicated and expelled from their positions. In that era, everything was allocated by the government. If you lose your work, you lose your means of survival. The only option was to be well-behaved and submit. Of course, it was not the same for the children of party officials, for most of whom there existed a special pipeline into employment in the cities, even if they had joined the rush to the ranks of the countryside. Their parents could find methods to fabricate excuses in the short term, then they would manage to return to the cities. The children of those officials convicted during the Cultural Revolution of being gang members, even those who spent a long time in the villages, were nevertheless, at a time suiting their parents, politically rehabilitated and returned to political circles, the experience of the revolutionary era of this paragraph is thus considered "gilded," and almost all were able to return to school, continue their studies, and join officialdom.)

We saw first-hand the cruelty and brutality of class struggle in rural areas and the ignorance, backwardness, and poverty of rural China in the 1960s. The arduous physical labor of the countryside really wasn't the most painful thing for our young and vigorous generation; what was painful was that the future was vast, but it lacked a tomorrow. The question that floated around the mind was whether one really was willing, in these cottages and sugar cane fields and rice paddies, shackled by invisible chains, to end one's life?

Given that there were only two pieces of land of freedom remained in China, and one of these would be Hong Kong, which being so near was almost within reach, why not try to reach it? The idea of seeking our freedom slowly arose within us. After a failed first attempt to cross the border by land via Danshui Township, Huiyang County, my brother Zhiyou and I began to plan to drive manually a small wooden boat (Shan Ban, 舢舨) across the waterway to Hong Kong.

Although Lingshan Commune in Panyu County is not far from Hong Kong (by water, 200 kilometers), in those days under the iron fist of the government, the plan had to be watertight. Strict hukou housing registration and militarization (making men of the so-called good social class become a People's Militia) were their effective methods of the so-called "Proletariat Dictatorship," and the very lightest accusations these Escapees would face was of the "treasonous defectors;" if found and arrested, they would either be thrown in prison, or they'd be turned over to the production teams or work units, being looked upon as class enemies, and come under severe scrutiny. In that time in the regions around and near Hong Kong and Macau, the Frontier Defense Army and armed People's Militia guarded with extreme measures and that the escapees would be killed with impunity. So, if we wanted to escape, it would be no easy task. We'd have to advance with extreme secrecy.

After many months of planning, Zhiyou, working on the production team, had, by means of the help from Xiyou's father (a poor peasant and former team leader who fervently sympathized with us, and treated us as nephews), successfully fought to be sent to Wanqingsha for work in land reclamation project, establishing the foundation of our Hong Kong-bound operation. Since Wanqingsha was located at southernmost end of Panyu County, at the mouth of the Pearl River, it was the closest point to Hong Kong (with regards to Panyu County). At night in Wanqingsha, if there was no moon, you could already see a halo of light over the sea. According to experienced local farmers, that would be where Hong Kong was.

We students had a very limited understanding of Hong Kong, only a very rough profile. Government propaganda told us Hong Kong was a society of decadent and decaying capitalism. True information about Hong Kong said the exact opposite, which we obtained from secretly listening to the Voice of America broadcasts and Hong Kong's radio broadcasts. Moreover, because emigrants from Guangdong were so numerous, and word of mouth spread among them, there was one point that was determined true: that the freedom we thirsted for was there.

I quickly reconnected with the jointly ambitious Fan Kang and Du Cai, and the two classmates joined our plan, and consequently Zhiyou energetically participated in his work diking, to win trust from the localities in order to screen inquiries into the water route to Hong Kong, and to understand the topography and the laws of the rising and falling tides. On the other hand, as planed I received Fan Kang from Guangzhou, and teach him how so he could practice his rowing boat technique intensively under the sun & the starry night. Once again as planned, we attended the farmers' market at Shawan, sold our end-of-year allocations of some grains & peanut-oil for cash, together with our other savings we managed to purchase an aged small wooden boat of eighteen feet in length. A little later, we also successfully strived to involve a local peasant, a descendent of a 'landlord', Pei Wen into our operation, knowing that and according to his own telling, he had many times before followed the production team's fishing boats south to the vicinity of the Ling Ding Island (a standalone island bordering Hong Kong) to fish. We hoped to draw support from his experience. Besides, He had showed us again and again that he rather go somewhere else looking for a new way of life than staying in Aowei being bullied by the poor peasant cadres, living a miserable life was worse than death… this naturally made him one of us, and we could entrust him to help hid and maintain the aged wooden boat we just purchased since we simply could not dock it in Aowei.

Time flies by, in accordance with our meticulously researched plan, we opted to set out before the Mid-Autumn Festival, because the nighttime falling tide would be longer than that of summer (the longest falling tide period is in winter), and also because the water temperature would not yet be too cold, that would lower the risk of being frozen to death in case of any one of us accidentally fall in the water. From June until September, we knew that the three-month preparatory period was insufficient to produce the result we wanted, and yet the time was urgent, most of all for Fan Kang and Du Cai, the two who knew nothing about boats' maneuverings, to train them from the beginning and to master it in three short months was no easy task, it's good that Zhiyou and I had secretly drilled ourselves early on, rowing the government-owned boat daily in & out as we please, we could do so unconstrained, and we also purposely taking opportunities for longer- distance trips to Guangzhou and back, so as to exercise and tested our physical strength and our technique. Fortunately, Fan Kang was kind of talented at sporting, and two months were not insufficient for him to learn rowing at a high speed, and eventually his technique was not much worse than mine. Zhiyou and I were inwardly cheerful; with Du Cai's rowing skill still merely at elementary level after three months, we were forced to give up on him, reckoning that with four or five people rowing in turn, we should already have enough.

With everything in our ingeniously concealed plan underway, all affairs running smoothly, we unwittingly arrived at the end of August. In line with our initial plans that we were to leave at the beginning of August in the lunar calendar, with the map that Fankang had exhausted his ideas to retrieve along with some cash and grain from Guangzhou, with a few ball-bladders and a compass that we had prepared… every night in our cottage, we would discuss the details of our routings and monitored the weather-forecast in Hong Kong… the closer that we got to the departure time, the more nervous we were.

All of our plans were unexpectedly changed in a moment of showing the kindness of thought from Du Cai.

One day in July, while Zhiyou was traveling to Wanqingsha, I was weeding in the field, and Du Cai was resting in my cottage, when an uninvited guest—Hu Qi, our classmate—paid an unexpected visit. Du Cai, unable to stop glib-tongued Hu from exploring, suddenly entrusted him with all of our plans! Hu was prepared before he came and wanted to join us and furthermore wanted to bring along his girlfriend Lu Sui. We were all immediately stunned. How could we hold seven people on that little wooden boat?! Even if we could accommodate this, the danger would still be great, and with a larger group of people, the safety of the operation would also be greatly affected. With a traitor-like-goal of fleeing to Hong Kong being so big of an issue in that time in China, amid of the nerve-wracking, enemies-all-around-us environment, an "operation" with so many people was exceptionally unwise, and we repeatedly advised Hu Qi not to bring his girlfriend, but he remained resolute and firm. In the end, we were moved by his romance and decided to take the risks. We made an audacious change, and somehow our plans after this change were unexpectedly successful. All our experiences of the many near escapes, alternating between hope and despair throughout the dark night, it was as if we had divine help from above after an endless night that changed the six young lives on that small aged wooden boat.

Because of Hu Qi's participation, many of our original plans had to be modified, for example, our original plan had us all, on the day of our departure, pretended to be sent by the production team to Wanqingsha, ostensibly for land reclamation (we'd already made our counterfeit certificates to support that), then together take the boat straight to Shisanchong, estimating our arrival in the evening. By then, the land reclamation team would have just stopped work, and everyone would be eating dinner, bathing, or taking a walk. And in this relatively confusing environment, we wouldn't be that conspicuous; and then we'd wait until after nightfall, around eight or nine, and then from there weigh anchor.

Now we'd become a group of seven people, including a girl. Of course, not only we couldn't squeeze into the boat with some construction material in it already and go straight from Lingshan to Shisanchong; and that might also make it become too big of a target. After discussing it, we all came up and agreed with a new plan, and this plan of dividing it into two groups would be relatively safe but would require that both groups be matched exactly both in time and place; Even with this being a big challenge, we were later able to accomplish it.

The date and time of our departure we chose as well, the 13th. of September, the night before the Mid-Autumn Festival…a night with no moon.

With the date chosen, everyone was to do his/her own work to prepare, and because of the sudden change in plans, my frame of mind and nerves remained tense ever since: from the beginning of August, I had been counting down the time, until, in the end, the day finally arrived.

"Tubin! Tubin!" From outside of my fshabby thatched cottage window, Pei Wen's urgent, muffled cry woke me from my sleep, my weary body still wasn't hearing the call, but I suddenly realized that dawn was not far away, and immediately sprang into action in the pitch dark, quickly putting on my clothes and feeling my way outside, and picked up an already-prepared bundle of bamboo outside the door as I passed through the lane. I crossed Aowei Village's sole little bridge and arrived at the gate to Aowei's distribution center. Pei Wen shined a flashlight at me, indicating the boat had already docked on the riverbank outside the shop door. I was careful to place the bamboo in the vessel without letting out a sound and quietly told him I had to return to my cottage to bring a pair of oars.

I quickly disembarked, three steps combined into two as I retraced my path, but I hadn't even made it to the bridge when I turned my head and saw Pei Wen hurriedly pushing offshore. I hastily whispered to him: Pei Wen! Pei Wen…but, hearing no reply, I continued on with my original path. Just a few steps later, a light flashed from the cow shed of the production team on the opposite bank, and I hastily ducked behind the distribution warehouse, crouching. At that moment in the dark, a person confusedly shined his flashlight in all directions, then slowly approached the cow shed from the east, and not long after, crouched, took out a cigarette, and began to smoke it.

In the light of the flashlight, I saw that the silhouette was that of the deputy production team captain, nicknamed "Mao Guazhu," ordinarily an arrogant person, but especially bullying to people of bad backgrounds: the so-called landlords, rich peasants, and counterrevolutionaries. People who belong to the class of the Black Seven would avoid him as if he were a G h o s t - E m p e r o r (Yama).

No wonder Pei Wen became suspicious upon seeing him and ran away in a hurry. It'd only be abnormal should he didn't make a quick getaway.

I was crouching there for more than 10 minutes, until Mao Guazhu extinguished his cigarette butt, stood up, and left. Apparently, he hadn't discovered us. But 10 or 20 minutes later there was no trace of Pei Wen, and I grew agitated, like a cat on a hot tin roof. "Shoot!" I inwardly wondered, "What could Pei Wen be planning? Could it be that Zhou Zhu (Mao Guazhu) scared him and he's ignoring our arrangement? After half an hour, I decided I could wait no longer, and rapidly returned to my thatched cottage, combining the two packages of the prepared items into one, carried it on my back, frantically locked the door, and left Aowei Village.

Quickly I walked along the riverbank to the sluice gate, still saw no trace of Pei Wen, arrived at the highway ferry crossing close to daybreak, about 4am, in order to avert suspicion, I temporarily refrained from crossing the river and continued on going south, following the river, and estimated that I would reach Yansha Production Brigade around dawn, and then planned again to cross the river. To save time, I jogged my way through, with the dog barking on & off from both sides of the road, passing by several villages. By the time I got to the Yansha ferry, it was already daybreak with the sky turning marble white.

Once on the other side, I went straight to Jiangjiaokou. When I saw Zhiyou, I was already drenched from head to foe and out of breath.

Together with Du Cai and Fan Kang, I briefed them and explained about my being late. After examining the unexpected circumstances, Zhiyou and Fan Kang told me that Pei Wen had arrived before me and had just left, with his saying that, while I was returning to the thatched cottage for the oars, Pei Wen discovered Mao Guazhu, got nervus and impatient and left in a hurry and wouldn't dare turning back. Before he left, he told Zhiyou that he wanted to consider changing the plan, even backing out from our operation. We now had no one to lead the way, and missing a pair of oars, what should we do now?! We had a simple discussion among us, and to us, Pei Wen's backing-out was not entirely a bad thing. Fitting seven people into the boat would have been dangerous anyway, and Zhiyou did have a basic grasp of the directions. However, leaving today had other problems. Even without the problem of missing oars, the boat still had issues: that boat that we had originally entrusted to Pei Wen and his relative, because it had been poorly maintained (one could say that my dear friend simply hadn't taken care of it), left out in the sun for long periods, some parts of the cabin had become dried up, partly decayed and when the boat's load exceeded five or 600 ib., water could permeate from there, evading blockage. The bow was also insufficiently secured; we feared that it wouldn't be able to withstand somewhat heavy wind and rough waves. Because of the concerns, before I arrived, Hu Qi had already been sent to the marina by the Dagang Hospital to look for a suitable boat.

I left them and walked into town to see how Hu was doing, for a while I saw Hu Qi flying by in a small boat, at first sight, I was inwardly screaming "OH, no!" that boat was just too *small*. It was only about fifteen feet long or less, and the cabin was pathetically shallow… If we already concerned with the original 18 feet long boat being small, then this boat was absolutely inadequate. At that moment, I truly questioned Hu Qi's judgement, including his choice of girlfriend: that Miss Lu Sui with whom Hu Qi insisted on bringing on board at all costs (cost of bringing hardship on all of us). Soon as we first reached the other shore (Hong Kong), she started talking nonsense to Hu about parting, and Hu Qi was apparently so upset, subsequently hu was vomiting blood over it, that would be another story we'd discuss later.

Back with Zhiyou, Fan Kang, and everyone, we quickly exchanged ideas and decided that Hu Qi had to return the boat to its original spot, and if by any chance he ran into the boat's owner, he must apologize and hope to avoid creating more trouble.

What's to be done? This is not something we could stop halfway. If we cancelled our journey then, we'd have the issue of picking a new date… two or three days later, the tides could become unfavorable, and the days' preparation would be wasted, we also feared not having a specified date would become a long delay… We discussed it for a long time without resolution. The minutes quickly ticked by, and soon it approached nine o'clock.

In an instant, clouds had rushed forth from the eastern sky to cover vast stretches, slowly blocking the morning light, and the breeze began to blow over the surface of the river. As the wind grew stronger, the churning waves lapped up three feet high onto the shore, and on top of that, it began to rain heavily. All of these left us escapees, still-indecisive party dumbstruck, only compounded our anxiety.

The strong wind together with the heavy rain, we were already soaked, if the rain continued unabated, even assuming all our preparations were adequate, setting out in the evening was not realistic. It seemed like the heavens had made the choice for us: After a quick exchange of ideas, we decided to postpone our departure by one day, and hoped to see if the weather would turn into our flavor; Since staying in Jiangjiaokou with no cover was simply ill-advised, Fan Kang and I took the boat into town and ensured it was safely moored, then we regrouped near the restaurant in Dagang Township, and, playing the role of diners, continued to study the postponement.

An hour later, everyone resolved as follows: in order to repair the boat, and yet not to delay our departure too much, we decided to set out tomorrow. Today we would take the boat to Hu Qi's dwelling in Dagang to repair it, which Hu Qi, Zhiyou, and Fan Kang would take charge of; furthermore, Hu Qi was to collect additional bamboo, Zhiyou and Fan Kang would row the boat with the bamboo to Wanqingsha, with land reclamation project workers as a cover. Du Cai would return to the production team and face his former teammates to retrieve a backup wristwatch (he wouldn't be able to get it), and I would return to Shangni Village to retrieve a pair of oars. The three troops immediately began their operations respectively and agreed that we'd all rendezvous under the Linggang Big Bridge the following day before dawn.

First, Zhiyou, Fan Kang, and Hu Qi bought some tung oil powder, bamboo silk, and so on for the boat repair work, then anchored the boat near Hu Qi's dwelling in Lingdong Production Team in Dagang Township. Pretending that the boat was accidentally damaged while carrying bamboo to a student/friend's housing project and require repairing, they turned the boat upside down in a secluded place, found a hammer and saw, iron nails and wooden boards, and started repairing the boat… Because of being exposed to the sun for a long time, the boat had a few spots, two fingers wide, where the wood was dried up/rotten; covering those spots with cloth and tung oil powder would leave them insufficiently firm, so the best solution was to sew out those pieces and then chock them with pieces of good wood. They used tung oil powder-paste to paste it up around, then nailed it on with galvanized-sheets, sealing them with additional tung oil powder/paste. Although these unsophisticated smiths had absolutely no ship-repair experience, the following evening would prove their methods were exceedingly well: a day and a night of maritime wind and waves, and the boat suffered not too much damage, with no leakages.

The heavens made it easy for us: after the afternoon rain, the sky cleared up, and by three o'clock the sun was shining again, allowing for the smooth advancement of boat repair, which was successfully accomplished before nightfall. Everyone let out a sigh of relief. With the bundled bamboo back in the boat and the boat anchored, they were well prepared for the pre-dawn shipment to Dagang Township; and it's all good for now.

As for me and Du Cai, at two in the afternoon, we took the bus back to our residences, parting at Jiubi Production Brigade. When I got back to Aowei, the first thing I did was to look for Pei Wen.

When I first saw Pei Wen, he was with his shameful face, while I was filled with rage and several times nearly broke out in anger, but I kept myself under control. What was the use of getting angry now? I did still speak to him in a belligerent tone to discuss the course of the day. Finally, I proposed that tomorrow before dawn, at three a.m., we would take the boat with the two oars to Jiangjiao. But he immediately had a distressed look on his face, hemmed and hawed without agreeing, then said that taking the little boat out would be difficult… and went on to say that he was afraid of an accident. Finally, he just told me that he'd decided to withdraw from our plan. At Pei Wen's admission I shrank back; I was caught entirely unprepared.

"Tubin, we'd been two good friends, so please forgive me. Staying here, my life would truly be difficult, and of course I'd thought about leaving, but I was never going to be able to leave behind my wife and children. If I leave with you today, you know what might happen; I'm worried that my wife wouldn't be able to take the pain if we fail. I would just add to the misery of the whole family. I've been considering this for three full days. Please forgive me for not going with you. I still envy all of you." Pei Wen hung his head after saying these words, not daring to look me in the eye, tears trickling out of his eyes.

"Don't worry! Our preparations are ample; I'd been convinced that we could make it. Thank you for your help and your guidance for all these times." I gave him a few sentences of light comfort, and promised that if we succeeded, we would connect again someday in the future. and I waited for him to return home. As soon as he stepped through the door, I immediately tried to clear up the cottage and tidied up my things. Not long after four o'clock., Pei Wen came back to me and said, "Tubin, tomorrow morning at three, I will take you across the river in a boat. You didn't need to swim, and that would be too dangerous! He seemed to feel regret for withdrawing from our operation, as I had originally planned to bring the oars and swim across the river before dawn, then walk to Dagang Township to meet up with Namping and the group.

"Thank you so much, I hoped I could someday repay you for doing that!" I said sincerely. "Nonsense, brother, it would be me that usually received your generosity often, and not a small amount of it. Now I'd exhausted my efforts doing the repaying…" After saying this, he took out a package of fried rice cakes and put them in my hand before he leaved, saying they were rations for in route usage at night time.

That night I tossed and turned, was unable to sleep.

Before dawn, at three o'clock precisely, Pei Wen and I put my things in the boat, then left my cottage and crossed to the other side of the river. The sky still pitch-black, you could just make out a hazy outline of the lone hut, the thatched cottage (Local peasants, in order to make room for us, the so-called intellectual youths, built huts a little way out of town. In fact, we slowly realized that offering shelter to educated youth was something peasant farmers were unwilling to do, on account of our taking up their resources and harvests. But in those days the government's command was not to be challenged, and not even with them being the country's master, and that they could only grumble in their own.)

As I got farther and farther away, I gradually became unconsciously disheartened. I'd been staying here for the past three years, and now that I was leaving, didn't know when I would have the chance to return. I didn't know if I would ever return. Even if I could someday return, I didn't think that a crude little hut/thatched cottage would still exist… not knowing that the boat had already docked as these thoughts streamed through my mind, Pei Wen and I shook hands and wished each other well: "Remember when you set out to bring enough fresh water, and when you reach Hong Kong, find some way to let me know that you arrived safely," Pei Wen said in a low voice.

"I won't forget, take care of yourself." I felt some ineffable sadness as I finished speaking and promptly took the paddles and jumped onto shore. I watched Pei Wen leave until his silhouette vanished into the center of the river.

I climbed onto the shore and groped my way through the plants/field, carefully keeping in the direction of Dagang. Fortunately, I didn't cross paths with anyone, and without stopping to rest, I reached Dagang right around five a.m.

Just before dawn, with the first sign of the morning sun, the boats, big and small, anchored by the river were all emitting wisps of smoke, the cool & gentle wind of early autumn left my sweaty, sticky body feeling comfortable, and with good spirits. I thought that this was probably the best weather of the year, just in time for us to leave.

A little while later, Zhiyou and Fan Kang arrived right on schedule in the bamboo-laden, just-fixed "new boat" at the meeting point. We carefully inspected the boat, and even though the weight capacity had exceeded 500 lb there was no sign of leakage; every part that had been mended was solid. We were quietly celebratory.

Before 5:30, Du Cai, Hu Qi, and Lu Sui each arrived in turn. Each person reviewed their events of the previous day in the same manner we'd already discussed, solicited with Zhiyou's opinion, and arrived at the conclusion that we'd split into two troops, strictly following the route map that he drew up: one by land and one by sea. Hu Qi, Lu Sui, Du Cai and I would form the land-route group; Du Cai and I would lead the way, posing as intellectual youth sent down by the Production team to Wanqingsha to work on the land reclamation project, and Hu Qi and Lu Sui, playing sweethearts (and they were, of course, really sweethearts) also as the same project workers, would follow us. Zhiyou and Fan Kang would take the water route; as if they were to deliver the bamboo for use as scaffolding in the land reclamation project, they'd follow the river going south and meet us at Shisanchong in Wanqingsha between eight o'clock and nine o'clock. At precisely six, as the fiery sun began its rise above the river, the two groups bid farewell and departed.

First, the four of us boarded the shabby ferry from Dagang to Wanqingsha. The early scheduled boat ride was packed with farmers, so we had no seats and stood shoulder-to-shoulder. To avoid exposing ourselves, we refrained from speaking, and pretended to enjoy the scenery of the river, but it was hard to hold on to the nervousness inside of each of us. We spent two oppressive hours of travel like this, until we arrived at Huangge station and a good portion of the passengers disembarked, giving just a little more room to move, but my legs were numb from standing. After leaving Huangge, the river opened up much wider, with the cows and horses on either bank becoming indistinguishable, and this would be the Pearl River Delta. To the northeast, it would be the Humen fort, a gaze to the south gave one the view of a vast expanse of water, with no land in sight. I couldn't help but feeling a little irresolute foreseeing about what it would be tonight when we'd be leaping out of the "tiger's den" … and what came next …

Around noon, the ferry finally arrived at Wanqingsha (Wuchong). Before the boat pulled up to the dock, we saw the dock packed with People's Militia inspectors, wielding rifles on the gangway, ready to inspect the disembarking passengers. They carefully inspected our identification, looking us "intellectual youth" up and down, their goal would be to uncover nonconforming outsiders from the inland. (Later, in Hong Kong, we would learn that on September 13 Lin Biao had died fleeing the country in what was known as the 913 Affair, and the Central Committee of the Communist Party of China had ordered all levels of frontier defense to ensure none of his allies escaped, and Guangdong was a lair of Lin Biao's accomplices. That day they'd lain an inescapable trap to arrest the remnants of Lin Biao's group, and we young folks had just happened to rush right into this sensitive moment.) Seeing the necessity of vigilance in the face of evil, our ingenious costumes and seemingly genuine identification, we concealed everything from their "sharp eyes," and they waved us onward.

It would certainly be worthwhile mentioning here that our suntanned skin and our vests with eye-grabbing big letters saying: "Panyu diking soldier", which we had as a legitimate cover that helped minimize much unwanted inspections throughout the route.

First the origin of our suntanned skin: in general, diking workers were much darker than farm workers, the reason being that in the diking zone, there are no trees or any places that offer shade as far as the eye can see. Being scorched by the sun day in and day out made them much darker all over. Because of this characteristic, Fan Kang, Du Cai, and I had intentionally tanned as much as possible in the months prior, so that now we were all very dark like the locals, Even Fan Kang, who had the lightest skin of all of us, was by then sufficiently dark.

As for the vests with "Panyu diking" printed on them, that was a random discovery that inspired us. Once when Fan Kang and I were returning our classmate Chen Tian to Nansha Township, as we were talking on the pier, I saw a young migrant worker wearing a vest with the characters "Panyu diking" printed on it, and a bright idea suddenly came to me: if we wore vests like this on our trip, how could they not be a good-luck charms? I told Fan Kang and Chen Tian my idea, and they both thought it was an extremely clever idea. We later used our crude means of production to make each person a vest, and the result was as clever as expected. We all felt like the vests were like our own protective charms, thinking there would be no need to feel anxious about being questioned when we met the people's militia or local farmers. We showed relatively little fluster, instead showing self-confidence, and we saved ourselves considerable trouble along the road.

We ate lunch in a public dining hall in Wanqingsha at around 1:30 in the afternoon. By then Zhiyou and Fan Kang had driven the boat to Wanqingsha and we met as planned in the same dining hall, but to avoid suspicion, we pretended they were strangers and didn't speak to them.

We stayed in the town until three p.m., then, seeing the sun begin to incline in the west, we continued our journey. We prepared to complete the most crucial part of the route—from Wuchong to Shisanchong. Hu and Lu went first, looking like lovers. Du Cai and I followed, maintaining a distance of 300 meters apart. If we came across anyone, we'd begin talking cheerfully between ourselves, and when we were in a secluded place, we'd stop and discuss the next step. We were concerned we'd underestimated our normal walking speed, and we'd arrive at Shisanchong suspiciously early, so we deliberately walked especially slowly, to stall for time.

The scorching sun was still high in the sky, on this side of the river, nothing but farmland in all directions, only a few shabby thatched cottages along the riverbank, if it wasn't the rice in those fields about to mature soon that showed a breath of life, everywhere you looked was just like desolate land. With the farmers, like the hard working ants, working laboriously in the field, and as far as one could see, the raised paths in the fields, shabby thatched cottages dotted the rough muddy road along the shore, everything seemed like something out of the Middle Ages, nothing letting on to the fact that it was now the 1970s. Between these working-ant-like people and the aloof central rulers, it's not unlike the slaves and slave-owners of the Middle Ages, where we'd been banished by the slave-owners to haplessly give up our lives at the farms to which we'd been sent, and now we were attempting to escape from behind this Medieval Iron Curtain to the paradise we'd desired for some time: the "heavenly Hong Kong."

With the seemingly protection of our heavily tanned skin and the eye-grabbing red letters of Pan Ken (番墾) inked on our vests, we passed through several villages without being questioned, with no obstruction along the way.

The sun set just as we were approaching Shisanchong as planned, and I couldn't help but get a little nervous. Awaiting ourselves for a quiet moment with no one around, we parted with our jackets and trousers and discarded the superfluous objects we'd been carrying, ready to go into battle with light attire. Du Cai and I wore only the vests and sport shorts with a towel hanging on our shoulders, looking like we were taking a walk after an end-of-the-work-day meal, trying our utmost to look leisurely and unrestrained, to hide our inner nerves, still following Hu and Lu from a distance.

By then, the sun had already hidden itself below the horizon, the curtain of night would pull itself on the backs of the clouds rushing past, and it became hard to recognize people from more than 20 or 30 steps away.

Seeing our opportunity, we hastened ahead to tell Hu and Lu to hurry to the meeting place (designated meeting location indicated on the road map drawn up by Zhiyou and to be memorized by everyone). At first Hu replied that it was too early, but after my urging over and over, they finally started to speed up, now maybe walking a little too fast... by then we could hardly recognize Hu and Lu from even ten steps away, out of the chaotic crowd of after-dinner- walking workers. Fortunately, our young eyesight was working well, nevertheless with the newly built dike base being bumpy and uneven, we had to closely watch for and follow the silhouettes of Hu and Lu in the crowd around them, and also to pay attention to the bumpy ground, as we sped up into jogging forward, our footsteps staggering along. After a while, we again ran into several People's Militia patrolmen carrying rifles, and slow down immediately and began thinking of replies to their questions, but thankfully, they didn't mean to come "visit" the four of us.

We speedily passed the land reclamation command section store and passed through Dongchong Commune's migrant worker sheds. From afar, these looked like backward, uncivilized, barbarous thatched cottages, utterly worn-out, many collapsed.... Just like any other devastation site of the hurricane, everywhere was in chaos.

With great difficulty we approached Hualong Commune's land reclamation migrant worker sheds, which should be the outermost worker-sheds in the newly reclaimed land base, passing by the workers sheds again, out there they were, in fact, the newly built foundation of a dike, which stretched out forward under our feet, along with the river water running toward the Southern Sea. Ahead of us amid of the pitch-darkness, the dike foundation looked like it was the road leading deep-down to hell…to the unknown?

Taking advantage of the situation with the scattered pedestrians around us, quickly we four had a simple and precise conversation… here we were, the meeting spot, DùCai and I promptly crawled along the dam to hide in a cluster of water plants on the muddy beach alongside the dike. Lying ourselves on the riverbed, the water now covering half of our bodies, we remained still in order not to make a sound, so passersby would not see us. Hu and Lu nestled up together on top of the dike, passionately whispering their love to each other, and again no one bothered.

30(thirty) minutes passed us by just like that, and with eight o'clock fast approaching, I saw there were no passersby, and wanted to move closer to tell Hu and Lu that it's time to start moving down, suddenly I heard a loud shouting from outside the dike. In a flurry, I leaned forward, carefully trying to determine where the sound's origin and content was, which turned out to be some migrant workers fishing off the dike. Du Cai and I had no choice but to remain silent still for the time being.

10(ten) more minutes passed by, with yet another voice which led us to determine that the workers were still there. Lying there in the darkness, we were extremely nervous and anxious, because by then there was only a short time remaining until our pre-set nine o'clock meeting & departure time (time to meet up with Zhiyou and set off altogether in his boat onto the open water, venturing for the last portion of our escaping journey). If by nine o'clock we had still not reached the meeting place, would Zhiyou and Fan Kang wonder about the condition of our group? besides, they couldn't stay at the meeting place for long, If they were forced to wait there for us, they would risked being discovered by the people's militia and or by the migrant worker walking by , and or compelled to depart… then the whole plan would no doubt have to be discarded.

With that playing out, even if we can retreat ourselves from the spot, more trouble would be waiting for us after daybreak… thinking this, I started to panic.

Time passed by second after second, my mind fixed on the excessively fast ticking of the alarm clock on top of me, I made a supreme effort to inhibit my nervous mind, looking to Du Cai, I saw he was just as anxious, and I moved my body toward him, and Du Cai in a low voice said to Hu and Lu that it would be too late to leave the canal from the top of the dike, that they should come and crawl down toward us immediately and together we'd crawl out through the grass plant, taking advantage of the now-rising tides to slide along. Hu Qi replied that it was still early, and that we should wait a little longer before doing so as we urged. Somehow with our repeat reminder, they just went silent with no response, soon, we knew that we could wait no more, and Du Cai and I exchanged glances: the situation demanded immediate action. After informing Hu and Lu the last time, we began to slide, with the tide just starting to rise, the muddy water was only one-half foot high, just enough for us to slide along, using both hands in the mud to pull the body forward like a mud fish. In a few minutes, we'd moved ourselves into two feet tall water plant bush and hadn't let out too loud of a sound.

Suddenly Hu & Lu trotted themselves down the dike, hand in hand, and still not lying on their stomachs, as if there were no one around, when they reached the mud beach, trying desperately to catch up with us, thus letting out a series of very loud splash, leaving the two of us at our wit's end by such foolish and deadly action.

I got up in a hurry and rushed back towards them to put a stop to their dangerous 'act', made them lie down on their stomachs, and quickly crawl deep into the water-plant bush, in which we temporarily cover ourselves, waiting for the right chance to move out further to meet up with Zhiyou's boat.

Just as we settled down, a bundle of powerful flashlight beams then came down from the top of the dike, and a voice shouted: "Who is that? Stand up…!" Fortunately, we were already hidden well in the water plant bush some 200 meters from the dike. After a confused flash of light, the voice went silent… we tried to feel each other through the darkness and was able to care for each other a little, then decided to crawl on toward the canal opening as fast as we could., By now the water level had risen to over one foot high, we were then half-swimming, half-pushing-through-silt to move ourselves along…

At this time our surroundings were completely dark and totally silent, with the only sound being the little splish splash of our swimming. Before too long we saw floating above the dike a navigation lantern, and we knew we'd almost reached the canal opening. Sure enough, we soon reached the end of the muddy beach, by now there's just one big, dark dam between us and our way out. We excitedly began climbing the dam, when suddenly a light flashed from outside the dam. We hastily lay on our stomachs, carefully watching and tracing the light, and saw two boats moored not far from us, on board with people whose voices we could hear…feeling tense immediately, with no other choice, we cautiously move to the other side of the canal, hid ourselves behind the little hill which was about 500 meters away from the two boats, and from there we examined our surroundings, waiting for Zhiyou and Fan Kang to arrive…still with those two boats mooring there, it did make us very apprehensive.

Still another ten minutes passing by, still with no trace of Zhiyou and Fan Kang, the four of us sat drenched in the water. It being early autumn, the evening air temperature was already pretty low, and, soaking wet with a sea breeze whistling around us, each of us couldn't help but shiver.

"Hey, Tubin, look!" Hu Qi suddenly cried out, "there's two silhouettes over there, it's Fan Kang!"

We all looked in the direction Hu Qi had pointed at, and sure enough, there was a little bit of shadow floating toward us, bringing with it the quiet sound of paddling. We held our breath and watched anxiously as the shadow floated closer and closer, already distinguishable as a small boat with two people on board, but we still couldn't be sure of it being our Zhiyou and Fan Kang. No one dared make a sound.

"Tubin, Tubin!" A soft cry came from the boat, which we instantly recognized as Fan Kang's. Each of us excitedly stood up. "Fan Kang, we're over here!" Hu Qi replied in a lowered tone. We all made fast for the boat.

"We've been waiting around here for quite a while, how could you all be this late?!" came a reproach from Zhiyou. Standing by the boat, we gave them a simple explanation of the cause and together we began immediately preparing to set off… First, we must dump the bamboo out of the boat into the water, and now with each of us being excessively stressed, end up dumping out the bamboo in too much of a hurry, making some excessive and loud sound/noise… Zhiyou and I tried hard to stop everyone… but it was already too late. A voice from the shore shouted out loud, "Who is that? What are you doing?" Along with the voice came the shining flashlight… As it turned out, like that in every established canal, even this newly built and half-completed canal already had a sentry mounded and concealed shortly after Zhiyou's last check-around,(the sentry was specialized in monitoring the would-be illegal escapees, Every sentry mounded was also allocated with automatic weapons to be used indiscriminately on rebels and those who didn't comply with orders.), and the light was already shining on us, the two boats not far from us had apparently had similar responses, and suddenly there was shouting coming at us from all sides. "People trying to cross the border! Capture them!" As soon as we heard these voices, everyone lost control and got up in a frenzy; Zhiyou and I tried to maintain order, but to no avail: the bamboo had not been dumped out entirely… Zhiyou, Fan Kang, and I had no choice but to let everyone on board the boat, continue finish dumping out the remaining bamboo, jumping back into the boat speedily and got into each one's positions accordingly and be ready to row(we'd planned beforehand that, once on board, Zhiyou would be the captain in charge, Fan Kang and I would take turns with the front pair of oars, and Zhiyou and Hu Qi would use the back pair of oars to row and steer). From there onward, the four oars all began rowing at once, plus the two additional single oars were helping push out from the mid-boat position…the small boat literally flew out of the Shisanchong canal, steering southward, dashing through the darkness on to the open water

At this point, the sentry mound militiamen, seeing their shouts went unanswered, raked their searchlights and machine-gun firing down on us, and the two boats moored some 500 meters away also turns out, were People's Militia motorboats waiting for orders... had now started their motors and were rumbling toward us. In a split second, the searchlight and the powerful flashlights began dancing chaotically tearing through the sky like a wild snake, interweaving with the bullets flying by us...together with the loud gun shots, the circumstances suddenly became extremely dangerous, Zhiyou and I exerted all our strength, brandishing our two oars with all our might to paddle toward the middle of the river, desperately attempt to avoid being shot at in the encirclement. Zhiyou suggested that since they would most likely chasing us toward the south-east direction(being the normal direction to Hong Kong from Shisanchong), we should for the moment navigate out of their expectation and rowing due south, and I immediately seconded, with only seconds after, we saw less bullets and searchlights dancing around us...continuously we braved with our death paddling due south for about twenty minutes...till the gun shot noise became much quieter and with no more searching light flying around us, and we decided to correct the steering toward south-east direction; I wouldn't know if it was because of the explosive strength doubling in the anxious frenzy, but we were somehow moving faster away from their motorboat! Or could it be that those not-too-good people's militia had simply gone the wrong way chasing? Or it could be the lack of moonlight that night helped us get out of the effective range of the searching light sooner. (this was why, in our meticulous plans, we had chosen the night with no moonlight from the lunar calendar month as the night we set out). On a night so dark you couldn't see clearly of the fingers on your hand, once we were outside the shine of the flashlight, we'd be out of their sight. Even then, we were still with the scare-thrilling feeling like a startled bird, every oar in every hand still rowed like a machine; our boat shot forward like an arrow leaving a bow. The heavy breaths of each one of us told us that we had just left "the gates of hell."

An hour later, we confirmed that no one had followed us, then let out a sigh of relief and high-fived each other in celebration of having escaped the checkpoint all together. (Much later, we would learn that that day we set off was just after the 913 Affair, in which Mao Zedong's legal successor, Lin Biao had been killed while fleeing abroad, and the Party, in an effort to prevent the lair of Lin Biao's accomplices—in particular Guangdong Military District commander Huang Yongsheng—from fleeing, had especially strengthened its defenses and patrols. We "attendees to this grand occasion" had nearly paid with our lives. Some would-be escapees on other boats that day were executed on the spot, and the great majority were arrested, repatriated, and sent to prison. We were in the fortunate crowd: with the blessing of heaven, we were able to escape!)

The boat was now far from shore, navigating the boundless, black expanse of the Pearl River Delta, the vast sea that could knock it over at any time; like a tiny leaf, wind and waves just a little stronger could flip the boat, the thought of which made each of us frightened. We fished out the compass we'd got ready and continued paddling south-eastward. Now the time approaching midnight, complete stillness on all sides, the river water was still at high tide but had begun to reced. The only sound was of the bow beating against the river water echoing out a *slap slap slap*, which pacified us somewhat. When we began taking out food and the fresh potable water, we discussed in whispers: "Would we arrive in Hong Kong by 5 o'clock as you had told me?" asked Fan Kang, to which Zhiyou replied: "Of course we would! At our motorboat speed, those idiots would chase and chase but could never catch up to us!" Everyone laughed at that, and the mood on the boat immediately became relaxed.

Suddenly, a few little fish leaped out of the sea as if they had wings into the silvery light, a few even jumped into the boat. We couldn't help but exclaim: "Wow, it's the sight of good luck! They all had the same fishy sound!" I don't know who suggested it, but we subsequently took all the little fish and put them back in the water, then took a little coin money and put that in the water also, so as to pray for a safe journey without incident.

On that night, the wind was mild, and after midnight the tide began to ebb. The four of us took turns with the four oars, plus Du Cai with a single oar, and the small boat maintained its high speed toward the southeast for about two more hours, until Zhiyou suddenly called in a soft voice, "Hey, did everyone see that faint halo of light in the sky ahead of us? According to the experienced old fishermen, Hong Kong would be right under that halo."

Everyone looked in the direction indicated, and sure enough, under the distant clouds was a faint semi-circular halo of light; taking a closer look, one could see that it actually also lighted up the cloud above in the same fashion as we had observed as we walked near a big city at night during the 'long-march' we embarked amid the cultural revolution, Nevertheless, now we were still amid the pitch-dark sea. And now that Zhiyou spoke of it, the halo did seem growing larger and larger, clearer and clearerby the hour and so did with everyone's sprit, it's growing ever stronger, everyone was feeling more excited with extra strength… the little boat flew like an arrow leaving a bow toward its destination: Hong Kong.

A while later, as we observed, the ring of light grew even larger, and we could gradually see the light's reflection on the clouds over the horizon. Aside from that, we were still in the middle of the open water surrounded by complete darkness.

"Lingding Island!" Again, it was Zhiyou that shouted softly, and he continued in a tone of evident excitement: "Look carefully straight ahead: a little island shaped like a curly bracket turned on its side. That's Lingding Island. We're getting close to Hong Kong!" We looked and saw a faint outline of a mountain top straight ahead of us.

"Whenever the skies were clear in Wanqingsha, we'd come survey this side, and the island we could faintly see had this exact shape. The experienced old fishermen said this was Lingding Island, behind which it wouldn't be too far from Hong Kong. And moreover, according to the map, that's the only one relatively large island in the Pearl River Delta," explained Zhiyou.

The others were silent, because no one was as knowledgeable or experienced in this respect as Zhiyou. Him, Fan Kang and I, who had made the map together for this trip, would know Lingding Island's general location, and agree with as expressed.

According to the map's instructions, we should keep to the left of Lingding Island once we reached there, and pass between Shekou and Lingding Island, then continue straight toward the mountain for the shortest route. Consequently, we immediately began to turn the boat due south-shouteast, and sprint with all our strength. But just as we started doing so, a strong adverse current pushed us back. At first, we thought it was just a random current, nothing terrible: we were young and vigorous and could push past in a spurt of energy, even if it took six paddlers working together to push past. However, we paddled hard for half an hour, but made no forward progress, and in fact the current actually was pushing us closer to Lingding Island.

We called out that this was no good; we could even see rocks protruding from the Lingding island, as we were quickly approaching… Zhiyou and I both knew that border guards were stationed on the island. If by any chance we stopped at the island, it would be very possible we'd be discovered, and then everything would be over. We actually trembled with fear at the thought.

We quickly discussed the situation involved and decided to fight hard with the current; there was no way we could allow ourselves being pushed to the shore, being captured with our hands being cuffed, At once, Zhiyou and I took the front and back ore, and Fan Kang and Hu Qi took the single paddles in the middle of the boat and immediately began paddling forward whole heartly. By now, the waves were clearly much higher and stronger than they had been in the first half of the night. The little boat was swaying in the waves; one could clearly feel the boat being almost unable to hold up; Seawater would, from time to time, splash into the boat. Du Cai and Lu Sui did the best they could with household utensils to scoop the water out of the boat, and we all did our part to work our way out of the jam of the odd current, eventually rowing toward Hong Kong. Everyone had summed up together with their left-over strength, trying to separate we from the danger zone, and the small boat slowly put some distance between it and Lingding island. It was still too dark to see each other's faces, but we could all feel each other's heavy breathing!

"I think we should go out into the ocean from the right side, then turn again toward Hong Kong Island." This time Hu Qi unexpectedly raised an objection to the course undertaking, "I disagree. Once we go out to sea, turning around certainly won't be easy." I immediately voiced my disagreement, and Fan Kang agreed with me, but Hu Qi stood his ground. Zhiyou, being the captain in charge, had swiftly put a stop to the dispute by agreeing, in a stern voice, with me and Fan Kang, and we decided to continue with the same route undertaking, Despite this, everyone was still terrified and anxious, yet we still made no sound, for fear the sound would find its way to the island and with us being exposed. The only sound we could hear was the crashing of waves onto the rocks on the shore of Lingding Island, a sound that suddenly became ear-piercing and frightening. Occasionally, a huge wave would hit the shore, and a sound would reach us as if trying to smash our heads open. We rowed like machines, the boat still rocking with the waves, and our nerves tensed like arrows on bowstrings.

We paddled pathetically for another hour and still were only just off the shore of Lingding Island. Our hands were aching, our legs were becoming numb, and the pits of our stomachs were swelling up. But our craving for survival kept us paddling forward like machines. Honestly speaking, by then everyone was feeling a little despair because we still had a large chunk of distance between us and Hong Kong, and it was already three or four in the morning and still hadn't escaped the Lingding island. With dawn approaching, and when that happened, we'd be sitting ducks.

At that point, the scene came before my eyes of two years previous, after my first attempt to escape via the land route from Danshui Township, Huiyang County failed, and I was imprisoned in a wooden "accommodation station" in Dongguan Prefecture: every day before dinner the demonic "disciplinarian" would send all the prisoners guilty of so-called "defection treason" to line up in the central grounds of the prison where he'd distribute a small bowl of coarse rice and a teaspoon of bean paste, then demanded each person facing the ground and barked at the prisoners: Stand up! Squat down! Stand up! Squat down! ... It wouldn't be long before some people, after a long day of bitter labor, with an empty stomach, would faint from hunger in succession: one, two, three... Sometimes I couldn't help but fall to the ground, and the disciplinarian "demon" behind me would rush over, brandishing an iron broom that hit one like hail. My instinctual reaction to the pain was to jump up like a string being plucked, my body leaving behind traces of scarlet blood... Thinking of this, I took courage once more. My mind admonished itself: I must succeed, I cannot fail! I must escape this current, no matter how; I must pass through that inescapable net called the "iron curtain" by the free societies!

The four of us rowing experts, plus Du Cai with the single oar, paddled mechanically, wildly, for an hour more, progressing a little farther, but still not breaking free from the adverse current. The sky was getting lighter and lighter, and seeing the lightness on the horizon, we were huffing and puffing like cows, turning our heads to see Lingding Island still held a fiendish death grip on us, refusing to let us go. Fear and despair were slowly swelling up in our chests.

But just as everyone was sinking into a silent despair, hope came to us: Du Cai was the first to notice the boat was moving, asking Fan Kang: "Do you think we're farther from Lingding than we were just a moment ago?"

Everyone in the boat turned their heads in the direction of Lingding Island, and it seemed that we were, but no one dared affirm it. But not long after, the boat seemed to resume its pre-midnight speed.

"We've done it!" cheered Du Cai and Fan Kang in unison, and we all felt the boat was indeed now quickly moving southeast, and Lingding Island, that loathsome mass of darkness, was gradually getting farther from us. For a moment, Du Cai and Fan Kang's excitement infected every one of us fellow sufferers, and the whole boat was brimming with an atmosphere of excitement. We began to softly encourage each other onward; we'd need to drum up our bravery to reach the other side.

Slowly, after this night pushing us to the verge of impasse, and then bringing us back from the dead, we realized: between the original whirlpool-like current coming from the east side of Lingding Island, and then the current from the west side, and the torrential waters upon our having arrived at the island's periphery just at the island's apex, even a motorboat at full speed would fear being unable to move a single step, and for our pitiful little man-powered boat to be capable of making any headway was extraordinary. In the end we were able to break free of the misfortune on Lingding Island since, thanks to the daybreak rising tide, the current had slowed down. And, as luck would have it, we were already approaching the northern extremity of Kowloon Peninsula. We estimated we had half an hour more of rowing left, and we'd have to get to the other shore rapidly. Otherwise, after dawn, we could be apprehended at any time by a Chinese boat.

At that moment, with a strength from I don't know where, four oars moving in tandem, no, make those five oars advancing simultaneously, sent this boat, once again, like an arrow leaving a bow, to Hong Kong. Soon Hong Kong Island was in view, and everyone on the boat threw up their arms in celebration. In that moment of joy, we forgot a whole night of exhaustion.

"Ouch!" Hu Qi suddenly arched his back and covered his abdomen with his left hand, "my stomachache! Zhiyou, you took over for me for a bit," he said, laying down his oar before he finished his demand… Zhiyou, who had just swapped out with him not long before, showed a look of astonishment, stood up immediately trying to grape the two oar from HuQi, just as that being completed many times throughout the night with no hiccups, except this time around HuQi anxiously letting go of the other oar and took a step forward at the same time, leaving Zhiyou with no choice but have to lean forward as much as he could trying to catch both oars while they were both hanging in the air, while changing of positions, the little boat swayed substantially, and then we heard a little "plop" when Hu Qi suddenly fell right into the water, just with his left hand barely hanging on the hard-to-grip left stern of the boat. It all happened very fast, in a split second, Zhiyou hurriedly gained himself a foothold, managed to grip and use both oars to stop the boat, but the boat was traveling too fast, and with the oars being right behind us, we all could already hear the echo of the creaking wood! We broke into a cold sweat—fearing the oar would snap in two! The boat was finally made whirled around and then eventually settled, Zhiyou did it! (With HuQi later claimed repeatedly that he owes his life to Zhiyou because of this mishap of his.)

Everyone hurriedly pulled Hu Qi back into the boat. Hu Qi's face was pale, a face of panic, the stomachache long gone out the window. Yet this whole time Lu Sui showed no more concern than the rest of us! After the event, Zhiyou would recall that at that time, he was truly unaware of courage, but was thinking only of the importance of helping, and never thought of the consequences of a broken paddle.

Poor Zhiyou, though, in saving Hu Qi, had put one foot on a rusty nail on the cabin floor and was bleeding. We promptly wrapped up his foot and temporarily stopped the bleeding. He resisted the bone-chilling pain and persevered with his lightning-speed rowing.

As we watched the island to the south grow larger and larger, we again began feeling nervous. A stillness fell over the boat, the crows let out no sound, and all we heard was the splashing of paddles and waves. By now the sky was marble white; the line of dawn had shot itself all across the sky.

We suddenly sensed a large, motorized fishing boat to our right that was speedily coming towards us, with seemingly excessive horsepower. In a split second, it was about 65 to 85 meters *from* us, and in the morning mist we couldn't make out what the boat was doing, but we knew it was anything but reassuring. For a moment, everyone stopped paddling and held on to the oars and other hard objects, ready at any time to fight the other people, we were so close to victory, we were unwilling to be defeated.

The big boat rumbled its motor toward us until we were side-by-side, then a voice shouted: "Illegal immigrants? Go back to where you came from!" That voice, overtop of the motor sound coming to us, scared us out of our wits.

Although we were prepared to act, we really hoped we wouldn't have to fight them. Then a miracle happened: the boat just kept going and left us there! Though, their huge wake almost flipped over our little wooden boat. Just like that, that matter of life and death was suddenly dispelled, This couldn't be anything but gargantuan luck on our side.

As we were recollecting ourselves, we pulled on to the rocky shore—the northern extremity of Hong Kong's west side, Lan Kok Tsui. After some disagreement, we decided first to hide our boat, just in case we had landed on the wrong shore, we'd still have the tools to continue fleeing.

(We had, in the past, heard from time to time that not a small number of fugitives mistakenly "embrace the motherland," having mistakenly fled not to Hong Kong, but to Shekou Township in Shenzhen, only to be captured.) But just as we'd hidden the boat, we heard voices from a distance shouting: "Catch them! Catch the fugitives!" (Later, we'd learn that those mischievous fishermen had taken a liking to our boat and were trying to scare us away.) The six pitiful youths, panic-stricken, all grabbed hard objects, grabbed our things, and took off in the opposite direction of the voices. With Lu Sui and Hu Qi in the front, followed closely by Fan Kang and Du Cai, while I supported Zhiyou in the rear, we ran through a short thicket toward the mountain for 20 minutes, and then seeing there was no one following us, congregated under a tree beside a big rock and rested.

Everyone was now gasping for breath, frightened and unsure what to do. The wound on Zhiyou's foot was still bleeding, so I looked for a particular common type of grass that I could chew into a paste and apply to his foot, and then cover with cloth, to temporarily stop the bleeding.

Everyone else rested and explored their surroundings: it was by now light out; the sun had been slowly hoisted above the sea. To the south, you could see overlapping ranges of high mountains; to the west, there was a cliff at our feet, and beyond that ocean as far as the eye could see; to the north, you could make out Lingding Island—that devilish island we'd almost landed on the night before—lying lonely in the sea. It was early autumn, a light wind blowing, the jade sea without a ripple, the first rays of morning sun shining down, and our little group couldn't help but be taken to the beautiful scenery around us. It was hard to imagine the boundless, pitch-black terror of the night before in this beauty.

Looking again to the south along the cliff and down the seashore, everything in view was still and silent, not a house or person in sight. After a lively discussion about where to go with everyone talking at once, we decided to climb the mountain in front of us.

The mountain in front of us had no tall trees, only shrubs. We walked for nearly two hours up the mountain, through which time.

The sun was burning fiercely overhead, our lips chapped, and our foreheads felt like cracking. When we abandoned the boat, we'd grabbed an inadequate amount of food and water, and now there was not enough to go around. We finished what we had before noon. Our bellies were hollow, our walking unstable and top-heavy, and we stood like mud unable to move. Actually, unable to walk further, we looked for a shaded area to rest a little bit. Fan Kang unexpectedly kept walking, and returned a few minutes later, holding up trousers as if he'd discovered the New World, running and shouting: "I really am in Hong Kong!"

"Really! This is Hong Kong! Hahaha!" Fan Kang grabbed my hand and pulled us backward. Everyone watched half-believing, half-doubting as he led us down to a spot halfway up the mountain, and pointed to a water pipe on the ground, on top of which was clearly printed the letters "HK". After each one of us had bent over and examined it, we broke out in shouts of joy, unable to hold in the excitement we were feeling, the absolute feeling of happy success that permeated through all of us. For a moment, the tiredness was completely forgotten. We high fived and held each other in a crying embrace.

Not long after, we made an even more important discovery: not far from the water pipe, we found a humble dwelling, inside which lived an elderly man, who, after asking us who we were, told us that we were indeed within the borders of Hong Kong's New Territories, in the Lung Kwu Tan and Lau Fau Shan areas. This exceptionally warm character showed us the route into town, and suggested we turn ourselves over to the police.

The place we had originally landed was Lan Kok Tsui, the northernmost point of Kowloon Peninsula, administered by the Lau Fau Shan Nim Waan police station. After saying goodbye to the old man, we followed the route he'd shown us toward the northeast, and midway along the path, we encountered a middle-aged fisherman, who, after respectfully asking our identities, called us "freedom-seeking patriots" and gave us his approval: "So courageous! Everyone on the boat is an educated youth. I've received I-don't-know-how-many illegal immigrants, but the ones who came over by boat all had *manggongzhu* (fishermen familiar with the route) leading the way. You're the first I've met to do it yourselves! Hearing his praise made us all a little elated, though we were unaccustomed to hearing things like "freedom-seeking patriots."

But this honorable man really saw us that way. As he praised us, he welcomed us into his home and let us eat our fill, before giving us exceptionally clear directions to the *chaiguan* (police station). That we'd only just climbed ashore and found such big-hearted compatriots really warmed our hearts and left us free of worry. The whole journey we'd suffered boundless terror, but now we were receiving a big morale boost from the old man and this fisherman in front of us. There wasn't one of us that wasn't feeling all sorts of feelings welling up in his heart. First we, with our sneaky plans, were called "defecting traitors" on the mainland, and now we were held up as "heroes" in a complete about-face of treatment. It dissolved any doubts we had in our minds: would Hong Kong or would it not accept us mainland youths brainwashed by the Communist Party?

After stuffing ourselves, everyone was in high spirits. A sweep across the sea and now we felt we'd soon become citizens of this free land. We said farewell to our benefactor, then left nervous, excited, and happy and hurried three steps at a time to Lau Fau Shan Nim Waan police station to surrender ourselves.

The police officer at the station spoke in the same tone as the fisherman in publicly praising us and quickly brought us into the Lau Fau Shan police station holding room, and one by one registered us, writing down our birthplaces, birthdates, occupations, political parties, et cetera.

Especially when asking about participation in the Communist Youth League or Communist Party, he was exceptionally conscientious, and we could clearly see that even on the topic of politics and political factions the British Hong Kongese authorities were sensitive. People very carefully took down our ages, which reportedly makes it easier to find work in this society.

The tedious registration procedure finally finished, the police officer gave us fresh "*acan*" (阿燦)mainlander)a simple warning, and I remember very clearly his last sentences: "For the younger generation (the youth), Hong Kong offers ample freedom and abundant opportunities, but it isn't the paradise that it's been called. Everything depends on you having your feet firmly planted on the ground and taking charge of your fate. I hope you value the opportunities that come your way."

Several hours later, we cheerfully entered the police station's "prisoner car," and were transferred to Yuen Long police office, watching through the prisoner car window at the scenery of Hong Kong's New Territories: everything was so fresh, from the finely lain asphalt road to the newly planned skyscrapers, to the modern clothes on the pedestrians. It all starkly contrasted to stiff, gray, old-fashioned China.

The Yuen Long police office building was, in our eyes, quite an imposing structure, with its solemn white plaster façade. At the building's main entrance were printed the two lions holding a crown of Hong Kong's ensign, and a portrait of a British woman hung there, too. We would learn not long later that this was who the Hong Kongese people called "the city matron" (or the boss's wife). We spent our first night in Hong Kong in the holding room of this building, and because we slept in the holding room and hadn't yet reached true freedom, we were tossing and turning restlessly all night.

The second day, the police officer told us: "According to the laws of Hong Kong, you are classified as illegal immigrants, so you need to enter through a special program to receive amnesty, and furthermore, you need at least one friend or relative in Hong Kong to vouch for you, then you can receive your audit and interview, and only then can you receive status as a legal resident. Just now my partner (my co-worker) has collected the names, addresses, and telephone numbers of the friends and relatives you listed and informed each one of them that they should come and collect you within a few days, so there's no need to be apprehensive, just be at ease as you wait." Then he went on: "For those of you without friends or relatives in Hong Kong, we have arranged for you to receive assistance from personnel from the Christian Church or the Caritas Center."

The holding cells were divided with iron bars, and each was about 50 square feet and could "hold" five to ten people. Most of the cells at that time were holding Hong Kong-bound "patriots," and the police officers were quite friendly, talking and laughing with us, making everything comforting and relaxed. Dinner was Western style: inside was a piece of steak. My roommate joked that "We come to Hong Kong and get a 'cut of steak'! If these foods were on the mainland, I'd eat this 'royal cuisine' my whole life!" Everyone laughed. The next morning, for breakfast we had cow's milk and bread, which was another fresh experience for us. I, who had never drunk cow's milk before, drank a sip and thought I was imagining things. It had no smell, and yet it had a sweet and fragrant taste. I thought to myself: in Guangzhou, cow's milk was no ordinary thing; it was rationed out. Only high-ranking party cadres could qualify to drink it, but in Hong Kong, here it was furnished in a jail cell. How could this place be anything but the rumored Heaven on Earth?

Detained in the Yuen Long police station for that time was emphatically not a difficult time, though every "prisoner" felt anxious, hoping for friends and relatives to come quickly. This was, after all, their last stop before freedom.

There aren't many coincidences in the world, but on our first day in Hong Kong, we ran into one: not long after "being sent to jail" and being distributed to cells, before we checked in, a familiar voice came from the end of the corridor: "Fan Kang, Tubin! It's Yang Zhong! Hey, over here!" We turned our heads in surprise and saw that it really was Yang Zhong reaching toward us from between iron bars and waving his hands, with an extremely cheerful look on his face. He was a close friend for many years, who after this death-braving affair, we never expected to see on the other side. The most atypical experiences are also the most unimaginable ones.

As it turns out, Yang Zhong and another classmate, Zhang Xianli had followed my lead out of Huiyang. (They later told me: if such a frail-looking person as you dared to do it, why couldn't they do the same and seize control of their fate?) They left from Dalang Township in Dongguan Prefecture, where Yang Zhong was living, pressingly trudging onward for six or seven days of hiding by day and walking by night, then another five or six hours of swimming with bare hands across Shenzhen Bay, arriving in the Hong Kong New Territories one day before us.

However, Yang Zhong told us, of the three people making the journey together, only he was lucky enough to make it to his destination. The other two had been discovered after being chased down by border guards just before beginning to swim out of Shekou coast in Bao'an County. The guards chased after them with big dogs and shot at them with machine guns, and Yang Zhong was lucky enough to escape straight into the water and get away from his pursuers. As to the other two, he didn't know where they were or if they were alive. As he told us this, Yang Zhong couldn't hold back his grief, and his eyes filled with tears.

Because of this coincidental meeting with Yang Zhong in the "prison," it seemed there were now more than six of us from the same high school class, on the same day, now here as "patriots"! It was clear that the thousands of us discontented, freedom-deprived youths who'd come here by water and by land, unafraid of the hardships, seeking only our dreams was clear to me then: my path was not walked alone.

Yang Zhong arrived in Hong Kong a day before us, so he left the prison a day before us. So, we were definitely getting out, but seeing Yang Zhong's brother, Yang Da (Yang Da also went about the same route, swimming to Hong Kong, a few months before Yang Zhong arrived) lead Yang Zhong out and seeing the look of joy on their faces, still made us jealous.

After two days, we "patriots" of the little boat finally breathed the air of true freedom, and as we were saying goodbyes, we were making plans for a reunion at a later time and place.

As for the date, we all agreed to wear what might be the most unsophisticated Western clothes in all of Hong Kong, but which we thought were quite impressive. Together we'd ride the Star Ferry across Victoria Harbor to Hong Kong Island, and then transfer to the streetcar and sit on the second level from Central District to the Western Ring, then from the Western Ring to Shaoji Bay, watching the busy, bustling, modern Chinese-Western crowd in the streets, feasting our eyes on the "Eastern Concrete Jungle" on Hong Kong Island, happy and excited at having arrived, with "Granny-Liu-in-the-Grand-View-Garden"-like awkward incidents of all kinds…

Some years later, four of the six of us would immigrate again, from Hong Kong to the United States. Both those who stayed in Hong Kong and those who continued on to the United States worked exceptionally hard, because here on the outside we had few friends and relatives and no higher education. To make a living, we had to work unskilled jobs in places like construction sites, kitchens, and clothing factories, and make a small living from that. We had successes and defeats, but we lived happily, worked hard, got married, never worried about the basic necessities, and all put our children through college and gave them a good education. Zhiyou, who was relatively young, even continued his studies at Hong Kong Pui Ying Secondary School, even though he had lost years of study to the Cultural Revolution and the Back to the Countryside Movement, and after progressing under hard study, he was able to qualify for the University of California, ultimately graduating from the famous UC–Berkeley with a master's degree. I spent five years in Hong Kong, working by day, taking classes and studying English by night, and I taking off-campus classes at the Chinese University of Hong Kong, finally immigrating to the United States and entering the business world.

# Escape: The Cost of a Life

*By Zhi You*

In the South of China, the weather at the end of May was blisteringly hot, reaching close to 30° Celsius at noon, the dazzling sun suspended high in the sky between a few floating white clouds. The villagers A Gui and Shi Wei were pedaling their bikes, with A Gui leading, on the road from Chongkou Village in Zhongshan Prefecture to Nanlang County. The yellow mud road was bumpy, and the bicycles' shaking was hard to deal with at times, and occasionally a truck would pass by and whip dust up in their faces.

Ming sat on the back seat of Shi Wei's old-fashioned Phoenix-brand bicycle, tightly holding on to his waist, despite the pungent smell of the sweat dripping down Shi Wei's back. Ming didn't care at all that Shi Wei's shirt was drenched with sweat and was sticking to hers. He could feel Ming's body shiver slightly, and he knew she was feeling a little nervous, and he turned his head and quietly comforted her: "Don't be afraid, you have me!" She simply nodded with a forced smile, her meaning being: "I'm fine, don't worry." But Shi Wei knew that at that moment he was just as nervous as she was… After all, this was a crucial moment in their lives.

Just then, a burst of wind hit them head-on, rousing Shi Wei from his thoughts. By then, A Gui's bike had already pulled ahead of theirs a little way, and Shi Wei pushed himself to catch up.

Ming was Shi Wei's girlfriend, and a top student at Zhixin Women's High School in Guangzhou. Her facial features were delicate and pretty, with a well-proportioned figure. She was one of the prettiest girls in Zhixin High School. They knew each other from having participated in the Cultural Revolution-era Flag faction (QiPai). Because they were with the same faction, and their family backgrounds were both bad, as their families were both Classified as "Black Five," they had similar viewpoints, and during the Campaigns, they were often together. From helping each other to admiring each other, their relationship quickly became one of boyfriend and girlfriend.

At the end of 1968, when all the middle & hig school students in Guangzhou were sent to Hainan Island and other rural areas and forced to become farmers & peasants…, Shi Wei and Ming though of a way, to feign illness to hide from the wave of banishment and became a vagrant in Guangzhou without work. Their parents were denounced and suffered terribly during the Cultural Revolution. Ming's parents were wealthy landowners in Fengshun County, Guangdong Province during the Nationalist Party era, and early on they were returned home by their work unit to be "remodeled," while Shi Wei's parents were considered urban bourgeoisie, and after being denounced were put under supervised by their work unit. Just when they were feeling dispirited, and didn't believe there was any way out, news came that many of their schoolmates who'd been sent to Panyu county had, after one or two years of farming in Panyu, one by one found ways to escape to Hong Kong. This was no doubt heartening news, and after serious consideration, they decided that rather than live a humiliating life in an environment where they had no independence, it was better to act boldly, and fight to change their fate. Shi Wei and Ming decided to follow in their footsteps, and they surreptitiously asked around about the way to seek their freedom and covertly practiced their swimming skills.

Finally in the summer of 1972, Shi Wei's classmate Mingde gave them some good news: a classmate who'd been sent to Dongkeng Village in Zhuhai had agreed to help: he could arrange to provide support for them locally and see them off at a place where they would "*maidu*" (the term of the era's escaping youths for starting an escape by climbing into the mountains) for several days in the mountains before descending from Zhuhai to swim to Macau. From Zhuhai to Macau, it was necessary to swim a stretch of inland sea, at least two or three hours, at most five or six hours, depending on the changing tides, and to avoid the border guard sentries located throughout the area. Shi Wei and Ming discussed more, and decided they would risk it. In almost a year of preparations, they found two basketball bladders, two pairs of practical rubber shoes, a compass, as well as several tools, and had the route as told to them by friends firmly in their minds.

Close to three in the afternoon, they arrived at Nanlang's public bus stop, found a bicycle storage stand and stored the two bikes there, and A Gui told the two of them to follow the other passengers onto a shabby bus going from Nanlang to Xiace, Zhuhai. When they stepped on board, they found the in-bus-People's Militiamen, and even though A Gui had already told them how to deal with them, Ming was still nervous, Shi Wei softly consoled her: "It's nothing, no matter what they ask, I'll just answer how A Gui told me." With those words, she relaxed somewhat, and Shi Wei's tone of voice also relaxed some.

The bus started moving soon after, and the militiamen one by one inspected the passengers' identifications, and when it was Shi Wei and Ming's turn, a middle-aged militiaman stared at Shi Wei. The man had a pistol attached to his waist, he wore an outdated People's Liberation Army uniform, and he had a fierce-looking face and two chillingly cold eyes; as they were clearly not locals, he adopted a suspecting tone and asked them: "What are you going to Zhuhai for?!" Shi Wei cool-headedly replied that they were visiting relatives. "Relatives in which commune? What's your relation to them? Do you have a certificate?" He didn't wait for Shi Wei to finish answering before firing off a round of questions in rapid succession, while Shi Wei fished out a forged certificate and A Gui rushed over and said to the man, this is my cousin, my mother lives in Dongkeng Village in Xiace. The fierce-looking guy saw that A Gui was a local and that he was with them (he'd just checked A Gui's identity), and he resentfully left them and checked the next passenger, and Shi Wei and Ming both relaxed a little. They exchanged a quick look before turning to look at the scenery outside the window, deliberately avoiding the "vigilant" gaze of other passengers (from the looks of it, they were all local farmers) ... Because of the man's interrogation, the passengers were all sizing up Shi Wei and Ming.

Shi Wei now understood the things his friends had told him… Most of the inhabitants of Guangdong's border regions had accepted the government's teachings, especially the so-called *pinxiazhongnong* farmers, who viewed outsiders with suspicion. They passed two endless, hard to bear, bumpy hours, until they finally arrived at Xiace station. As they were getting off the bus, A Gui said to Shi Wei, in a deliberately raised voice: "Cousin, your aunt has been waiting for us at home for a long time, so let's not waste time!" He pulled them down a secluded side path to avoid any new problems from arising.

Immediately afterward, he found three good friends riding bicycles to take Shi Wei and Ming to Dongkeng Village, and there easily found Mingde's friend—his classmate Li Yi, a short, but strong and capable young person, whom they were all meeting for the first time. He seemed very enthusiastic and simultaneously invited them to sit and reassured them that they need not worry. He saw the worry on Shi Wei and Ming's faces, and said frankly, "Just be at ease here, you're very safe. I have a very good relationship with the production team here, and they would never bother friends of mine. You're already the third group of '*maidui*-ers' that I've helped this year, and all the friends who've accepted my help have had good luck; the other two groups arrived on the far shore without a hitch, plus one group that didn't make it, but nevertheless safely retreated, and you'll be no exception. I'll be waiting to hear good news from you."

According to the original plan, Shi Wei and Ming would spend one night there and set out on the evening of the second day, but Li Yi suggested that they leave that same day, because the sky that night would be clear with a bright moon, it would be most suitable for crossing mountains; according to the weather forecast, it would last for a few days, so you two should make use of it, because the weather on the southern coast was fickle, and could change at any time.

The house Li Yi lived in was far from the village, backed by the mountain. After the sun set, very few people would go there. Li Yi prepared for them an extremely lavish dinner, with fish he'd caught himself, chicken he'd raised himself, and vegetables he'd grown himself, and the four of them ate around the little wooden table, and Li Yi and A Gui drank a little *baijiu*. Feeling a little tipsy during dinner, A Gui started talking, and gave a toast: "This glass is to offer best wishes to Brother Wei and Sister-in-law Wei, that they go with the winds at their backs, and safely reach their destination! Seeing you '*zhuocao*' (which is Cantonese for "flee") without fear, and I can't conceal from you that I admire you, as unfortunately I have both parents and a pair of young children, and I'm the son of landlords, and I wouldn't dare, alas… Come, have a drink, so some day in the future you won't forget our brothers here!" When he finished speaking, a few tears were glistening in his eyes, and his deep red face exposed to a pained smile. A Gui's slim face was filled with wrinkles, making him look older than his true age, and it was clear that in those years in the countryside, A Gui must had suffered no small number of hardships…

In the era when he was a "Bad Wealthy Rightist," A Gui suffered the kind of hard luck and miserable plight living and working in the countryside that go without saying. When he was sending them off, though, he revealed a little: "The harvests the past few years have been very bad, and between Land Reform, the Three-Anti and Five-Anti Campaigns, the Great Leap Forward and Three Red Banners, and the Three Years of Great Famine, together with the Cultural Revolution we've just been through, farmers haven't had one good day in all that time. People are bewildered. That we suddenly have years of crop failures in a region as populous and affluent as the Pearl River Delta, and that even the respected so-called leading class of *pinxiazhongnong* farmers don't have enough food to survive, it doesn't even bear speaking for us of the Black Five. When the days are a little bitter, we all suffer through them equally well, but the hardest thing to bear was the torment to our spirits and the insults to our dignity: in the countryside, ever since the Communist Party had arrived, people were split into three levels: poor peasants and tenant farmers were the first level, lower-middle peasants were the second level, and Bad Wealthy Rightists were the third level; since we were in school, during every government movement, we were considered a part of the less-good third level, and when our parents were denounced, we had to go along with and denounce them. In that period, we, the children were considered targets of surveillance; whenever someone did something bad in the village, we were always the first to be suspected. And every day we'd stand on the grain-drying platform and wait to be assigned work with no dignity. Good work, relatively light work, like driving tractors, catching fish, and looking after livestock, always went first to *pinxiazhongnong* farmers and their children, and from there on down, until the lowly, difficult work was assigned to us so-called "Bad Wealthy Rightists" and their children; we'd get heavy jobs like scooping manure, digging fishponds, carrying dirt… My parents' generation could hardly endure it; we had to accept this humiliating and unjust treatment no matter what?! My little sister grew up to be pretty and charming. There was one evening two years ago in the sugarcane fields she was raped by the no-good son of the production team leader, and my father strongly pressured me to keep my head down, but how could you take it and being bullied & humilliated like that?! Seeing that rotten kid so immensely pleased with himself, I wanted to throw my knife at him several times! But I thought of my family, and I just had to bear it, and my sister and mother could just cry desolately on each other's shoulders at home, shedding tears in secret…"

Sensing the atmosphere was off, Li Yi consoled A Gui, "Well, isn't that why Brother Wei and Sister-in-Law Wei are fleeing? Come, we're all one when we're leaving! Brother Wei, I hope A Gui's words have given you added strength. This route is arduous; it'll be at least three or four days, and you'll encounter many difficulties, just don't give up! Remember, you must travel by night and lie low by day, walk by mountain roads, and rest as much as you can during the day, to regain strength. The moonlight is very good the next two days; you'll be able to walk quickly."

As Li Yi told them this, while he was packing up the leftovers on the table, and quoted: "The wind blows, the river freezes; once leaving the expeditionary hero never to return!" He said that every time he saw friends off, he would encourage them with this wild babble, and with a laugh, he said that the last sentence was simply saying that he hoped they wouldn't be picked up and be returned, and that they'd safely reach the other side. Shi Wei and Ming felt the solemn and stirring atmosphere and, since they were after all about to set out on the journey, couldn't help feeling nervous.

Soon after, Shi Wei started putting his baggage in order, taking care to prepare the goods and rations: the ball bladders, compass, and food were indispensable, as well as gloves (because he'd been hasty, he'd only packed one pair), an old Shanghai-brand wristwatch that his father had given him, a set of clothes that he'd prepared for Ming to switch into, two old military-use aluminum canteens… After thinking a little, he put the wristwatch on, and tucked the compass into his shirt, and stuffed everything else into his backpack, Brother Li Yi and A Gui took them to the base of the mountain not far from the back of the house, and Li Yi pointed south to the unending string of hills under the moonlight and continued on to the mountains behind them, telling Shi Wei and Ming that they had to follow the mountain route to the southeast, and that behind the Baisha Mountains were the Xiangzhou Plains: "You'll have to fight to cross them in the dark, find a place to hide in the mountains before dawn, and then start again when it gets dark. Avoid places with villages, find the highest concealed spot you can hide in the daytime, and read the route map over and over. I'll stop pestering you now, so you can make up time on the route. Take care of yourselves!" Shi Wei and Ming waved goodbye to the other two and quickly walked uphill for ten minutes before they saw Li Yi and A Gui returning to the house.

As to the feelings of gratitude and loyalty between the two of them, Shi Wei and Ming were extremely appreciative, and after arriving in Hong Kong, Shi Wei often thought of them in dreams. When they first reunited with Li Yi several years later in Hong Kong, they closely embraced each other right away, their eyes brimming with tears of excitement. Because of the gravity of the reunion, a union of life & death, Shi Wei remembered it well. Then they faced the sky and broke out in a joyous laugh that everyone had been able to reach freedom. After that, it didn't matter what problem Li Yi had; if Shi Wei knew about it, he did everything he could to help.

Just after starting out on the mountain path, Shi Wei and Ming broke out into a wild run. From nine o'clock until they got tired at midnight, they'd walked who-knows-how-many miles, only thinking about hurrying as fast as they could. They sat and rested on a big rock in a patch of short shrubbery, drank some water, and planned how they should walk the next portion. The sky was clear, many stars were out, the snow-white moonlight sprinkled over the woods, the crows were making no noise, and there was no sound to be heard except the distinctly hurried breathing of the two people. They looked into the distance from the mountaintop at the winding mountain range illuminated by the moonlight. Like flickering belts of silver, the creeks interwove vertically and horizontally into a picture-perfect landscape like nothing they'd ever seen before. Shi Wei couldn't help but exclaim: "How beautiful! What a pity, it's hard to leave a place like this, the mountains and rivers of the homeland that gave birth to me and raised me, and yet tonight we're going all out to leave her behind!"

The first night, their energy was relatively high, and they thought only of hurrying forward on the route, so after resting just a short while, they continued again.

The mountain they were on now was a large one, and it would take at least a full night's time to cross it. After crossing it, there was a flat zone of several kilometers, and Shi Wei and Ming rested a little while, then squeezed through the mountain's woods, avoiding the regular mountain road, climbing with difficulty, snaking their way forward. Shi Wei did all he could to make a path for Ming, helping her onward, sometimes carrying her, and they continued like that until the sky was marble white and they were halfway down the mountain, at which point they could walk no farther.

Shi Wei pushed into a patch of shrubs about human-height and found a rock to sit on. Ming was gasping for breath, with soybean-like drops of sweat hung from her face, and she was leaning on Shi Wei. Shi Wei fished out a small towel, and helped her wipe the sweat from her forehead, face, and neck, and tenderly kissed her forehead, saying: "Ming, are you tired? Lean on me and rest a while!" Ming raised her head and looked at Shi Wei with deep emotion, then nodded and held on tight to his waist, asking: "Really, Brother Wei, are you afraid?" She displayed a concerned expression on her face. As Shi Wei wiped off the sweat on his own face, he replied firmly: "No. There's no need to be afraid. If other people can do it, then of course we can too. You can rest easy with me by your side." At that moment, Shi Wei looked calm as he comforted his girlfriend, but in actuality, how could he not be worried? He certainly wasn't one bit calmer within himself! Looking out at the endless sea of forest and mountains in front of them, the vast and obscure route forward, where was their destination?

Because of ruggedness of the mountain forest, Shi Wei's body had gashes in many places from branches and rocks, and, though the cuts were shallow, he still felt stabbing pain, though he bore them without making a sound. Accepting that the next two days would be under these kinds of circumstance, he had to just take some peppermint leaves and chew them up and put them on the wounds, to guard against inflammation. At first it hurt a lot, plus the soles of his feet blistered, his joints were swollen and aching, and they weren't getting any better. He simply couldn't take it. But he said to himself, "I've got to just grit my teeth and bear the pain! On the route, he and Ming would constantly encourage each other. As their bodies adapted, they slowly became numbed to the pain, and by the third day, they started to get used to it. They began to understand that when people are courageous enough, they have some kind of faith that they will go on, and the body's functions display a magical capability to exceed the limits of what they can undertake. When they later crossed the bay, they proved this to be true.

They didn't speak much because of the exhaustion, and soon Shi Wei was leaning against a tree trunk next to the rock, with Ming leaning against him, both in deep sleep. When they woke up, the sun was already high in the sky. Shi Wei quickly looked at his watch; it was already nearly 11 o'clock in the morning on the second day.

The two of them got up and stretched, shook the dust off of

themselves, looked outside and then quickly pulled their heads back in. Since they were not far from the base of the mountain, there was a group of women tilling the soil, and they could dimly hear the sound of them talking.

They had to quickly find a place to hide in the trees uphill, where they found a relatively safe place to sit down and, as their stomachs were empty, Ming took some coarse grain biscuits out of the backpack to eat and some water to drink, then they looked out again, and saw that the workers had left, probably having returned home to eat lunch. They could see clearly now seeing the sea of mountainous forest behind them, and they could tell that what they'd walked the night before had been no small amount, which made them pretty proud of themselves.

After resting for a while, they looked out again. The sky was completely clear now, without a cloud for ten thousand *li*, and the visibility was so high, the sunlight lit up the whole earth. They could see that below the mountain lay plains they estimated to be ten-some kilometers across, the plains' golden paddy fields spread southward, behind which there was cluster of mountain peaks, which must be the Banzhang Mountains they'd been told about, several hundred meters tall. Supposedly there was a reservoir in the mountains, and to the east of the mountains was the sea (the mouth of the Pearl River). Shi Wei and Ming had to cross these plains and arrive at those mountains that night, and during the day, they'd rest in the Banzhang Mountains; the next night they'd cross Banzhang and arrive at the sea and swim to Macau.

Shi Wei mentally plotted the route and timing, carefully looking and visually exploring forward from halfway down the mountain to see if there were any alternative routes. He spent about the greater part of an hour until he decided upon that night's route and continued to hide and rest with Ming. He hoped they could muster up enough spirit and strength to cope with the night's march. Because he was so nervous, and it was broad daylight, Shi Wei couldn't fall asleep and had to force himself to close his eyes and rest. He endured it until the evening, then he woke up the deeply sleeping Ming, so they could get ready to go.

The sun had sunk behind the mountain for a little bit now, and the racing red clouds and golden paddy fields formed a beautiful painting. The distant farmers carrying their tools stopped working for the day in twos and threes and returned home. They took advantage of the afterglow of the setting sun and hurried down the mountain. By the time they arrived at the base of the mountain it was dark, and they continued along the route.

Shi Wei and Ming avoided the major road, and chose a small, relatively minor path, to avoid meeting a villager on a walk at night; this small path was a shortcut from the east to the mountain ahead, and it was also relatively close, so they ended up saving one-third of the time they'd estimated it would take to reach the base of the mountain. Though the route was swift, they didn't dare to make too big of a noise, avoiding saying anything to each other. On this path, on one side was a paddy field, and on the other was a sugarcane field, which just happened to shield them.

The moonlight was not bad, but the muddy pavement was potholed and bumpy, and the two of them stumbled along the road. They walked haltingly for about four or five hours, when suddenly a shimmering band of light appeared in front of them, and Shi Wei, alarmed, blurted out: "Isn't that a river?" Ming was also staring at it, and it turned out to be a small river, the rippling water flashing moonlight, and she answered in a trembling voice: "Yes, what do we do?" Shi Wei quickly realized that at this moment, he absolutely could not be cowardly. He answered immediately: "Don't worry, haven't we already prepared to cross the sea? This little stream is no problem to us, come, let's take advantage of the fact that it's still early and cross."

Ming was infected by her boyfriend's steady tone, and her confidence grew. They quickly walked forward, hand in hand. Soon they reached the river, and Shi Wei first took the backpack from Ming, then descended to the river and tested its depth. He walked about ten-some meters, already the center of the river, and the water still hadn't reached his chest, so he returned to Ming on the shore and said: "It's not a problem, the river isn't very deep; we can slowly wade across it!"

The two of them took off their outer clothes, and stuffed them in the backpack, and Shi Wei led the way, holding the backpack high in the air, while Ming held on to his swimming trunks and followed him as they slowly waded across. Because the night water was chilly, they couldn't help but shiver once they got to the other side, but since it was summer, after all, they adapted after walking a little while.

When they were crossing the middle section of the river, Ming seemingly tripped over something, and she fell over into Shi Wei, swallowing a little river water. Luckily, she didn't choke on it, or she would have made noise. Shi Wei quickly wrapped his left hand around the backpack and used his right hand to hurry and pull Ming up, but Ming was already soaking wet all over. Fortunately, they arrived at the southern riverbank about half an hour later. When they got there, Shi Wei at first wanted to stop and let Ming tidy up before walking again, but Ming unexpectedly courageously insisted on continuing forward. She said: "I'm fine, it's important we continue! We have to keep up the pace, and if we delay and don't reach the mountain before the sun rises, we'll have problems." The two of them shook the water off their bodies. Ming swung her head back and forth, and didn't change clothes, just draped her jacket over her shoulders and continued on. More or less an hour later, they reached the base of the mountainous area.

It was near dawn now, and the sky was slowly getting lighter. Shi Wei said to Ming, "How thrilling! If we hadn't taken this shortcut, we might now be only halfway across, and we'd have to hurry and we'd be in big trouble!" The two of them couldn't help but embrace and kiss each other in celebration. They then hurried up the mountain and found a secluded spot and changed out of their muddy clothes. Shi Wei first urinated by the grove, and just as he turned around, he saw Ming slowly taking off her clothing, exposing her naked body. Ming's figure was slim, exquisite, and appealing, and under the hazy first rays of sun, it was like a masterpiece of God.

He stared blankly for a moment, with a strong urge to run over and kiss her. This thought flashed through his mind, but then warned himself: "Wei, what time is this? Escape is what's important!" And he turned his head and quickly changed out of his wet clothes. Ming also quickly changed out of her clothes and came over and picked up Shi Wei's clothes and shoes and hung them with her own on a branch nearby to dry, then she told Shi Wei to sit on the stone next to the big tree. Ming lay down and nestled against his chest, kissed him, and said: "Wei, I love you, but we're too tired today, and we need rest, huh?" Waiting for the person below her to say something, she was already lying still on Shi Wei. As Shi Wei gently caressed her soft-as-silk waist and back, she quickly fell asleep; he was glad he hadn't acted impulsively just then, otherwise... He was incredibly tired right now, and he followed his girlfriend into sleep, leaning against the tree trunk and snoring.

As he was dreaming, a sudden sound of muddled footsteps woke him up, and a distant sound of voices that seemed to be swearing: "Fuck his mother! They're escaping, those treasonous, defecting sons of bitches, all day they were escaping toward this mountain. I'm itching to get to use the mortar, I'll blast them apart!" Shi Wei quickly dragged Ming awake and packed the clothes, and they sneaked into a mountain cave nearby. After a while, the sound moved away from them. At that point they realized that it was noon on the second day, and the scorching sun shone down on their bodies, making them feel it's might; the clothes they'd just collected were already dry, so they put on underwear, drank some water, and ate some food.

Shi Wei and Ming discussed and decided to take advantage of their having recovered some strength, and continue climbing for a while, to strive to get to the base of the mountain and the seashore by the time it got dark. Tomorrow night could be the most crucial part of their operation, and setting aside a lot of time would always be beneficial, but the mountain they'd just climbed clearly had People's Militiamen searching for illegal emigrants, and they had to walk a comparatively problematic route to avoid them. So, Shi Wei and Ming progressed slowly, snaking through the undergrowth. The mountain path was precipitous, the trees densely packed, and they met poisonous snakes and wild animals, but luckily, they hid from each one. The two of them had gashes in many places on their hands and feet, but fortunately they were all superficial wounds, and they pushed forward unfettered, with tenacious determination.

Shi Wei had Ming put on the gloves and helped Ming climb forward as much as he could, but at approximately two o'clock, Shi Wei was not careful and fell, with the backpack, into a cave in the mountain and nearly pulled Ming down with him. Just at the pivotal moment, she quickly-wittedly grabbed a dried-up tree trunk by the side of the cave and avoided misfortune. The cave was about four or five meters in depth, but fortunately Shi Wei landed on his feet, and had grabbed onto a branch as he was falling, and so softened the impact of his fall, and only suffered minor injuries to his knee. Shi Wei tried to prop himself up with his feet to get free, but the walls of the cave were too far apart. He took two steps before falling back down again. He tried several more times with no success, until his legs were tired, and he felt paralyzed on the cave floor. Ming started crying above, and when she extended her head to look at Shi Wei, pearly tears fell into the cave onto his body. Shi Wei, sitting and resting on the cave floor, consoled her, "Don't worry, we'll find a way. 'Heaven never bars one's way…'"

After a while in which Ming had not looked down at him, Shi Wei called for her twice with no response, and he started to get worried for her, but what use was it? He was at the bottom of a well! While he was worrying helplessly, Ming was carrying back a bunch of tree vines. She leaned her head over the hole and said in a loud voice: "Brother Wei, we'll save you! I'll try using this!" And with strength that she didn't know she had, she let loose one end of the vine and wound the other end of the vine around the dried tree trunk by the cave, held it firmly in her hands, and told Shi Wei to climb up the vine. Shi Wei quickly put on the backpack, firmly grasped the vine, and pulled himself up with difficulty, step by step. Ming watched him until he was standing firmly on the ground, then hugged him and cried as she kissed his cheek, mumbling: "You're okay, you're okay, you scared me to death, my brother Wei…" The two of them embraced each other closely for quite a while, hating to separate.

With some difficulty they crossed the mountain to the east, but two or three kilometers in front of them was another mountain peak, behind which was the sea (they later learned this was Dabu Mountain). But how could they cross the zone between the two mountains in the daytime? Shi Wei and Ming discovered a sugarcane field, not far from the base of the mountain and extending to the small mountain by the sea, that could screen them, and from the base of the mountain, they hurried cautiously with heads down into the field, but by the time they got to the other side of the sugarcane field, their two bodies were riddled with the scars of sharp sugarcane leaves. Thanks to their haste, they quickly reached the top of the mountain, and about two hours later, they saw in front of them—was that not the ocean?! Looking east from where they were standing, at a distance not far from them, was a vast body of water, extending without end into the distance, glistening blue, which the slowly sinking sun lit up with a submarine twinkle. Was this the smelting-gold setting sun about which poets write? How spectacular!

They took advantage of the short period while the sun was setting to rest, and when they woke up, they had regained a significant amount of energy. Shi Wei stood up and looked at his watch, looked at the afterglow on the horizon, and said to Ming: "Let's take advantage of the sky not being black yet, and strive to get to the base of the mountain, then wait for it to get black before we cross the highway and get to the sea, okay?" Ming nodded, and propped up her exhausted body to get ready to leave, and Shi Wei saw how exhausted she was, and thought: "For a big city maiden, no more than twenty years old, who'd never left home, even one who'd suffered many torments because of the social status of her family, can her body take these few days of following me and bearing hardships?" He spontaneously took pity on her, saying: "Okay, let's rest a little more, and when we're feeling better, we can start again. Come, sit, I'll massage your back and shoulders and calves for a bit, to make you comfortable and regain strength."

Shi Wei sat her down on a dried up log, and first crouched in front of her and kneaded her calf, and then moved around her and got ready to massage her back, and as Ming watched him, her eyes filled up with tears, and she suddenly grabbed his hand and gave him a deeply emotional kiss and said: "Brother Wei, thank you for loving and cherishing me so dearly, but our time is pressing! I'm fine. I support myself with thoughts of our future and what's ahead. Don't worry. Come, let's walk!" She suddenly jumped up and pulled Shi Wei into a run. Shi Wei was excited by her sudden jumping up and the staunchness of her willpower and jogged behind her.

When they arrived at the base of the mountain, they made use of their time by eating and drinking their fill, and then resting a little, before getting to know the surrounding terrain and choosing the route they would later take. Although it was not yet completely dark, the moon had still not risen. Shi Wei looked at his watch. It was 6:15 in the evening. He looked at the compass, and due southwest, he could dimly see some buildings, which appeared to be a village. As the sky got darker, that direction lit up. Shi Wei guessed that that was their destination—Macau. Ming saw it now, too, and pointed excitedly, saying: "It is, it must be."

Unfortunately, they couldn't just walk straight up and confidently present their ID cards to enter this land considered a part of China but instead had to sneak through the mountains and enter the sea and swim several hours to get there. Is it anything but sorrowful?

Shi Wei and Ming couldn't just descend the mountain and go, as the northern checkpoint was straight in front of them, strictly guarded with unfeeling soldiers; it would be throwing their lives away. They had to go into the water from a remote area to the east, but even then, they could run into border guards on patrol. They were both prepared and encouraging each other for the trip setting out from the bottom of the mountain, walking for about an hour down the rugged, forested mountain, and a little north to a spot near the sea. From there, it was about 300 meters to the seashore, and the two of them walked with difficulty, bending at the waist, and found a relatively concealed spot to hide and rest for a while as they waited for a suitably safe opportunity to run into the ocean. Shi Wei untied the backpack, and gave the remaining biscuits to Ming to eat, and then they took the guava they'd picked along the way and two bananas and split them, and drank some water, and kept some candy in the backpack.

Crouching there, they could just barely see some activity on the thoroughfare by the shore: at intervals of about half an hour, two people that looked like border guards would walk by, and then half an hour later, walk back the other way. Shi Wei judged that from this timing, they were carrying out an assigned patrol, so he and Ming decided that after they passed by the next time, they would act. Another half hour passed, and two soldiers did walk by, so, holding their breath as they waited for the soldiers to pass by, Shi Wei and Ming got ready by throwing the backpack under some underbrush, and put the things that were inside in a plastic bag and used a rope to tie the bag tightly to Shi Wei's belt, and each of them inflated a ball bladder. By now it was already after midnight. Ten minutes after the border guards walked back past, the two of them, backs bent, slowly made their way to the sea. Just then, a cloud was floating by and covered up the moon, and suddenly the sky went black; it really was a blessing from Heaven! Shi Wei hurried to the shore, took off his shoes and tied them to his waist, and took a nylon cord a little more than a meter in length and tied one end to his waist, and the other end to Ming's waist. Just as they were about to leave, the bright gleam of a searchlight shone their way, and the two intimidated people immediately dropped to the ground and hid in the grass. After a while, when there was no movement, they swam into the ocean.

The breeze was still, and the waves were quiet when they set out, and because they were still close to the shore, they had to be very careful not to let out too loud of a sound, so as not to alarm the patrolling soldiers on shore. Only after they'd swum more than a kilometer away from shore did they dare take deep breaths of air. However, the waves out there were a little bigger than the waves by the shore. Shi Wei asked Ming: "Can you, do it?" Hearing her respond yes, he immediately relaxed. The tide at this time appeared to be moving southward, and without too strenuous an effort, they left the dangerous section, and Shi Wei said to Ming: "Now we are fundamentally free; from here on, we'll be relying upon ourselves and our luck; we've got to make extra effort!" Ming also encouraged him at the same time.

After they'd swum about two kilometers from the shore, they looked in the direction of Macau and could already see the silhouettes of buildings and the halo around the city, and they prepared to take a curved route, far around where they supposed the China-Macau border to be, then winding around into Macanese waters. But where was the border area? They didn't know where Macau began! So, the whole night, Shi Wei and Ming spent making a large circle, and after three hours, they still hadn't arrived at what they were sure was Macau, but by then they had clearly over drafted their energy, and it was getting harder and harder to move, their hands and feet too weak. The wind and waves were also stronger now than they were before, and with Shi Wei dragging Ming along by his side, both holding tightly to their ball bladders, they took a short rest, and Shi Wei encouraged Ming, saying, "We're almost there, don't worry, let's rest a bit, and then continue! Ming asked in a small voice: "How much longer? Will we make it?" Ming evidently could swim no more, and what could Shi Wei do? He could only say it wouldn't be much longer. By then, they'd been swimming for more than three hours, and their energy was used up and their stomachs were empty.

Just as they were deeply worried and hungry and tired, Shi Wei remembered that there was still some pieces of candy and a bit of a biscuit in the plastic bag, and he quickly took them out, and they both ate, and Ming's spirit improved a little. They decided they would swim at an angle toward the southwest and climb ashore whether or not it really was Macau.

At this point, Ming could no longer swim, and Shi Wei had to carry her, tightly holding the inflated basketball bladder, and swimming west with all his might. Soon Shi Wei felt that Ming was paralyzed on top of him, seemingly without breathing, and he immediately stopped and moved her head back and forth with his hand, until she half-opened her eyes, and nodded her head, and he relaxed slightly, and said to her: "You should stay propped up; we're almost to shore." With that, he swam as fast as he could to shore.

With the weight of two bodies bearing down on Shi Wei's one exhausted body, he advanced forward at a snail's pace, even using all his energy. After about half an hour like that, even Shi Wei couldn't take it anymore, and he began to lose his head. He turned his head and looked at Ming, with her eyes closed, and tears rushed forth like from a spring. "I can't give up! There's just this little bit left," he said to himself, summoning his courage to swim a little bit more. He gradually saw the lights of buildings in distance, and his spirits rose, and he moved a little quicker, striking the water as his life depended on it.

The darkness that came before dawn had passed, and the sky turned marble white.

Panting, Shi Wei continued across the sea, and a while later, he saw a spot with a pile of rocks, and slowly made his way over, not suspecting that there would be a person on the shore beckoning him over! Shi Wei was now utterly beaten, and needed someone's help, thinking just make it to shore. But he saw someone on shore wearing what looked like the apparel worn by the police in the Hong Kongese movie *The House of 72 Tenants*. "Could he be about to arrest us and take us to the police station and then send us back?!" With that thought, Shi Wei began swimming away in a great rush, but the policeman calmly called out from the shore: "*Houshengzai* (young man), where are you going? From the looks of it, you have no more energy; if you swim back out there, you'll die! Come up here, I'll help you, my name is 369; even though I'm Macanese police, I won't arrest your brave people. I've already helped countless young people like you."

Shi Wei looked at this man from afar. He was about 40 years old, thin, medium height, with a full beard, and he looked like an honest man. Without much choice, still straining to carry Ming, he crawled ashore. 369 quickly came over and lent a hand, setting them down on a rock. Ming woke up little by little. When she opened her eyes, she said: "Who is he?" Shi Wei replied in a big voice: "Our savior! We're in Macau!" 369 continued to say: "It's impressive, that you swam for hours through the strong wind and big waves of the middle of the night; that I was able to pick you up makes you very lucky; it's truly admirable! Alas, that with the government of that side, the people have no way to make a living!"

Then he asked if they had any family in Macau, and Shi Wei responded that he had an aunt, and asked for help notifying her. "Of course, of course, I'll do that later," he said quickly, "but first we have to get you a change of clothes and something to eat. You look like you won't make it much longer. You wait here; I'll bring a car over." Not long after, 369 came back in a taxi, and in a few minutes, they were in the Areia Preta residential neighborhood. The taxi driver refused to accept money, and Shi Wei and Ming thanked him. The three people went into the basement of an old, two-story house, and sat down in the lounge. 369 first let them into the room to change their clothes and then went to the store next door and bought milk and bread and told Shi Wei and Ming to eat till they were full. The two lucky people were moved to tears, and they kneeled in front of 369 and thanked him for his great kindness and virtue. 369 hurried to help them up and told them it was nothing extraordinary, he was only doing the very least he could as a fellow citizen.

Two hours later, the aunt that Shi Wei hadn't seen in over ten years had rushed over and was taking them to her house.

A month afterwards, Shi Wei's aunt put money into helping them find people to take him and Ming, the "*qushe*" (Cantonese for illegal immigrants who'd snaked across the border via fishermen's routes), to Hong Kong, where the two of them started their new lives in a free society.

# Life is Limited, and Freedom is Priceless

*By Ocean*

I took a bus from Guangzhou to Huizhou, by the time I arrived at my slightly dilapidated old home on Shuidong Street It was already 6 o'clock in the evening , and the afterglow of the setting sun shone on the worn-out gate with pilled-stained-paint, while everything around seem so aged and dispirited, being by then the young master of the house, even after a long journey, I was still pretty much in good spirits, and immediately after dinner, I began sorting out and organize the things that I had brought back from Guangzhou……and reclining leisurely on the aged lacquered-worn long rosewood bench in the living room of this old house, and slowly examining every detail of the house in the dimming twilight throughout the remaining in the evening, this old house was one of the countless properties owned by my grandparents who ran their business " Chen Shaoji" some 49 years ago, and the rest were just simply being confiscated. Although this house is relatively small and now even looks a little dilapidated, it still revealed traces of the former grandeur, down under and from the outline one can tell that it used to be a very imposing building, with a total area of about 4 or 500 square meters. As my eyes fell on a photo of our family, my thoughts brought me back to the childhood memories of the time I spent here, thinking that the joyous time of the three generations of grandparents and grandchildren together under one roof was far too short, and just in a few years, we were scattered all over the places, with the family was totally ruined; and now that I was about to leave my home, my beloved parents and embarked on a dangerous journey with uncertain live and death, and even if I succeeded, I really didn't know when I would have the opportunity to come back, just thinking about it, I couldn't help but shedding streams of tears.

The following day was the Chong-Yang Festival, and for a long time before the Cultural Revolution, these old Chinese tradition rituals had been celebrated with thousands of years of traditional customs that the new government called them the "feudal remnants", had been "thrown into the garbage heap of history", and no one dared to mention it publicly, but among the people, there were still someone who would secretly commemorated and passed it on.

At noon , my friend Chen Yingbai also rushed from Guangzhou to meet up with us, I had bought some vegetables and small river fish in the farmer market in the morning, and originally wanted to buy some pork belly to make braised pork with preserved green mustard , but during this period the meat supply being very tight, the pork usually sold out very early in the morning, and people with the government-issued meat ticket (which was issued according to each family 's head-count rationally) had to go to the butcher shop in the farmers' market really early in the morning to queue up, and often only a small number of people in the front could have a chance for the pork.

End up I had to order more small fish instead and still managed to cook a much more sumptuous lunch than usual, and the two of them devoured it to their heart's content, with great satisfaction!

Chen Yingbai, a friend I met in Guangzhou, dropped out from high school, also did his best to avoid being sent to the countryside , and like me, he too was a jobless vagrant. Over- heard a few fellow Huizhou natives talking about the border-crossing on an occasion the previous year, I walked over to engage , didn't expect that everyone was so like-minded on the topic and we hit it off almost instantly, and after several exchanges into the conversation, sharing the same aspiration we soon became good friends, and agreed to "wearing-grass" (an euphemism for escape to Hong Kong) together if there exist a good opportunity to do so. Chen Yingbai was one of them in the group, a tall guy, burly, more than 1.8 meters tall, had a hearty personality, and was a man who is anxious for justice and righteousness.

I, was an unemployed drifter from Guangzhou No. 33 Middle

School in 1966 and encountered the Cultural Revolution, and after the suspension of classes until 1968, followed the school to the countryside to Duanfen Commune, Taishan County, Guangdong Province. With the pre-existing stomach problems since I was a child, had only been in the countryside for a little over one year, I was misdiagnosed with a small part of my stomach with a stomach-bleeding trail and had my stomach cut off, and had to return to Guangzhou to recuperate for a few months with no permit to do so. And yet, because of doing so was not in conformance with the governmental policy at that time, I had to make it up, somehow with the relevant departments simply ignored a good numbers of my application letters submitted to make up for the approval to return to the city , I, unremittingly, end up having to go through the mess using my parents' relationship with the Standing Committee of the Guangzhou Federation of Industry and Commerce in the past, finally found a person in charge of the relevant department in Guangzhou, obtained the approval to move officially my hukou(city resident-ship) back to Guangzhou in 1972, but was with no job assignment, and I immediately became a vagrant again when upon my return. During this period, luckily, the body gradually recovered. However, seeking a job in Guangzhou was really difficult , with my many job-application turned down repeatedly, it's the period while Mao Zedong and the Gang of Four were still struggling with the existing bureaucratic system that was then said trying to take the power away from them, it's the all the ultra-leftist ideology by then, the main theme of class struggling were extremely unfavorable to these young people who were being divided and classified into five categories, not to mention the assignment of work to their children, and even the works of their parents were sometimes precarious. After two years of doing nothing, I began to worry about my future.

During the time of my stay in Guangzhou, I learned that many of the students from our school, the Guangzhou No. 33 Middle School had been escaping to Hong Kong and Macao for some time. This did inspire my thinking to try the adventure, and not too long after, with a few meetings with these like-mined friends, I too embarked on the road of no return, escaping to HK for freedom.

With the same group of people, I once tried to escape to Hong Kong in Dansui in the prior summer, but unfortunately with only a few kilometers away from Boluo County, we were interrogated by the para-militia, and it took a lot of lip service to get ourselves out of the situation, so we had to return to Huizhou and wait for another opportunity

After a short stop in Huizhou, I, again returned to Guangzhou immediately. I continued to keep in touch with my fellow travelers and practiced my swimming at the Pearl River Swimming Pool every day and sometimes crossed the Baisha River from Guangzhou all of the way to the South Nam-Hai Town to exercise my physical fitness and endurance.

One day at the end of September 1974, the two brothers Zhou Baozheng and Zhou Yanwu, who were among the group, suddenly came to visit and told me that the two of them had set off from Huizhou and were able to get themselves close to the coast of Daipeng Bay, and only being tracked by the well-trained K-9 dogs and caught by the border-petrol after 8 or 9 days of difficult journey. With 3 months in prison, they had been tortured half to death and was only released at the end of year prior. Now that they had basically recovered, while still had a relatively fresh memory of the route taken last time, and wanted to try that again before the winter came, here they were, feeling me out see if I would be interested in participating.

I thought to myself that this was such a good opportunity, how could I let it slip away? Without saying a word, I immediately agreed, and also asked to accept Chen Yingbai to go with us together. The two brothers also readily agreed, however this time they requested that we needed to start from my hometown Huizhou, because their own hometown was closely monitored by those people in the street committee, I patted my chest and claimed that there was no problem, and I would arrange it accordingly and immediately.

So, I, Chen Yingbai and the Zhou brothers went separately to get prepared and agreed to set off on the day of the Chong Yang Festival (the Double Ninth Festival).

Just shortly after 2 o'clock in the afternoon, the Zhou brothers came to my house on time, so did Chen Yingbai, I entertained them to rest for a little while and explained some details of today's departure and prepared to leave. In order not to be too ostentatious, we were divided into two batches, one before the other; Yanwu and I led in a group, and Yingbai and Baozheng in a group thereafter , the first stop was to go to my grandmother's house in the annex city which was on the way, to say goodbye to my grandmother, and retrieve some of my belongs that I had prepared f some time ago or a special trip like this .

My grandmother was already in her seventies by then, although being in her old age, she did seem to have a very tough body, with her kind-heart, a smiling face under the gray silver hair, and her speech was elegant and organized, and she must have been a nice gracious young lady.

My ancestral family was in Huizhou, and it was already a well-off family on the well-known side of Huizhou City during the time of the Republic of China, and almost half of the properties on Shuidong Street belonged to the Chen family. My grandfather and father successively managed the family business, Chen Shaoji, and dominated the shopping area. In 1949, with the change of government, and they, like all the capitalist landlords throughout the country, lost their fortune overnight. My grandfather died unjustly, leaving my grandmother to live alone in the city. The branch of my parents' business in Guangzhou was also forcefully transferred into "co-op" mode and eventually to the government.

When my grandmother saw us, the youngsters, she saw us and knew that we were going to go on a long journey. She quickly beckoned us into the house and sat us down to rest, fetched some fruit from the kitchen and urged us to finish it , and then asked me about my current situation and the destination of the trip. After I told her the real planning, the old woman's face changed sharply, and she immediately pulled me into the room for detailed questioning. Knowing that the grandson was determined, she began to worry about our preparations and carefully checked all the young man's belongings. Then take out foods like dried sweet potatoes and fried rice crackers from the storage at home and ask the young people to bring them along. Grandmother usually loves her grandsons the most in the family, in her age, knowing that his grandson is going to endure a long and risky journey soon, would be in need of auspicious prey, even if he escapes successfully, they probably would not see each other most likely indefinitely, she hugged me real tight and advised: Xiang'er, the road from here to the seashore would be dangerous, be very careful, always remember that life is precious, safety first, and the tears are dazzling down, falling on my elbow. I also knew at the time that the parting with my respectful grandmother, might be the moment of life and death, but I could only try hard to hold back my tears and comfort her softly: Grandma, be rest assured, there were four of us, we would definitely help each other on the way, and would also listen to your advice: to put safety first.

Tracking the time, for us to come out of my house, take the bus and get off at Ma'an Commune, walk to the Dongjiang River, it should be already be in the evening, find a hidden woods and by the water, quickly take off the clothes, wearing only underwear, stuff all the clothes into a big plastic bag and tie it tightly, and rushed into the Dongjiang River…… Four strong youngsters arrived on the opposite bank in less than 20 minutes. Immediately put back on our clothes again and continued on his way.

That night, the four of us went up the mountain and ran all the way through the rather dense mountain forest and arrived at the east side of the Town Yonghu before dawn the next day. During the night run, we found a hidden place in the mountain-forest so we can rest throughout the day time, and continued the trip at night, (it's a must, for the escapee to march on at night and rest during the day to avoid being exposed and being caught.) shortly after climbing over a not too high mountain, it began to rain with the wind blowing hard, it soon turned into a horrify storm, and we all got soaky wet, had to hurriedly look for a shelter somewhere, fortunately we found a cave to hide out till the wind subsided, and every one of us had prepared a set of dry clothes in the back pack, however, with the heavy rain pouring down together with strong wind roaring and squeaking throughout the forest and the torrents, we just could not sleep at all throughout the dark night, seeing nothing but feeling rather scared......

The storm continued until the afternoon of the next day (later we learned that this was a strong Category 2 typhoon called Elaine, 10/23-10/31. The second encounter was Tropical Storm Phil Faye, 10/31-11/05.), we all managed to rest up a little bit, by the time the night finally fell upon us, I was the first to wake up and immediately woke up everyone to continue on with our way. Looking ahead, the nearby mountains stretched so high and down to the south, and there seemed to be with no end to it in the darkness, we looked at each other.

And thought, how could we get out of these!? Zhou Yanwu saw everyone's worries and said: You don't have to worry too much, we had walked through these side last time, we could just walk around the foothill of the mountain in the east, although it would take a little longer time l, but we can avoid the risk of climbing up the mountain road. With that said, he led everyone along the path on the side of the mountain. It was a very fortunate night, there were no accidents along the way, and we arrived at the middle of the mountains before dawn and climbed to a hidden spot in the middle of the mountain before sunrise so as to get ready to rest. Just as I was lying down the mat and preparing to lie down, Zhou Baozheng suddenly shouted: Oops, honeycomb! I got stung, hornet! Ouch, it hurt! He hugged his head and face in pain and just stood there. Then a swarm of hornets swarmed and buzzed above the heads of every one of us, caught us off guard completely, and instantly, everyone fleeing away with heads in our hands, and the hornets just keep chasing after us relentlessly, Just for a little while, everyone's head, face, hands and feet were stung by wasps, and we just couldn't help but shouting , screaming, crying loud with our heartbroken, by the time the wasp finally stopped at a distance, we looked at each other, and our heads and faces were all red and swollen, and our hands and feet were full of bloody wounds scarred with burning heat, and we each quickly applied the wounds with the panacea that we had brought along with us, but to no avail. We just could no longer tolerate the trauma anymore, rushing back to the hill-side-stream that we passed by while running down the hill, taking off the clothes and soaking ourselves into the water, washing off the wounds desperately. The cold water of the stream did help reduced the pain a little, and everyone was complaining about Zhou Baozheng's accidentally poke through the honeycomb this time, but we just didn't even know that things could be even worse yet, so I whispered, there were already several para militia with guns pointing at our direction not far from the creek , we were quietly surrounding by them. By the time I noticed, it was too late to try to escape, so we had to surrender ourselves, and be captured obediently.

Soon the four of us were tightly trussed up and escorted to a house in a nearby village, where we were interrogated by their captain. We had no excuses but to admit that we were trying to get close to the border...... to Hongkong; The para-militia then untied us and locked us up in a mud-brick house, with locked gates, and waited for the next morning to be sent to the public security station in a nearby town. The para-militia was rather humane, bringing them two meals a day. The mud-brick house, though dilapidated, has a very strong gate and only two windows with iron branches. Soon after the four of us entered, we began to discuss, since there was still one night left, should we find a way to escape? The idea of hitting the doors and windows seems to be out of play, is there any other way? After discussing back and forth for a long time still with no results, everyone was very frustrated, anger at ourselves, and we all had no appetite in the face of the lunch that was delivered to us, and barely eating any, we were very tired and lay down on the ground to rest, after all, we all had tossed ourselves around for a whole day and a half. I too, try to lay flat in the corner of the wall and looked at the roof in a daze, thinking to myself, how could it be so bad for us all...? At this time, the wounds of the wasp were still hot and feeling stinging, and just as I couldn't sleep, Suddenly, my eyes were casting on the roof tiles, and I had an idea, and I knew what to expect. And I saw that Chen Yingbai next to me didn't fall asleep either, so I gently moved closer to him and told him what I thought of. He looked at the distance between the iron window and the roof and nodded in agreement with my idea. So, everyone was woken up, ate the dinner that was served earlier, and tried to rehearse my escape plan, and agreed that it was feasible. But with the para-militia still being present out there, we had to wait until late at night when they were sleeping, so we waited with bated breath until midnight to make sure that the para-militia outside the door was not moving around anymore, the tall Chen Yingbai stepped on my body when I bent down myself and climbed up to the window, and then reached out to the tiles on the beam, carefully uncovered the tiles one by one, and created an opening large enough that his body could slip out, so one by one, we all got to the ground, Chen Yingbai gently walked around to the front of the house, and did not see the para-militia guarding us, so the four of us quickly left the village by taking advantage of the moonlight, returned to the place where we were arrested in the morning, retrieved our clothes and equipment, and hurried up back to the mountain as quickly as we possibly could.

On that night, the four of us were frightened of being caught again, we charged forward desperately and walked quickly toward the southeast direction unconsciously in the dark. Before dawn, we had already come to the mountain range near Sanhe. We all felt very tired, so we found ourselves a place to rest halfway up the mountain. Sanhe this area is mostly lofty hills, one after the other, with rather dense forest, at dawn I only feels that I was simply surrounded by mountains. So, I asked me of my group: Have we taken the wrong path? The three looked at each other, with no answer, not even the Zhou brothers, the experienced escapees who had a failed run not too long before. I then took out a compass from my bosom, opened a simple map, pointed in the direction of Dansui, and said: If we want to go south through Dansui and go down onto the seashore from the coast near Kwai Chung, then we must go south tomorrow, and tomorrow we will first find a way out of these mountains.

Finishing with the discussion, we each lay down to rest.

I got up at noon and ate something and continued to sleep until sunset.

I originally had planned to get out of this group of mountains in one night, but I didn't expect that after going around and around in the middle of the night, it still seemed to be in the same valley. In the dark night, we groped our way forward aimlessly in the woods, overcoming thorns by thorns, going up and down the hills, the more anxious we were, the more that we couldn't find our sense of direction, the mountains were like a gossip map, a puzzle, and the compass seemed to be invalid, and we had no clue until dawn. At this time, everyone became so tired, that we had to find a place to rest in the middle of the mountain and to wait for the sun to go down again…

The next night we continued to toss in the mountains, never could find a way out, when everyone was about to give up, I suddenly thought of a way, suggested that we should just climb up the highest peak, we look down from there for a place where there is a light then that would be place where we should be heading to, regardless with the north and south…..to go to that place, at least it would certainly led us out of this mountain range first, and we could talk by then… When everyone has nothing better to suggest, let's just do it! The peak was estimated to be several hundred meters high, climbing to the top will take a lot of physical strength, fortunately we all managed to reach the peak, sure enough, looking to the southeast, we vaguely, but really see some looming lights, everyone can't help but cheering, admiring my wisdom.

For the next four or five days, every night we had to face not only the risk of being caught by the border petrol/para-militia, but also the dangers of the moving through the wild and dense forest, the rugged terrain, i.e., you would encounter poisonous snakes and beasts, falling into a 'pot hole/pits' and or even over a cliff… and you could only move slowly, fighting every step of the way on these rugged mountain roads in the jungle, everyone was scarred with our clothes were torn broken, our body were riddled with scars, bruises… and yet no one among us had ever complained, silently we charged forward, help and encourage each other, and it was our belief that everyone of us would get out of this desperate situation in one piece!

And we did, after passing through the relatively lower mountains to the west of Huiyang Dansui was the plain area near the town Pingshan, and everyone knew that we were probably not far from the sea. Although everyone was tired after a long journey of more than 10 days, there was the first sight of the encouragement of the hope of success.

It would still be quite difficult to think about the Pingshan residential area that we needs to bypass through in the evening under the moonlight, as we had planned we just had to twist our way through, as we came near the village by the mountain before day light, we ran at time, almost trotting our way through the wood, just as we were about getting out the wood , all of a sudden everyone was dumbfounded seeing five or six figures with gun-like objects on the wood path in the front, we were about to flee in different direction and heard someone shouted out loud "don't move..!" along with the gun-clicking noise, knowing that for sure the guns were real. I whispered to everyone: it's important to stay safe first!

At the time everyone also understood that even if we were unwilling to, we just had no other choice but to raise our hand and surrender!

But, when these armed para-militia started walking toward us, two of them stepped out asking in native Cantonese "were you all Escapees from Goungzhou?…How dare you still walking around in broad daylight?

I, and every one of us knew by then we had no excuses but to admit as what happened to us last time around, so I approached them and state that we were just totally lost after running around for the last 10 days or so and were extremely tired now, please just show your being passionate…and let us loose this time ……thanks, and thank you thank you……and started to bow/Kao tow……with one of us three actually on his knee already……

At that time, the two turned around whispering to the rest of their group in HAKKA dialect for a while, then the two approached me again, saying in Cantonese: why were you all being so careless……because you all were just extremely lucky to bump into the kind hearted people like us today, and I had asked of the captain for a special favor on your behalf, and he had agreed to let you all go free this time……just hurry up now to go say thanks to the captain …; and leader of the para-militia actually approached us and nodded and signaled us to leave quickly, and before they turn around, the two waved and whispered to me: be careful now, it would be the shoreline once you climb over the mountain ahead… saying thanks repeatedly, we all could not believe what we just heard, being so moved and suddenly we all couldn't help but broke into tears!

And we rushed ourselves into the woods, up to the mountains ahead of us!

The mountain ahead, should be one of the highest that I have ever encountered along the way, it took us half a day to climb halfway up, and after a break at noon, the wind began to blow again. at dusk, the rain and wind became stronger and stronger, and by the next morning the storm turned so violent with the wind just danced wildly, whistling across the mountains and forests, the torrent roared down from the mountain almost instantly, the thunder and lightning roared continuously, and we, the 4 youngsters from the big city who now hiding in the caves had never seen such a terrifying scene of the nature, and we were absolutely silent, sitting on the ground with bated breath awaiting for the violent wind and rain to pass us by quickly. The cave that we temporarily hid in was relatively shallow, not enough to shelter us from the storm, everyone's clothes were almost soaked, the temperature at the beginning of November was already below 20 degrees, everyone was just shivering with the cold, the Zhou brothers propped up a piece of plastic sheeting they brought with them, it only help a little, everyone could barely be sheltered from the torrential rain fall, and had to try to stay warm as much as we can with each other.

It was only till the third day that the wind and rain gradually faded away, Taking advantage of the wind and rain being subsided for a while, we began to climb over the peak, and from the peak down to the south in the middle of the night, we could faintly see a halo at where the southwest sea-islands connecting the mainland area , the Zhou brothers claimed, that would be our dream place Hong Kong. Seeing that "success" being still far away yet it's indeed in sight, and we couldn't help but feeling really excited with the thinking that the goal was almost within our reach, so we hurried down the mountain, and before dawn we had come to the foot of the mountain and found us a hidden place close to the seashore to hide and rest, and be ready to make the final sprint into the sea at night.

It felt like the long day was extra-long, and finally over, with the red sun gradually falling toward the horizon, and the crescent moon was slowly climbing into the air, and the shadows swayed in the calm waves of the sea, and I, with every one hid in the bushes on the western coast of the Kwai Chung area and waited with bated breath, with the food and belongings being almost exhausted during the 13-day long journey, we all decided to finish eating the left-over as much as we can, and managed to gather the fiercely protected item, the live-saving item, the "the bulb bladder" and the related items so that we can make use of them as needed, soon as I finally made sure that there was no one around us, I walked quickly to the beach and threw myself into the sea, taking advantage of the moonlight, with the Zhou brothers leading the way, and we successively followed behind to swim quickly toward the faintly recognizable Dongpingzhou Island in the southeast. For the first hour, the sea was relatively calm, so we quickly moved away from the coast, and not until it was judged that we should be relatively safe by then. Everyone began to pause for a little rest, and talking in whispers, and everyone estimated that we should be able to reach our destination in about three or four hours, and began to relax a little……However, once everyone slowed down a little, we all began to feel the biting cold of the chilling seawater, among us Chen Yingbai's body hypothermia was more serious, so everyone decided that we had to continue to move forward at a faster pace in the hope of maintaining a steady body temperature. Doing so for less than half an hour, the sea began to swell and stir up with stronger wind and waves, and I Immediately instructed everyone to gather together close as much as possible as we move forward so as not to be scattered and or washed away and be easier to help out with each other if needed. However, with the wind speeding up and the waves became much stronger, and suddenly, struck by a huge wave, the four of us were scattered, and subsequently we could never be gathered together again in the rough ocean water, by then I could vaguely see the Zhou brothers far ahead, and Chen Yingbai was nowhere to be seen. I tried to search the surrounding sea, but to no avail. At the moment, with the evil waves around, I was afraid of losing the opportunity to catch up with the Zhou brothers, so I had to give up the search and desperately break through the waves in freestyle, narrowing the distance between myself and the Zhou brothers.

In this way, amid the Taipeng bay in the dark night, I fought with the vicious waves for about two hours, and the momentum of the wind and waves slowly weakened. I gradually felt physically exhausted at the time, feeling the freezing-cold sea water biting-piercing throughout my entire body, holding up with the bulb-bladder and panting while searching for traces of my fellow Chen on the sea. Finally, I saw that there seemed to be two shadows floating up and down on the surface of the sea about 200 meters away, and behind the two shadows was a huge figure of an island in the back, and yet there was still no sight of Chen Yingbai, as I mustered up the remaining strength to swim desperately in the direction of the shadow, and in about 20 minutes, I finally had a round up with the Zhou brothers. But what I saw was that Zhou Baozheng was actually dragging his younger brother moving forward slowly on the water, and not long thereafter, the younger brother became unconscious, and he could only carry his younger brother on his back, holding onto the two bulb-bladder and paddle slowly. It looks like his brother was hardly breathing by then. Even so, Zhou Baozheng still seemed very determined, and even trying to encourage me while slowly moving forward, comforting me with intermittent words: Do you see the island in front of you? This should be Dongpingzhou, let's hold on no matter what! Obviously by then, I just could not hold on to it anymore, my limbs were sore and numb, and I couldn't quite hear his words...... Nonetheless, it's with his encouragement, I immediately thought of my mother and grandmother, and thought of the benefactors I met two days ago who had captured and released me, with all of these happening throughout the past few days, it was obviously to me that the ancestors (or my mother?) who had been blessing me/us with the spirit of heaven, and I couldn't and shouldn't have given up at the critical moment. So, we continued to muster up the courage to keep paddling our hands and feet, and the three of them finally approached the island beach in the front. Zhou Baozheng was using his last bit of strength to drag his younger brother to the shore before falling collapsed to the ground, and me too passed out while trying to land myself on to the island……

When the three of us woke up, it was already noon, we found ourselves lying in a fisherman's house on the island.

With the help of the fishermen, the three of us were successfully sent to the Yuen Long Police Station in Hong Kong the next day and finally met with the relatives and friends two days later and were officially freed.

However, Chen Yingbai still had no whereabouts and news of him since then, which has become a pain throughout my life.

## Mo Xibin, a student from Guangzhou No. 33 Middle School

I, Senior to my schoolmate He Xibin at the Guangzhou No.33 Middl school could not locate him when I was in Guangzhou last time, even his family was silent about his where about when I visited them, they even suggested that I might have gotten the last name messed up with another person's.

The Bald Head(nickname of a common friend of many); It should have been Mo Xibin, not He Xibin, while there was another Classmate with "He" as his last name, called: He Guoqing who was in the same class with Mo Xibin, He and I had afternoon tea the other day, and He claimed that he would be able to get a copy of Mo Xibin's photo for us which did not fall through, but I know where He Guoqing lives, which was: Woolong Hill top.

Mo Xibin lived in Deyuan Fang, Nanhua West Street, Guangzhou, and studied in Xizha South Primary School.

We were in the same photography class back then in The Youth Palace Located behind the "Haitong Park" Now that Mo has die since

1971, a long, long time ago……

Mo Xibing, student at The Guangzhou No.33 Middle School, the 66th. Class into the school year at 6th class of the 3rd year (while I was in the 5th class of the 3rd year (the sophomore year in the middle school))

He, so was I, was also sent to the Duanfen Commune, Taishan County, He could have die trying to flee to Hong Kong in the year 1971, so claimed by some of his fellow classmates.

And after that, no fellow student from the Guangzhou No 33 Middle School has heard Mo's message again, whether it is the schoolmate in Guangzhou, from Taishan, from Hong Kong, from anywhere…..there has been just no news Mo Xibin at all, in short, Mo Xibin seems to have disappeared into the thin air, of course, there is an ominous premonition in the heart of the family, he should die like other escapee friends !

Even so, but how he dies, no one knows!

Until 45 years later, when I returned to Guangzhou for my class reunion in 2016, I found out how Mo died:

It turned out that Mo Xing's "escape trip" (driving a small wooden boat to HK), a total of eight people, was unfortunately spotted by the border patrolling people (para-militia) at the exit of the Pearl River (where the river running in to the south China sea), Mo Xibin and the rest of the six people were all grown up by the Pearl River, with excellent swimming skill, and they immediately jumped into the river trying to flee from the scene, The para-militia, on the other hand, opened fire immediately, and seven people died in the water, being rushed out of the sea and didn't even leave any trail of the corpse at all! One of the remaining people didn't flee simply because he did not know how to swim, and he was scared to death, ending up with memory lost for a few years!

It has ever since then, there had been no news of his whereabout at all, Mo Xibin, just vanished into thin air……so claimed by his family!

Decades later, with the slow recovery of his memory capability the survivor of the shooting tragedy would have the opportunity to tell the rest of the Mo Xibin's family of the shooting tragedy. It just so happened that a classmate surnamed He, who was working in the same commune together with Mo before Mo Xibins escaping venture, met Mo's uncle on the street once and told him about the shooting tragedy, and now everyone knew how Mo died!

Like Mo, he was shot and killed on the way escaping to Hong Kong, some could fall to death while climbing a mountain; some was bitten to death by a poisonous snake; someone was bitten to death by a shark in the sea, and still someone drowned in the angry sea!

I wouldn't know how many, and I wouldn't even know how to count them ……when my group of four(4) , walking 13days to the coast, trying to swim to Hong Kong's Tung Ping Chau Island, with one disappeared, it was late November, the water was freezing cold, and I believe that he would also be dead in the sea!

If none of us told the world what happened to all of the escapees who died crossing the border, they all would disappear into the thin air, just as what happened to my classmate Mo Xibin, no one would know that such seven young lives were lost like this!

I remember a reporter once said as such: "Human blood is not rouge"! We advocate the erection of a memorial to commemorate the victims who lost their lives on their way escaping to Hong Kong for freedom!

# I am Just a Little Bird

## By Xi Man

In the summer of 1964, I was about to graduate from junior high school at Guangzhou 33rd Middle School. Instead of continuing to senior high school, I applied to Guangzhou First Chemical Technology Vocational School. My teacher, a father-like scholar, made an effort to see my mother and tried to persuade her to change my mind. He argued that, based on my academic performance, I should stay on a more scholarly path by finishing high school and then advancing to university. I couldn't agree with him more; continuing to university was my dream. However, I was more aware of my own situation. Since my grandfather owned land before the Communists took power in 1949, my family's political status was classified as "landlord," which placed us in one of the "Five Black Categories," effectively rendering us with an untouchable social status. Attending university could only be a dream that would never come true. Not being able to receive a full college education has been a lifelong pain. The best I could hope for was to learn a skill at the vocational school and get a job in the city where I was born and raised. I didn't think I was asking for too much.

I was accepted into the vocational school, and the first semester went by smoothly. One day, during the first week of the second semester, I was summoned to the principal's office. The principal wasted the first few minutes on current political revolutionary propaganda, and then he said, "Our country needs good youth to go to the rural areas to work, and you are honorably one of the lucky ones." I naively asked, "Can I choose not to go and continue my studies?" He replied, "If you don't obey the decision of the authority, we can't allow you to stay in school."

It was crystal clear: I had no choice but to obey the authority—leave the school and go to work in the countryside.

Many years later, at the Confucius Temple in Taiwan, I saw the Confucius quotation "There is no class separation in teaching" printed on the entrance door. I was deeply moved, and tears welled up in my eyes.

The principal tried to comfort me by saying, "It is not that our school is abandoning you. You are still considered a student of our school." (Two years later, during the Cultural Revolution, we fought for our return to the city based on this "promise.") That was a lie. Even in my teens, I highly valued education. I enjoyed going to school and learning, even at the vocational school. But in 1965, at the age of 17, my opportunity for education was brutally deprived from me—forever! It was so unwilling and so helpless. Was I destined for this?

In fact, the problem was not just the termination of my school education; I was facing the possibility of losing my city identification. Now, I might turn from a city boy into a peasant, forever becoming a third-class "citizen."

On the morning of February 7, 1965, we bid farewell to Guangzhou. Our bus slowly pulled away, and I stuck my head out of the window. It started to drizzle. My mother stood in the rain, waving goodbye with one hand while wiping her eyes with the other. I couldn't tell if it was tears or raindrops dripping down from her forehead. Heartbroken, I pulled myself back from the window, sobbing.

After seven hours of a bumpy ride, the bus brought us to the Da Huai Farm in En Ping County. Thirteen boys and one girl from our Chemical Technology Vocational School were assigned to the rubber plantation team. It was a very desolate place; there were no people for several square miles, and even trees were hard to find. But at night, the moon was bright and clear, and the stars were beautiful and scattered across the sky. It felt like a place far away from civilization.

The rubber plantation team was an experimental project initiated by the Provincial Agriculture Bureau. It was an attempt to move rubber plantations north to a higher latitude.

In the 1950s, China aimed to produce the rubber it needed to reduce and eventually eliminate rubber imports. Large-scale rubber plantations were established in Hainan Province. The Provincial Agriculture Bureau wanted to try it out in En Ping County, even though it was at a higher latitude. In addition to us 14 newcomers, there was a student who had just graduated from a tropical plantation school and a rubber plantation technician transferred from a farm on Hainan Island. There were also 10 street youths whose high school education had been terminated due to their families' political status, and who had been "persuaded" to relocate to our farm just a couple of months before our arrival. Additionally, a few local peasants were also part of the team.

Using the most primitive hand tools, such as hoes and shovels, along with our shoulders and bare hands, we moved huge piles of dirt and rocks to level the hills into terraces. We started the plantation from seeding, nurturing, grafting, propagating, and transplanting. The work was tough and tiring at first, but I got used to it in about a month. Luckily, there wasn't a single Communist Party member in our team, so we were able to escape the boring political indoctrination. We were paid 18 RMB a month (about half of what a young worker made in the city of Guangzhou). Eating in the farm canteen cost two-thirds of that, so besides taking care of my stomach, I still had 6 RMB left.

There was no electricity, and after the sun went down, it was complete darkness and silence. However, I wasn't going to waste my youth this way. With a kerosene lamp inside my mosquito net, I spent a year finishing high school courses in literature, mathematics, physics, and chemistry. With the little pocket money I had, I indulged myself with subscriptions to a few literary and scientific periodicals. Even in the 1960s, I had read about scientific topics such as fiber optics and genetic modification. I also used my spare time to record the growth of rubber plants under different amounts of sunlight, rainfall, and temperatures. Life wasn't that bad until one day when the party secretary from the farm decided to come to our team to exercise tighter management. From then on, political meetings were held daily, and "class struggle" became an everyday topic. I became a target for the party secretary simply because I focused too much on my studies and paid too much attention to the plantation business. He demanded that I redirect my attention, from deep down in my soul, to closely follow the party line of class struggle. The so-called "class struggle" was so abstract that no one knew what it was. The almost illiterate secretary himself never impressed me as someone who knew what he was talking about. All I could imagine was that one must do exactly what he asked and echo exactly what he said. That was aligning closely with the party's line. I knew I could never do that. I already had a hunch that political problems might follow me everywhere from then on.

Then came the middle of 1966, marking the beginning of the so-called "Proletariat Cultural Revolution," a Chinese political movement initiated by the then-great leader Mao Zedong, which turned the country upside down for ten years.

Are we still city folks? We saw that the chaos might turn out to be an opportunity for us to reaffirm our identity. When our school principal persuaded us to go to the countryside, he told us it was the city's policy that we would keep our city HuKou (Urban registration). Now, at the beginning of the Cultural Revolution, we went to the Guangzhou municipal office to confirm that this was the case and to find out when we could return to the city. To our surprise, the city official informed us that the decision to allow us to keep our city HuKou had been a mistake. The mistake was corrected right after we left town. In other words, our city HuKou had been stripped, and we could not return to the city anymore! What a blow!

Why was it such a big deal to have a city Hukou, or urban registration? It is the food coupon and the possibility of a salaried city job. Peasants in the countryside did not have that.

We immediately returned to the farm and demanded that the farm officially send us back to our school. Due to its geographical isolation, the officials at the farm didn't know much about what was going on. When we handed them the Cultural Revolution documents, they didn't know what to say or do. Some of the leaders were survivors of past political campaigns and understood the unpredictable nature of those campaigns and the serious consequences of any wrong move. They said nothing. The top official pulled me aside and said, "You guys are too young and naive. During these kinds of situations, it's best not to make a move. You should just wait and see." He was afraid of making a wrong decision that might cost him his job.

But we were faced with the possibility of losing our city registration, and nothing could be worse than that. We didn't have much more to lose. In October 1966, along with a couple of guys who stayed behind, over 600 of us gathered at the municipal office, demanding permission to regain our city HuKou and return to our schools. This became known as the "Student-Worker 600" movement in 1966.

We had a few meetings with the city officials. In one of those meetings, one of us showed the officials his personal file. There was a registration record indicating that the handling office was the "Guangzhou Industrial Committee for the Elimination of Counter Revolutionaries." What? Are we all "counter revolutionaries" now? Mayor Zhong Ming was speechless. It was later discovered that the city didn't know which office had jurisdiction over our case, and the seal of the "Committee for the Elimination of Counter Revolutionaries" happened to be lying around; someone just picked it up and used it. How ridiculous! The city finally decided it was a mistake. All students should be allowed to return to the city and to their respective schools.

We returned to the vocational school, but the whole country was in political and social chaos, making any study impossible in schools across China.

In the autumn of 1968, the most turbulent part of the Cultural Revolution came to an end. High school students from 7th to 12th grade were all considered high school graduates. About 5% of junior high school students were allowed to collectively advance to senior high school, while 90% of high schoolers were sent to the countryside for "re-education from the poor peasants." The number of youngsters forced to leave the cities was estimated at 17 million. Fortunately, the majority of our vocational school graduates were allowed to stay in the city and were assigned city jobs. A small number were labeled "troublemakers" during the Cultural Revolution and were sent to the Hainan Agricultural Farms.

Since we had once been sent to the farm, we could not be reassigned to city jobs. However, the Da Huai Farm in En Ping County also refused to take us back, stating that we had already left the farm. I was left with two choices: 1) Stay home and risk being unemployed for the rest of my life, or 2) be sent to any rural area our residential committee deemed fit.

At this juncture, talks of escaping to Hong Kong began to circulate in some circles.

I had no choice but to follow the orders from the residential committee. Seven of us—six boys and one girl—were sent to the Meitan Production Team of Huzhen Commune, Boluo County. The village was next to LuoFu Mountain, by the Dongjiang River. The girl's name was Kam, she was from a finance School. Kam later became my girlfriend and eventually my wife. The villagers were quite nice to us. Upon our arrival, we were given plenty of grain, cooking oil, and sugar. We were never discriminated against, and they highly valued our educational background. A couple of months after our arrival, three of us, including my sweetheart Kam, were selected to teach in the village school. The village leader probably thought I was the most educated because of my thick glasses, he approached me first and tried to persuade me to become a teacher. It was definitely a much nicer assignment than working in the fields. I kindly turned down his repeated offers. I was grateful for their kind consideration, a bit of guilt has lingered with me ever since. However, my eyes were set further down south-Hong Kong.

## Running for the Sea

All the Chinese students who were sent to the countryside were called "ZhiQing," meaning "Youth with an education" or "educated youth." The ZhiQings in the area surrounding our village were largely from the 5th Middle School of Guangzhou. We all got to know each other quickly. The main topic of our enthusiastic discussions was escaping to Hong Kong. In 1971, I got my chance to try my luck. With the help of

ZhiQing from Huangjiang, Dongguan, I made it up to the hills without any problems. My debut was with another young man. The two of us followed the textbook procedures exactly, hiding during the day and advancing at night. We survived one typhoon and even escaped a search operation conducted by the local militiamen. After we crossed WuTong Mountain, we reached a strategic spot from which we could clearly see the lights of Hong Kong. It was about 10 PM, and the tide was right. We entered the water and began to swim toward our freedom. After swimming for about 30 minutes, my partner began to slow down. He seemed to have lost his strength and begged me to wait for him. I had no choice but to go slowly. When we were about 200 meters from shore, my feet touched the ground. The sky lit up quickly with the morning sun. All of a sudden, a patrol boat sped up from behind and stopped between us and the spot we aimed to land. We missed it, obviously. However, I had no regrets about slowing down to be with my partner.

We were taken to the local garrison's company headquarters, then to the battalion's headquarters, and finally to the regiment's headquarters. A few days later, we were taken to a prison-like collecting shelter in Shenzhen, designed to house escapees like us. We were locked up in small, primitive prison cells. I was so tired and exhausted that I lost my appetite. All I wanted to do was lie down and close my eyes for those days. Four days later, after several transfers from Shenzhen to Zhang Mu Tou, we finally arrived at the BoLuo County collecting shelter. I was finally able to regain my senses. In the local prison, I was welcomed warmly by a group of friends. They even arranged a good sleeping spot for me. We spent a lot of our time exchanging experiences. Each of us told our own story: where and when we started, where we had been, what the terrain was like, what we encountered along the way, and the details of when and where we entered the water, including the current conditions, and so on. It was like a daily seminar. Ten days later, we were released from the county collecting shelter, fully educated.

After comparing notes with our cellmates, I realized that our village was an ideal starting point. The village was near a node on the Guangzhou to Huizhou highway, and there was a bus stop nearby. One significant advantage was that our village was just barely outside the sensitive border area, so no special permit was required to get there. From where we were in Hu Zhen, we could reach the mountain range within a few days without too much trouble.

The news spread quickly. Our Hu Zhen Mei Tan village became a hotspot for future escapees. During the spring of 1972, many people came to visit us to carefully study the terrain. At the beginning of summer, waves of them came and went. By rough estimates, there could be close to a hundred people, of whom I only knew a handful. Each escapee had to carry enough provisions for roughly ten days of travel in the mountains. The dry food typically came in the form of dry flour stir-fried with sugar and lard, lumped together the size of an avocado. The job of going to the store to buy flour naturally fell to the only female member of our group, my sweetheart Kam. She had a well-respected job as a teacher at the local school and was good-looking and well-liked by the villagers. If one of us boys frequently patronized the food stores for large quantities of flour and pork fat, it would have inevitably drawn attention and turned into suspicion.

Kam knew exactly what my ambition was. She and I were also slowly falling in love with each other. There was no doubt that she would like to be in Hong Kong with me. However, the danger of the journey and the long-distance swimming at night in the high seas scared her. Failing was one thing, but there were also stories of people going missing or losing their lives. By rough estimates, the death rate could amount to about 5 percent or more. It was not an easy decision for her to make.

Just a few days after May 1972, I decided to try again. Non-stop heavy rain had been pouring for several days, and the Dongjiang River swelled to a dangerous level. The current was flowing so rapidly that the ferryman refused to take me to the other side of the river. I had to abandon the journey.

Kam was relieved to see that I returned safely. She also started to ask me detailed questions about the escape. I could sense that she was struggling internally.

Two weeks later, to my happy surprise, my sweetheart Kam finally made up her mind. She decided to take the risk with me.

"Four-eyed is going to do it with his girl." (I was nicknamed "Four-eyed" due to my spectacles.) The news circulated in the nearby villages and among the ZhiQings from the Fifth Middle School and other schools. Friends mobilized to prepare for our journey, just as we had done for others.

It was May 23, another farmers' market day. Before dawn, the three of us—Kam, Sam, and I—walked 15 minutes to the town of Long Hua. Four friends with four bicycles met us as planned. One bicycle was loaded with our provisions and took off. The three bikes carried the three of us on their back seats across the Dongjiang River, past Qiaotou town and straight to Qingxi town. By the time we arrived in Qingxi, it was already afternoon. We met our local contact, Little D, and handed him our provisions. He was going to deposit the provisions at a prearranged spot for us to pick up later, as it would have been too dangerous for us to carry the supplies ourselves.

The three of us relaxed in a small restaurant, waiting for Little D to return. To avoid arousing suspicions, the four taxi bikers turned down our invitation to eat with us. We bid farewell: "See you all later in Hong Kong." In fact, what we had done so far was standard operation; I had done the exact same thing a few times for other escapees before.

We had some good meals in the restaurant, but it was getting late, and people began to leave town to return to their villages. Little D was not showing up, and we were all a bit worried but didn't dare to show any sign of anxiety. To act normal, Kam and I got close to each other, pretending to be a couple having a good time. To prepare for the possible questioning by patrolling militiamen, we made up a story that we were ZhiQings from Qiaotou who had come to the farmers' market. We claimed our bikes had been stolen and that we were waiting for friends to pick us up. Since we had nothing with us, there was no reason for us to be suspected.

Finally, Little D showed up. With a glance, we exited the restaurant.

We kept a distance of about 50 meters behind Little D and got onto the eastbound Zhang-Hui highway. Fifteen minutes later, we switched to a little dirt road. With a signal from Little D, the five of us quickly disappeared into the sugar cane field beside the road. We hid in the sugar cane field until it was completely dark. Little D returned with our provisions, along with two local young farmers. The six of us set off on our southbound journey right away. Passing a small village, we made our way up to Nan Mian Mountain. The first part of Plan A was completed successfully.

The first two days went smoothly. Kam followed me closely as we rested during the day and walked at night. On the third day, it rained, providing a good opportunity for us to collect drinking water. There were no bottled waters back then, and it was impossible to carry enough water for ten days. We had to rely on rivers, streams, or whatever nature bestowed upon us. We found a cave to keep ourselves dry and strangely encountered two groups of escapees, each consisting of 20 people. The rain lasted almost the entire day. When it got dark, everybody picked up their gear and started to roll.

All of a sudden, I lost control of my legs and felt dizzy. I couldn't even stand. I decided to keep the trouble to myself and told the others, "You guys go. I'll stay. If it gets worse, I'll surrender myself to the authorities; I should be able to get some medical care. Those two groups of 20 are experienced; you should stick with them. I won't blame you." Little D, Sam, and the two young farmers had no better choice, so they did exactly what I asked. But Kam didn't want to leave me behind alone. She made up her mind to stay with me.

Ever since that moment, we have been together for our whole lives, never apart. We must be destined.

After the others left, Kam found a big flat spot. She laid out a plastic sheet and helped me lie down. Then she found some clean water, mixed it with salt, and told me to drink it. She took out a piece of ginger, peeled it, and told me to chew on it slowly. Pretty soon, I felt heat surge through my entire body. It wasn't a fever; it was rather comfortable. I was very tired, so I tugged another sheet of plastic over myself and fell asleep.

When I woke up a little later, I saw that Kam was holding a corner of the plastic sheet to shield my head from the drizzling raindrops. I was still powerless, but I could hear her heartbeat—it was a bit rapid. In the mountains at night, sounds of the wind blowing, the rain, the insects, and even the howling of wild animals mixed together like a serenade. It was soothing. Little raindrops sometimes fell on my face; they felt cool and comfortable. When they fell on my lips, they tasted sweet. That was a comfortable and serene feeling I hadn't had for a long time. It was like my mommy coaxing me to sleep.

When I woke up again, the sun was already up. I felt completely recovered. I asked Kam how it was last night, and she said, "It was the scariest night I have ever experienced. I felt we were surrounded by lots of wild animals, and I did not sleep at all." I realized she had stayed up all night to be my guardian angel. How lucky was I to have her! Thank God, and thank Kam.

We gathered our stuff and located a safer spot to hide during the day.

At noon, all of a sudden, there were loud noises—people shouting all over the place. We were shocked and scared. There were also sounds of gunshots. Were they hunting or shooting at some escapees? There was no way for us to find out. Luckily, the noise faded away, and it became peaceful and quiet again.

At nightfall, we resumed our journey. With only the two of us, we were much less likely to be detected, making it easier for us to maneuver. In the entire mountain forest, we could only hear our own footsteps and occasional whispering. When we were tired, we sat down to take a break. I raised my head to look at the bright moon and the stars, then lowered it to gaze at the beautiful woman I was deeply in love with. What a beautiful life! What a beautiful moment! For a split second, I forgot we were in a fierce fight for our lives and our future.

"The long night is passing by, the sky is turning bright. Sincerely wishing you the best, my girl. I hope from now on, You and I will never forget this charming night." — Lyrics from the Russian folk song "The Night at the Outskirts of Moscow."

We went down Nan Mian Mountain, through Long Gang Plane. On our way, we navigated around two militiamen checkpoints and survived two patrolling squads. Kam was very scared at the beginning but adapted quickly.

On the third night, we reached the top of Da Gu Mountain. Just as we got ready to take a break, a low voice called out from the bushes in the dark, "Old Four?" It scared the hell out of me! But in a split second, I relaxed. Besides being nicknamed "Four-eye," I was sometimes called "Old Four," which also referred to my near-sighted glasses. Two pieces of glass plus two eyes equals four. That told me whoever called out that name must be someone who knew me well. Sure enough, five guys emerged from the bushes—they were friends: B Boy, Sunny, Chu, and Big Head, along with a young man from Dongguan whom they had met some time ago. (Although many people came through our place to initiate their journeys, I hardly knew their names. People were usually referred to by their school names, such as Fifth Middle, Sixth Middle, and Eighth Middle, and so on. When we met again many years later, people also identified themselves by their school names first.)

We were all thrilled to see each other in such a place and at such an occasion. They pulled out a can and opened it to treat us—it was braised pork. It was delicious, packed with protein. What a brotherhood! After we devoured our treat, we continued toward Mei Jian Mountain. At daybreak, we split into smaller groups and found our spots to hide for the day.

At nightfall, it was time for us to move again. B Boy said he had seen two men with rifles on their backs walking up the hill earlier. I suggested that we should go over the ridge and quickly go downhill without stopping. Everyone agreed. B Boy took the lead, followed by the young man from Dongguan, with me in third place. Following me were Kam, Sunny, Chu, and Big Head. (B Boy was the youngest; he was still in elementary school in 1966 when the Cultural Revolution started. His maternal grandfather was a high-ranking official of the Guo Min Tang in Taiwan. His parents faced brutal persecution during the Cultural Revolution and both committed suicide. B Boy wandered the streets all day with a knife in his pocket, figuring he had to be tough to survive. People in the neighborhood felt pity for him, and he was always invited to eat at the neighbors' homes.)

As we proceeded, I somehow sensed that something was off. I tried to prepare Kam for the unexpected. I told her, "If anything happens, just run. Don't stop. They have only two people, and they can't catch us all. There is a 10-second time delay between when they push the bullet into the chamber and when they fire; that is enough time for you to get away."

We reached the ridge and started to go downhill. Strangely, B Boy started to lead us back up to the ridge. Just as I was about to ask him for the reason, two bright white flashlight beams pierced through the darkness and landed on us.

"Who is that? Everybody freeze!" Followed by the loud and stern order was the unmistakable sound of bullets being bolted into the chambers of their rifles. In a split second, I quickly turned around and tried to signal Kam to run with me. But I was shocked to find that Kam and the people following me had all disappeared. I had no choice but to run. Just a couple of steps away, I jumped into some thick bushes. Damn! I was free-falling! Luckily, I only fell about 12 feet and landed between two big boulders. I held my breath, not daring to make any move. Through the coverage of the thick bushes, I saw three figures standing at the spot I had just jumped from. B Boy was being held by two armed militiamen.

"How many of you were together?" one asked. "There was one more," B Boy responded.

"Watch this guy; I'll go get the other," one militiaman told the other.

Five minutes later, he returned with another person—it was the young man from Dongguan. I felt a bit relieved that it wasn't Kam.

The two armed militiamen took their captives and left. Soon it was calm and quiet again. B Boy and the Dongguan man took the hit to save us. Thank them. I got out of the bushes and moved toward the spot where Kam had left me, but I couldn't find anything. By the time I reached the bottom of the hill, it was bright. At that moment, my own fate felt insignificant compared to Kam's safety. I desperately called out Kam's name as I wandered around the forest. "Where are you, Kam? Are you okay?" The valley echoed my cries. I didn't care if I got caught again; I could always try again. But Kam was so kind and innocent. What a terrible thing it would be if something bad happened to her!

At noon, I had to quit the search. I calmed myself, thinking perhaps she had also escaped the turmoil. The sea was not too far away. Hopefully, she could get to the water, cross it, and land in Hong Kong. God bless Kam!

When it was completely dark, I began to move south. Without Kam next to me, I couldn't care less; it actually made me feel more relaxed. Going over the hill, I could see the sea separating Hong Kong from the mainland. I stopped at mid-level and found a place to hide for the day. In the daylight, the surrounding area became much clearer to me. About 5 kilometers to the right, there appeared to be many buildings, which must be Shatoujiao. There were also buildings about 3 kilometers to the left, likely Yantian. Directly in front of me was a parabolic-shaped small bay. There were two rows of one-story housing; it must be the barracks. I dared to move lower until I could hear the sound of the waves. I was at the innermost part of the bay, like the origin of the parabola at (0,0). About 400 meters to my left seemed to be an outpost of the border guards. About 500 meters directly below was a cactus field. Beyond that lay the highway. South of the highway, there was another patch of cactus. There was about 10 meters of sandy beach between the cactus and the water. No one seemed to be on the highway all day, except for a few vehicles. It was very quiet.

When it was completely dark, I abandoned everything that was no longer needed and moved in front of the cactus that was as tall as I was. I took off my clothing and wrapped my head with it to protect myself from the thorns of the plant. I went through the cactus and ran across the highway, then passed through the second cactus field. Finally, I sprinted toward the sea.

I took a deep breath and swam underwater. Two breaths later, I had gone out comfortably far enough. I removed my long trousers and shoes, inflated the football liner that I had prepared as a flotation aid if needed, and swam forward as fast as I could. A few boats passed by, but they didn't bother. About an hour into my swimming, my feet touched the ground. A few minutes later, I landed on the soil of Hong Kong, the British Colony. Theoretically and practically, I was at that moment formally free from the jurisdiction of the Chinese communists! I looked back at the dark silhouette of the mainland and thought, goodbye; I don't care to set foot on that land again. I turned around to walk toward a bright future.

## A page was turned

A few days later, I was informed by friends who had arrived in Hong Kong earlier that Kam, Sunny, and Chu had made it successfully. It was the happiest moment of my life when Kam and I reunited in Hong Kong. After we both found our respective jobs and settled down, we got married. Within three years, we gave birth to two beautiful girls. In 1979, Kam, our two girls, and I immigrate, a country we've deeply loved. In 1991, our third daughter was born. All three of our daughters received excellent educations, earning their doctorate and master's degrees in law, architecture, and engineering. Kam and I had our opportunities for education taken away from us, but our daughters made up for what their mom and dad had lost in China. A couple of years after we settled in California, Kam and I started a plumbing business, which has been running successfully for the last few decades. Our family is thankful and grateful to this great country, and we pray to God to keep America great forever!

# Indomitable, Swim to Freedom

*By Old Guy, Pan*

## 1. 1966

For China, 1966 was an extremely unusual year. Why was it unusual? Because it marked the beginning of the "Cultural Revolution." This so-called "Cultural Revolution" started in May of 1966 and essentially ended in 1968. The Cultural Revolution turned upside down the social order that the Chinese Communist Party had established since coming to power in 1949, delivering a brutal blow to nearly every family in China. The economy was on the verge of collapse, and countless people suffered, died, or had their families shattered. During those two years, China's high school students were used by Mao to carry out the revolution to purge government, party, and army leaders he didn't like.

In 1978, the Third Plenary Session of the 11th Central Committee of the CCP characterized Mao's "Cultural Revolution" as a catastrophe, highlighting its absurdity and destructive power.

I was 15 years old in 1966 and was in the second year of middle school (8th grade) at Jiangmen No. 1 Middle School. With the onset of the Cultural Revolution, schools were closed, and both teachers and students were busy participating in the revolution. Many of those storming into action during those years were middle school students. Since my father was a factory worker and a Communist Party member, our family was categorized as one of the "five red categories." This gave me substantial political leverage to participate actively in the revolution. However, I was never able to fully embrace Mao's philosophy of class struggle and practically sidelined myself from the revolution. I did not join those so-called "combat ranks." However, I seized the opportunity for free train travel and successfully made my way to Shanghai, though I missed out on going to Beijing and, of course, did not see Chairman Mao, which was the most fashionable thing to do at the time.

While later, everyone with normal rationality acknowledged that the Cultural Revolution was an utterly absurd farce, at the time, not a single individual or organization dared to speak out against it, including the so-called "national leaders" or generals of the armed forces who fought and won the revolutionary war with Mao. Those leaders and generals suffered greatly, some even losing their lives, during the few years of the Cultural Revolution. Since the world began to recognize the Chinese, particularly in modern times, the intelligence of the Chinese people has been increasingly acknowledged globally. Yet, the absurdities of the "Great Leap Forward" in 1958, with its claims of harvests of "10,000 pounds or more of grain per acre," and the Cultural Revolution, along with various political movements in mainland China after 1949, were no less ridiculous than "The Emperor's New Clothes." In this vast country, not even a naive child was there to stand up and tell the truth to expose the lies!

For someone like me, a teenager, the Cultural Revolution decisively marked the end of my opportunities for education in China.

## 2. Going to the Countryside

In 1968, perhaps Mao had had enough of his madness, or maybe he had achieved his political goals by purging his rivals and was ready to wrap things up. It was time to hide the bow, eliminate the running dogs, and clean up the mess. However, he faced the problem of handling tens of millions of high schoolers. The way he used them in the two years of violent revolution had matured those youngsters in a very rebellious way. He could not send them back to school or simply allow them to stay in the cities. The economic destruction of the past two years made it even more impossible for the cities and towns to provide jobs for the tens of millions of them. So, Mao came up with the idea of sending these urban youth to the vast countryside, letting the peasants feed them. He issued the "highest directive" stating, "It is very necessary for educated youth to go to the countryside and receive re-education from the poor and lower-middle peasants." At the end of 1968, China launched the grand "educated youth up to the mountains and down to the villages" movement. In order to deceive the youngsters and persuade them to leave the cities, Mao's authority also glorified the movement as "The Great Strategy of Anti and Prevention of Revisionism," meaning to prevent China from becoming like the revisionist Soviet Union. Except for a small number—about 5%—of junior high school students who were allowed to stay in the cities and continue to senior high school, most students from grades 7 to 12 were considered graduates and scattered to rural areas and farms throughout China, relying on farmers to feed them.

The 5% who didn't need to go to the countryside were children of families with good status. They were allowed to stay in the cities and continue to senior high school. Almost all of those kids were given city jobs or continued to universities after just two years in senior high school, regardless of what they had actually learned. The 95%, no matter how unwilling, had to leave the cities and start their lives as peasants and farmers.

My father was a factory worker and always took pride in being a "Chinese Communist Party member." He firmly believed that I would definitely be able to stay in the city and continue my education, avoiding a move to the countryside. Just when my father was feeling self-satisfied, he received a notice from the factory: his son would not be staying in the city but going to the countryside! This was a thunderbolt out of the blue. How could this be?! At that time, the word on the street was that a sensitive member of the newly established Revolutionary Committee believed my father's history was not clean enough and recommended removing me from the list. The term "not clean enough history" referred to my father's forced labor in Indonesia during the Japanese occupation in World War II, where he was caught and made to work as a cook for the Japanese army. Although this was certainly unfortunate, he had already confessed to the authorities. It was completely illogical to remove me from the list. It was a serious matter—his son's future! My father insisted on reasoning with the military representative. However, even though I was just a teenager, I was wise enough to know that in that absolute totalitarian society, there was no room for reason and no legal basis. Even the President of the country could lose basic human rights and dignity, let alone us lowly citizens.

Despite my father's continuous disgruntles, I took the family residence booklet in hand, went to the local police station, and canceled my city residence registration.

On November 7, 1968, I became one of the over 17 million educated youths (EY) sent to the countryside after the Cultural Revolution.

Looking back decades later, I have to admit that going to the countryside had its positive aspects. Young people spending a few years in a harsh rural environment could benefit from the training, but that should have happened after their desired level of education. Moreover, they should not be forced to spend their lives in any place; they should be allowed to choose the profession they liked. However, at that time, the slogan was "root yourself in the countryside for a lifetime." In 1968, no one could foresee Mao's passing. If Mao had truly "Long Lived", the policy of sending EYs to the countryside would have continued. Not only could we not return to the cities, but our descendants for generations would have been condemned to being peasants. At that time, the material life of urban residents in China was already quite impoverished, and the peasants were in destitute. They were glorified by the government as the most revolutionary "poor and lower-middle peasants," but in reality, they were systematically relegated to the status of China's underclass. They were essentially trapped; moving to the cities was absolutely impossible. If we had rooted ourselves in the countryside, generation after generation of our family would have become de facto underclass.

By 1972, I had already spent four years in the countryside. Over the years, my father's repeated teachings to me were always the same: I must humbly learn from the poor and lower-middle peasants and must not do anything that goes against Mao Zedong's thoughts. This was the sorrow of the Chinese people. They had no personal values and could only parrot fashionable political slogans. I understood what he meant: comply, don't cause trouble. That was the life philosophy of the majority of Chinese people during that era, as the cost of not going with the flow was too high. As for what "Mao Zedong's thoughts" meant, not even an expert scholar with a higher education could explain it logically, let alone a factory worker with just an elementary education. If I pretended to conform to the so-called "party lines," I might gain favored treatment and increase my chances of transferring back to the cities. In those years, sporadically, some educated youths were occasionally allowed to leave the countryside. But the competition was fierce, and I knew I couldn't be one of them because I refused to act as a party-line follower. In the years that followed, I endured the hardships of manual labor. My labor capacity had reached the level of a first-class young male peasant; I could carry almost 100 kilograms on my shoulder. But rice farming didn't yield much profit, and the villagers were extremely poor. A good peasant barely made enough to buy food to feed one person. Fortunately, my father provided me with more than ten yuan each month, which helped me get by. But I couldn't rely on my father's support forever! Even the children of peasants dreamed of moving to the city, let alone us young people who grew up there. Like countless other EYs at the time, I certainly couldn't resign myself to being a farmer for the rest of my life. The question was: how could I get out of there?

## 3. Seeing Hope

In Guangdong, a coastal province, everyone knows that not far to the southeast lies a place called Hong Kong. I had long known that the preaching about "two-thirds of the world's population living in dire circumstances" was nonsense and never took it seriously. Almost everyone knows that people in Hong Kong not only enjoyed a materially superior lifestyle to ours but also experienced political freedoms akin to Western countries. In 1970, a girl EY (Educated Youth, the name generally given to those whose education was terminated and sent to the countryside after the Cultural Revolution.) attempted to sneak to Hong

Kong had failed and was captured and sent back to the production team. This was my first encounter with an escapee at such close quarters. It was her prescient father who took the excellent opportunity of the 1962 exodus to take his eldest son and daughter to Hong Kong. Now this delicate young woman of barely 18 was being forced to become the most primitive, hardest-working farmer for the rest of her life, barely making enough to survive. What else could be more ridiculous than this? Determined to reunite with her father, brother and sister in Hong Kong was undoubtedly her best choice. But faced with such a vivid example, the three of us stronger EY boys not only did not awaken but probably even mocked her capture with a certain feeling of schadenfreude. Perhaps it was due to regional differences; people from Guangzhou and Jiangmen, the town we were from, had different ways of thinking and understanding, probably a small-town-mentality. Of course, besides broader knowledge, boldness, and relatively flexible thinking, Guangzhou EYs were assigned to locations near Hong Kong, such as Panyu, Boluo, Dongguan, Huiyang, and even Bao'an, which were adjacent to Hong Kong. Those in these areas could even see the particularly bright night sky to the south at night, making them more likely to have the inspiration to escape. In contrast, Jiangmen EYs were mostly sent to rural areas in Xinhui and Sanshui Counties, and most students of our high school went to Muzhou Commune in Xinhui County. There were hardly any cases of EYs escaping in the entire commune.

In 1969, my cousin, who had been sent from Guangzhou to work in the countryside in Dongguan, made his way to Hong Kong. When I learned about this, I felt nothing—perhaps I thought it was too far away from me. In 1972, my aunt told me that my cousin, who was one year younger than me and used to spend every Chinese New Year with me, had successfully escaped to Hong Kong. It was barely a year after he was sent to the countryside, also as an Educated Youth (EY) with only elementary schooling. At the same time, his older sister, my other cousin, was actively arranging her own itinerary. The news of my younger cousin's departure greatly shocked me. The actions of him and his sister finally awakened me thoroughly. It was an epiphany! Going to Hong

Kong was indeed the correct path! I made a firm decision to learn from my cousins, to learn from the Guangzhou EYs! I later learned that as early as 1968 and 1969, some foresighted Guangzhou EYs purposefully arranged their relocation sites to areas like Dongguan and Bao'an to facilitate sneaking into Hong Kong. A good friend told me that when the authorities just started persuading, she readily agreed to go to Dongguan without needing much persuasion. A 20-year-old girl, seeing through the essence of the authoritarian regime cloaked in beautiful attire, meticulously planned to risk crossing borders to seek freedom. Knowing she couldn't change it and couldn't afford to confront it, she could only stay far away. What else could be better for her than being assigned to a border area close to Hong Kong? After arriving in Hong Kong, this friend not only became economically independent but also continued her education. By the 1970s, almost every EY who had been sent to the Pearl River Delta from Guangzhou knew about the act of escaping to Hong Kong. Many thought about it, many went, some were caught and sent back, and some even disappeared without a trace.

Upon returning home, I couldn't contain my excitement at the dinner table and revealed my cousins' endeavors to my father. Of course, my father sensed my inner thoughts during our conversation. But he didn't express any opinion. Deep down, he certainly wished for me to reach Hong Kong safely like my cousins, but he also knew that this venture wasn't without risks; getting caught was just a minor issue compared to the possibility of losing one's life while attempting to cross perilous seas. It was the struggle between immense temptation and danger that left him undecided. I couldn't worry about all that; the idea of going to Hong Kong had firmly taken root in my mind. The only thing troubling me at the time was that I didn't have close relatives willing to support me upon arrival. Although I had grandparents and uncles in Hong Kong, they weren't wealthy. They were working hard in Hong Kong, rarely having the leisure to return to Guangzhou for a vacation. Since they moved to Hong Kong, which was around the time I was 8. I had never spoken to them as an adult, let alone discussing this serious issue with them.

However, this minor challenge couldn't deter my dream from

fermenting. I started to refuse to participating in the hard labor that was wasting my youth, often sneaking away to Guangzhou, the capital of escapees to immerse myself in the culture of escaping, to find ways to get out. Three male EYs from our production team, Michael, Ball, and I, lived together in the same house. It seemed they had awakened to the idea earlier than me and were scheming separately to find a route. In April or May of 1973, Michael told me he had found an arrangement. With envy in my heart, I saw him off at the Guangzhou Baiyun Road Guangzhou-Kowloon Railway Station. Three weeks later, I received his triumphant letter, adorned with a postage stamp bearing the image of Queen Elizabeth II. Excited and jealous at the same time, my determination to go to Hong Kong grew stronger. Ball also became active. He faced several setbacks but finally made it to Hong Kong at the end of 1973.

News of friends reaching Hong Kong kept coming as relentless stream of blows mercilessly struck my nerves, tormenting my soul with envy and jealousy. Wang Qiang, a good friend from the same factory dormitory area as me, had become a popular figure, earning the favor of EYs and locals alike, and even becoming the secretary of the local Communist Youth League branch. When he returned to the city, he would eagerly inquire about any new directives from the central government or Premier Zhou Enlai regarding the future fate of us EYs. In reality, he was just eager to know if there was any hope that our exile would end. As the dream seemed increasingly distant, he also realized that hoping for the central government to transfer him back to the city from the countryside was practically hopeless. I also told him that I increasingly lost faith of being transferred back to the city as a possibility. Regarding the issue of escaping, there were rumors that Premier Zhou Enlai had changed the categorization of sneaking into Hong Kong from "treason" to "illegal visiting." This change undoubtedly ease many people's concerns; even if they failed, the punishment would be relatively light.

Some nights, we were walking along the riverbank, gazing at the flowing river, searching for inspiration to escape. The current situation and our mission were clearly laid out before us. Wang Qiang sighed with helplessness about the current situation but gradually became more determined to go to Hong Kong. As for concerns about support, we thought: let's cross that bridge when we come to it; perhaps things would naturally fall into place when the time came.

Besides determination, the most crucial aspect of going to Hong Kong was having support in the border areas. This support could come from EYs or local farmers, and naturally, the closer to Hong Kong, the better. At that time, Huanggang in Bao'an and Shekou were ideal landing points along the Hong Kong border, very close to the point of entry, but special border passes were required to go to those places. Ordinary people couldn't obtain border passes, so most had to depart from places far from these sensitive border areas, such as Boluo, Zhangmutou, Shilong in Dongguan, Huizhou, Danshui, and so on. These routes involved traveling days and nights, traversing mountains and ridges, and evading the search of militia. Generally, it would take about two weeks to reach the crossing point. Before entering the water, many had to pass through the national defense highways guarded by border soldiers equipped with military dogs. Many were caught by several military dogs and arrested. Besides military dogs, those traveling to Hong Kong's eastern route also had to worry about sharks. After overcoming the arduous mountain roads and the military dogs on the national defense highways, many ultimately perished from the freezing cold seawater or fell prey to sharks. Unfortunately, we didn't have connections even in places like Boluo, Dongguan, or Huizhou, let alone Bao'an. Apart from directly going to Hong Kong, about 20% of people took the route through Macao. The only problem was that the Macao authorities had an agreement with the mainland to repatriate illegal immigrants. Therefore, one couldn't stay long in Macao and had to go through an additional process called "Qu She" (snake sneaking) to reach Hong Kong. The ideal landing crossing points in Macao were Qianshan, Wanzai, and Tanzhou in Zhuhai. However, entering these places was also difficult and required border passes. Most people could only start from the north of Zhongshan or Zhuhai and travel days and nights for about a week to reach places where they could cross into Macao. I hadn't heard of anyone being bitten by military dogs in Zhongshan or Zhuhai. Furthermore, due to the large outflow of river water, there were fewer sharks in the waters near the mainland side of Macao.

Whether in Hong Kong or Macao, such connections were hard to come by, and they were more of a matter of luck than anything else. Even the best subjective initiative might not be of much use.

## 4. The First Trial

Where there is a will, there is a way. Ever since my revolutionary visions took shape, I started seeking out and mingled with some people who had already taken action in their pursuit for Hong Kong. Around mid-1973, two female EY friends from a small escapee circle invited me to join their plan. It was a Macao-route through Zhuhai. For such a godsend opportunity, without hesitation, I decided to go along.

One summer day that year, my younger brother gave me a ride on his bicycle to Shiqi Town in Zhongshan County, where I bought a bus ticket for Dajinding in Zhuhai with a fake ID. Before noon, the two women showed up to take the same bus as agreed. We pretended not knowing each other and got on the bus separately. After more than an hour, we arrived at Dajinding and got off the bus one after another. I noticed some militiamen carrying rifles patrolling near the station, and the atmosphere was tense. The two women walked in front, and I followed behind. After entering a bamboo grove, I saw them enter a public restroom. Since I couldn't aimlessly continue walking alone, I had no choice but to enter the men's restroom on the other side. After a few minutes, I came out of the restroom, ready to meet up with them and continue the journey. But the two women were not in sight. Mindful of the militiamen outside the grove, I didn't dare to call out. In that environment, any unusual move could attract the attention of the militiamen, so I had to linger around the restroom for a while. But even after looking around the grove, the two women were nowhere to be found. Could they have gone forward? Prior to setting out for our journey, I hadn't had the chance to meet the local liaison in Zhuhai and didn't know how to make the contact or get provisions. But since I had come this far, what else could I do but move forward? Perhaps if I quickened my pace, I might catch up with them. So I sped up and walked until dark. As hope of catching up with them faded, I became increasingly confused and my resolve began to waver. Seeing a sugarcane field by the roadside, I plunged into it, temporarily escaping reality. Squatting in the field, I pondered the situation at that time and the actions to be taken. In fact, the reality was quite obvious: no provisions, no reception in Macao, and continuing further probably meant no way out. I finally decided to spend the night hiding in the sugarcane field and retreat the next morning along the same route. There I was, squatting in the sugarcane field all night.

As dawn broke the next day, I walked northbound along the road, heading back home. After walking for two hours, not far from the hometown of Dr. Sun Yat-sen in Cuiheng Village, I saw a checkpoint set up by several militiamen interrogating passersbys. They also saw me, and it was too late to hide, so I had to pass by them with a bold face. Needless to say, they quickly found out what I was doing and sent me to the Jinzhong Detention Center. My maiden voyage ended in prison.

I later learned that the two girls didn't succeed either. They had hidden behind the restroom in the bamboo grove only to avoid passing pedestrians and never entered or used the restroom as I had thought. While I kept walking forward trying to catch up with them, they spent almost two hours searching for me around the bamboo grove. What a coincidence! After five days and nights of crossing mountains and rivers, the two fragile girls persisted until they reached the water. Due to exhaustion and fear of the waves, they prematurely used their floatation devices, and were spotted by a patrolling militia boat, and caught. Had we not separated they would surely have been able to preserve their energy more effectively; also, had I been there at the time, we wouldn't have needed to use the floatation devices, more likely to have evaded the patrolling militia.

## 5. The Second Trial

After two months of detention, I was taken back to the production team in the countryside. Shortly after, news came that Ball had also successfully reached Hong Kong. The news stabbed me hard once again. I didn't tell the production team about the successful escape of Michael and Ball. This way, I could at least continue to receive their food rations. The grain rations in the production team were at the government-set price, 9.80 RMB per 100 catty, while the black market price was 30 RMB. The Pearl River Delta in Guangdong had fertile land and was considered wealthier than other provinces. However, grain shortages was still a problem. There were at least two weeks out of a year that people would run out of grain. A black market for grains was then inevitable. Selling at the black market price of 30 RMB, I could earn twenty yuan RMB. At that time, each of us received about 600 catties of grain rations per year, so with the two of them combined, I could have sold 1200 catties in the black market and earn 240 yuan per year, which was a huge sum. But I wasn't that aggressive. I only sold 200 catties and made 40 yuan RMB. At the same time, we EYs received pork rations each month. I of course took advantage of their shares. That and some extra money, my material life wasn't too bad, at least I was able to maintain the minimum level of protein in-take on a daily basis.

However I now had to start all over again, struggle to find any connections along the border.

Ever since going to the countryside, I was upset that my education opportunity was disrupted at the age of 15. I had only two years of middle school education. Was this how my life would be? What about my dream of going to university? At the very least, couldn't I finish just high school? In the second year of middle school, we studied algebra, just completing factorization of quadratic equations and function graphs. The study of calculus I had dreamed of all along was now out of reach? This realization filled me with fear. As long as I could seize the opportunity, I wanted to learn something to enrich myself. But it was not fashionable to study academic subjects, doing so would be frowned upon. Therefore, I didn't dare to look for textbooks on mathematics and science to study. English was the only subject I thought of and had the opportunity to flip through some books here and there. There was an EY from Guangzhou No. 7

Middle School who showed me an English textbook compiled by Peking University. I borrowed it for a while; pronunciation and phonetics were no problem for me. What troubled me was grammar that I hadn't learned well in the second year of middle school. I kept dwelling on the first few chapters and couldn't progress.

During workdays I tried to find ways to escape from the meaningless labor. Every night, I would turn on the radio I somehow acquired and tuned in to Voice of America on shortwave. The program "English 900" was heavenly attractive. One time the cadre named Gao Jian who was responsible for supervising the EYs, happened to come to our production team. The floorboards weren't soundproof at all; I was sure he couldn't understand the Mandarin broadcast of Voice of America, but he could detect that the tone wasn't right, so he shouted loudly from downstairs: "That's enough, immediately stop that reactionary thing!"

There was a local young girl whose father was a famous doctor at the village health center. She graduated from a nearby junior high school prior to turning twenty. The girl came from a "noble" family and was considered educated. Through the loose floorboards, she might occasionally hear me listening to the "English 900" program on the radio. As a young intellectual of the time, she might have consciously despised the political rebelliousness and developed a liking for its trendy and fashionable nature. The fact that I was studying English might've impressed her. One evening, after she finished recording work points, she came up to my floor and actually asked me about the usage of English articles. Although my grammar in the second year of middle school was a mess, I could still manage to answer some of her questions. Because my pronunciation was pretty good, correcting her English with a rural accent was an easy task. We were sitting very close to each other. Observing her lips as she pronounced words, I noticed a barely perceptible hint of a mocking smile, but her eyes betrayed her, revealing a look of trust and admiration. Looking at her seemingly affectionate eyes, I suddenly felt dizzy, confused for a moment, and couldn't control myself. I reached out and held her hand... Suddenly, she stood up abruptly, rudely pushing away my hand, and said sharply, "Damn you!" before hurriedly running away and downstairs.

I was embarrassed, regretful to death. The next day, I seized an opportunity to sincerely apologize to her. She was a little shy but very genteel, softly saying: "It's nothing, never mind."

I guessed that she wasn't really extremely angry and didn't mean to curse me. It was just an instinctive reaction by a completely inexperienced girl in fear. Fortunately, I appreciated her firm stance. Had she not firmly rejected my decadent bourgeois intentions and instead allowed me to hold her hand, then even hug her into my arms, a 23-year-old male like me might not have controlled myself. Had she been half-hearted and let me do what all young men like to do, then I would have been in trouble. Moreover, from her indifference the next day and her shy, softly expressed forgiveness, I sensed that she harbored no grudges against me. Had I continued to entangle with her, dragging her into the river of love would not have been difficult, young women in the countryside marrying an EY was still relatively desirable and even fashionable at the time. Objectively speaking, to rural young women, a 23-year-old young man with almost a junior high school education from the city, and basically mastering all farming techniques, was quite an ideal marital choice. If I had intentions to root myself in the countryside, becoming the son-in-law of a famous doctor in the village could be a high probability. Fortunately, I came to my senses that night.

That was my only experience with the opposite sex in the land where I had lived for twenty-four years: I only touched the hand of a rural young woman with a junior high school education, and I didn't even succeed! This was a lesson! After experiencing this painful encounter, I vowed never to let myself fall again.

I quickly pulled myself back onto the right track. My revolutionary spirit was obviously vigorous.

In the summer of 1974, Wang Qiang, who used to confide in me, saw me go once and became envious. Another EY friend Cheng Yu, also expressed interest. With these two additional comrades joining, we decided to form our own group. Since we had no contacts to go directly to Hong Kong, we had to go through Macao. We decided: if there were no conditions, we would create them. On the first or fifteenth day of the lunar month, the sea water would recede at midnight. On the first day, there was no moon, the outgoing tide was weaker; on the fifteenth, the water flow was much stronger, but the moon was high in the sky, making it relatively risky. We decided to take the conservative route and chose the first day. The plan was to take public transport south to the middle of Doumen County, find a place to hide and wait until dark, then head east to the Modaomen waterway. After dark, we would swim eastward from Modaomen. This method required swimming for two nights. The target for the first night was Hengqin Island across from Zhuhai, and we would hide on the island during the day. On the second night, we would swim to Macao from Hengqin Island. Swimming thirty kilometers of waterway between Doumen and Hengqin sounded daunting. But in the summer, the rivers filled with plenty of rainwater flowed quickly toward the sea, reaching speeds of up to five kilometers per hour. After testing in inland rivers, we found that we could cover thirty kilometers in less than six hours. We figured that we would reach Hengqin Island in five hours on the first night, and it should be easy to swim the rest on the second night. At that time, everywhere we went on public transport needed a pass from the production team. The blank passes were pre-printed with ink, and the clerk filled in the contents with a fountain pen. We saved used passes for future needs. We created new passes by soaking them in hydrogen peroxide in a plate, steaming them in a pot, and the fountain pen writing would disappear, leaving only the ink part, and then we could fill in whatever we wanted.

In June, we decided to take a gamble. We took a passenger boat from the commune, Muzhou Town, southward to Baijiao Town in Doumen. At the station before Baijiao, we disembarked using a rowboat to bypass the Baijiao terminal, where militiamen conducted inspections. After leaving the boat, we needed to find a place to hide and wait until dark to head east to reach the river section where we could enter the Modaomen estuary. We saw a cement bunker on a small hill; we quickly climbed the hill and entered the bunker. After a short while, it started to rain, and we heard someone bringing a ladder and climbing up to the roof of the bunker. I understood it was because of the rain, someone came to collect the crops being sun-dried on the flat roof of the bunker. Shortly after, this person came down the roof and wanted to open the door to bring in his crops. Cheng Yu hurriedly used his shoulder to hold the door shut. What a dumb move? This guy obviously knew the bunker well. If we shut him out, would he alert someone and get us all in trouble? I pushed Cheng Yu aside with one hand and opened the wooden door with the other. The person stumbled and almost fell into my arms. When he saw the three of us, he was also greatly startled. I guessed he probably quickly realized who we were. He apologized humbly, and wanted to leave in a hurry. But I was not going to let him leave so easily! I grabbed his wrist and didn't let him go, while comforting him that we wouldn't harm him. Wang Qiang also quickly took out his ration coupons and several pieces of Chinese currency, stuffing them into his hand. Seeing that we meant no harm, the man relaxed. But of course, we didn't hide our secret from him and instead told him everything. The man said: "I myself have been bullied for many years because I'm from a well-to-do peasant background. If I had the audacity, I would have escaped long ago." Since that was the case, I decided to take a chance and believe him. I asked him to return to his shack and cook us some food.

He left. In less than an hour, he brought us food; he had slaughtered a chicken he raised and cooked a pot of white rice for us. He only asked us to send him a bottle of peanut oil after we arrived in Hong Kong. But he never told us his name and address.

We successfully entered the water and reached the main channel on time at around 12 midnight. After swimming for half an hour, I made a fatal mistake: at around 1 a.m., I saw a boat with dim lights in a distance, wondering what that was. I turned my head around and shouted loudly to urge my two companions who were falling behind to catch up. All of a sudden, the boat turned on its thundering engine and the mother of all lights turned on. That boat was lying in ambush waiting to hook us. As a result, none of the three of us could get away. They tied us tightly to the guardhouse outside and let the torrential rain and hungry mosquitoes take turns tormenting us all night. The next day, two militiamen carrying "Type 79" rifles tied us up with a rope and took us to the Doumen detention center, where we were detained for about a month before being transferred to the Xinhui detention center. Before August, the three of us were escorted back to the production team.

## 6. The Third Trial

While still in detention, Wang Qiang and I thought it over and realized that Macau was not as unreachable as we had initially imagined. We learned from our fellow inmates that we were caught by the notorious so-called "Fifth Perimeter Outpost." However, they were just outfitted with a boat anchored in the middle of the river. On a dark night like that, if we quietly advanced and bypassed that point, the hurdles shouldn't be too great. So we decided to give it another try immediately.

Cheng Yu had been bullied by other detainees in the detention center. Some one literally urinated on his face while sleeping at night. It was a large cell and there were hundreds of inmates and it was impossible to find out who did such a horrible prank. In fact Cheng Yu didn't even tell us about it until we were released from prison. Had we known it, could it be possible for us to beat the hell out of the guy to revenge it? Yes. If we had known who the guy was, the three of us could probably have jumped him. Just probably. I have to admit, none of us three were the fighting type. But it deeply traumatized Cheng Yu. He withdrew.

One day in mid-August, just over two weeks after we were released from prison, Wang Qiang and I decided to give it another shot. Following the same method as before, we still took the boat south from Muzhou, hiding in the same location after disembarking. We even let the same man from the shack cook dinner for us again, and we made the same promise to send him a can of peanut oil. After dark, we followed the same route to the Modaomen River estuary. From the hiding bunker to the Modaomen River, we had to pass through several villages, many fields, and streams, covering a distance of two or three hours.

But as luck would have it, that night we encountered particularly tight ground patrols. Dogs barked intermittently, and flashlight beams flashed here and there, indicating a "situation." Old Wang and I, moving through fields and streams, were extra cautious. As a result, we delayed getting into the water. By the time we finally reached the riverside, it was close to 1 a.m. In theory, at this hour, the ebbing tide would have slowed down, negatively impacting our swimming speed. We figured without four or five hours on the first night, we couldn't swim the twenty kilometers to Hengqin Island opposite Macao before daybreak. Getting into the water at this time would be futile. So we retreated to a sugarcane plantation to wait for the second night.

The next day, the scorching August sun made the plantation hotter than a steamer, but we persevered, enduring the torture of the intense heat without daring to leave to find water. Perhaps our fate was not yet sealed; just after we successfully endured the most painful afternoon hours of intense heat, around four o'clock, several militiamen wielding clubs suddenly appeared in front of us, looking fierce and menacing. They shouted, "Where are the others?!" I was puzzled, where could the others be? We had obediently hidden in the sugarcane plantation, so how did they manage to pinpoint us so accurately? It turned out that there were others hiding on the nearby hills, unable to bear the heat, they came down to find water and were spotted by the militiamen, leading to a search. By chance, they found us hidden in the plantation. If we had known this earlier, we might as well have gotten into the water the night before, and perhaps we would have had a better outcome.

## 7. Had to break out of Jail

In less than two years, I got caught three times. These three cases were no joke. If I were caught again, I worried that the case would be upgraded to a "criminal" level, and it wouldn't be just an "internal conflict among the people" anymore. With this in mind, I opted for a made up "false identification". It meant that my name, address, and workplace were all fake. I randomly made up an address from a certain commune in Taishan, along with a fake name. At that time, China didn't have a system to verify authenticity, but you had to escape or break out before someone found out your true identity. That way, one case could be completely wiped out. However, if you couldn't find an opportunity to escape or got caught, you would definitely face harsher punishment.

From the moment of escort, I kept looking for a chance to free myself. However, with my hands tied and two armed militiamen, I had no way out. After walking for two to three hours, we were taken to the Doumen detention center and thrown into a cell with twenty-some others. Prison inmates were let out every morning to wash by the well. Meals were also served outside in the court yard for lunch and dinner. We queued up, squatted in the open space, waiting to receive and eat our meals. There was also a chance to bathe by the well at night. The two daily washing sessions appeared to be the most free moments for us. I noticed a low wall about seven feet high with sharp glass pieces on top. I thought to myself, If I could find a gap when the guards weren't paying attention, I could throw something up there and use a ten-foot run-up to flip over. The problem was, I couldn't know what was on the other side of the wall. If it was a cliff, even a twenty to thirty-foot fall could be fatal. I abandoned the idea of climbing the wall.

While I was painstakingly searching for an opportunity to escape, I noticed three guys in our cell were always huddled together conspiratorially. One afternoon, one of them, a tall guy, walked to the corner of the "toilet", got up on the low wall, and reached up to push the tiles above. "Oh, my God! They're thinking the same thing as me!" But no matter how hard he tried, he couldn't move those tiles. Seeing his frustration, I stepped forward and offered to try. After assessing that I was shorter than him, the guy hesitated for a moment, and with a hint of disdainful smirk on his lips, he stepped back from the low wall. I got up, lifted my feet, hooked the beam with my left hand, suspended myself in midair, like a monkey hanging from a tree, then extended my right arm and exerted a force, loosening the tiles on top. Everyone in the cell watched the situation unfold in silence. When they saw the light coming through the loosened roof, they all softly exclaimed in unison. Everyone understood what was happening and the seriousness of it. After completely resetting the loosened tiles, I silently descended from the low wall.

After dark, I went back to the low wall and carefully moved away the loosened tiles, creating a hole about two feet square, then came down. It was somewhat risky to be the first one to climb out, but as the hero making the hole, I naturally had the privilege to choose when to go out. One guy volunteered to go first and crawled out. He peeked in and whispered, "It's clear," then disappeared into the darkness. I followed suit. Wang Qiang followed me. And along with four other cell mates, we decided to travel together. I had no idea how many people all together got out that night.

Within half an hour, we felt our way onto the northbound road. At that time, it was impossible to continue fleeing. We just wanted to return home. The six of us marched in a hurry, with me at the back. After walking for about half an hour, suddenly, several bicycles came up from behind and passed by us. In the darkness, I could see that they were carrying rifles on their backs. An ominous thought flashed through my mind, and with a "crash," this group of people suddenly braked in front of us. "Oh no!" Before they had a chance to speak, I instinctively shrunk my body and rolled into the bushes beside the road. Below was a small creek only a few inches deep. I quickly sank my body into the mud, leaving only my face exposed. The people above waved flashlights, shouting, cursing, searching, causing a commotion for about ten minutes before taking their five trophies away. Worried about an ambush, I laid in the mud for at least half an hour before daring to come out. That really scared me out of my wits, turning me into a genuinely scared bird. After climbing out of the mud, I found that I had lost one of my shoes in the chaos. The torrential rain that followed washed away the mud on my body, but the confusion and fear left me disoriented. In the pouring rain, I was bewildered and terrified, so I had no choice but to hide in the green curtain of the south — the sugarcane field, spending the night there.

## 8. On the Run

It was a clear day the next day, with not a cloud in the sky. The August sugarcane was so small that it couldn't even be eaten, but the leaves were just tall enough to block the rare cool breeze, and short enough to let the scorching sun bake every inch of the land. At noon, the farmers carrying sprayers to spray pesticides passed by me, spraying me all over, yet they didn't notice me.

Although it was hot, I could breathe a sigh of relief and figure out the direction. After nightfall, I felt my way out of the sugarcane field, walked through the fields, waded through small brooks, and headed towards the highway. Once, as I approached a clump of banana trees, I suddenly heard the very distinct sound of someone hitting banana leaves behind the trees. I quickly retreated and lay behind the ridge to wait and see what was going on. A minute or two later, seeing no movement, I moved forward again. When I reached the same point, the sound came again. I jumped behind the ridge again. At this point, the word "ghost" flashed through my mind. I calmed down and walked forward. "Okay," I said, "if you're here to catch me, just come out and catch me. If you're a ghost, please tell me what you want me to do for you, don't play around." After saying this, I stood still for about a minute, letting "it" think it over. Not hearing anything, I continued on my way, and the sound didn't appear again.

After reaching the highway, I crouched down to observe the situation. Occasionally, a "Gongnong Ten" hand tractor roared past, as if it were charging towards me to hunt me down. I didn't dare to walk along the highway, I found a gap to run across it and continued along the mountain path. That night, the foot without a shoe was cut in several spots by rocks and thorns. I sat on the ground intending to alleviate the pain. With my eyes open, I seemed to see around me inmates sitting in the same barn, and I actually started talking to them. By that time, I had been on the run for twenty-four hours, no sleep, without a drop of water, or a grain of food. Although I hadn't eaten for 24 hours, I didn't even feel hungry. I was too concentrated on evading catch. But now I was truly exhausted. Humans accustomed to group living find it very uncomfortable to be alone in panic for a long time. It could probably be one of the reasons that cause schizophrenia.

A minute or so later, I got my senses back and I continued walking on the mountain in the faint light. Suddenly I felt stepping on some hollow and in a split second, my chin slammed hard into my knees, causing my chest to ache so much that I blacked out for a few seconds. Looking back, it seemed that I had fallen from a small cliff about ten feet high. I continued walking with a limping gait, but misfortune struck again as I fell into a knee-deep quagmire. Trying to get out, I suddenly sank waist-deep. Too frightened to care about the mud, I immediately tried to lie down as flat as possible and half crawled, half rolled to drag myself out of the quagmire. Unaware of how much time had passed, I walked for another couple of hours, in pain, tired, and hungry. Suddenly, not far away, I saw a dark patch that looked like a sweet potato field. I approached it eagerly, feeling like a starving ghost. I reached out and indeed felt sweet potato vines, so I dug my hands into the mud, only to find a few thin roots. Nevertheless, I picked a few slightly thicker ones, wiped off the dirt, and sat down to enjoy my first meal in thirty hours.

With a sense of alert, I still had to avoid any place with human traces or light. In the darkness, I once again lost my direction. When I reached a hilltop, it suddenly started pouring rain. Helpless, I sat on the hilltop, using the excuse of being lost to give myself a chance to rest. The pouring rain washed away the mud on my body, and it felt like a water blanket had been draped over me, blocking the chill wind. In comfort, I fell asleep with my head on my knees. I didn't know when the rain stopped. When I woke up, it was around seven or eight o'clock, and another sunny day. From the mountain top, I could see that I was near the Doumen Brigade, in close proximity of the border with Xinhui County, which was actually where I wanted to go. Since I had lost one shoe and wearing only one looked suspicious, I threw away the other one. Wearing the nice cloths that was prepared for Macao (after landing in Macau, one had to wear fashionable clothes for disguise to evade the Macao police, and I spent about thirty yuan to buy two sets of clothes from a Hong Kong visitor),

I walked down the mountain barefooted. Occasionally, EY-looking young men rode past me on a bicycles, some looked back at me with strange looks. In the Pearl River Delta region in the early 70's, it was rare to see EYs dressed in old military uniforms, wearing military caps, and dressing like Red Guards. Instead, they gradually developed a rebellious consciousness by expressing themselves through their clothing and appearance. Progressive in their thinking, both male and female EYs liked to wear clothes imported through Hong Kong and Macao connections and would also apply popular hair gel. Therefore, just by appearance, I could judge who could offer me a helping hand. I was quite confident that I could convince someone to take me back to their place, let me take a good bath, eat a ton of food, sleep well, and then lend me some money so that I could openly take public transportation to escape from that troublesome place. I had several impulses to ask for their help, but the words kept slipping from my lips, thinking that I had already escaped from danger, and I would rather save the glory of a successful escape entirely to myself.

## 9. Got Recaptured

I shouldn't have been so confident. Perhaps it was not the end of my suffering. I was leisurely walking, feeling satisfied, when suddenly a big hand heavily smacked my shoulder. I turned around to see the stern smile of the head of the detention center, Mr. Guo. "Head Guo," I reluctantly called out to him. My instinct at the time was not to provoke him so as to avoid a beating. As it turned out, it just happed to be a day that our jail transferred prisoners to another detention house, the truck driver stopped to eat, and the truck happened to be parked at a three-way intersection I had passed. Mr. Guo was sitting next to the driver's seat watching me walk by. It was just a strange coincidence. After escaping for a day and a half, I was caught again. How a rotten luck that was? Perhaps he was busy with the transfer, and my cooperative attitude saved me from a beating. He tied me up tightly and had a transport bicycle take me back to the detention center. My fellow inmates from the second cell could be seen peering through the gaps between the few round logs at the door. They were amazed that I had been caught after being out for so long.

That evening, I was ordered to embrace a tree about 16 inches in diameter with both hands handcuffed, deprived me of food and water, as a form of punishment. The tree was outside the windows of the women's cell. It was a hot August night in the South, and we men naturally slept with bare chests at night. For security reasons, the male guards often peered into our cell through the few door pillars. The female inmates, however, had to wear only underwear to cover sensitive areas, trying to stay cool. Through the windows, whether I liked it or not, the movements of the female inmates in thin underwear on the beds cruelly invaded my sight. I had never seen such exposed women before. It was unbearable! I couldn't keep my eyes shut — the scene in front of me made me uneasy, yet I couldn't keep my eyes closed either. I wasn't sure if the guards had purposely added this torment for me.

Later on, my cellmates told me that twenty people had escaped that night, but fifteen were caught no more than four hours later, and I had become the sixteenth. Four guys successfully freed themselves.

Capturing eighty percent of escapees somehow satisfied the detention center. The next day, all escapees were gathered to have our heads shaved. After the ceremony, the guards brought sixteen pairs of handcuffs for each of us. Some pleaded with the guards to loosen the handcuffs, but the guards only made them tighter, leaving the pleaders regretful. Seeing it, I decided not to bother. In the next three months, in all aspects of daily life from brushing teeth to eating, bathing, and using the restroom, we were never separated from the handcuffs.

One time, there was a fight in the neighboring cell which left someone severely injured. It was a serious matter, so the detention center decided to hold a criticism meeting to educate the fighters and escapees. We were taken outside the cell kneeling in a row on the gravel ground. The guards, in order to enhance the intimidation, even crossed our handcuffed hands behind our backs and waved a stick in front of us while shouting instructions. One of the guards didn't like the way he was looked at by the inmate next to me, he jabbed a stick at the guy's face, causing him to fall to the ground in pain, face covered in blood, snot and tears. The guy had to endure it without complaining or showing any sign of displeasure. Otherwise, the punishment could be more severe. The rest of the guards made loud noises with their sticks, occasionally hitting our shaven heads. I had always been obedient in prison, knowing how to behave to avoid unnecessary punishments.

Since then life became very calm. With the handcuffs on for over three months, I experienced a rare tranquility in life. I knew they wouldn't release me anytime soon, and I had nothing to worry about in the present, tomorrow, or the day after. After the jail breakout incident, the detention center added a layer of bamboo nets on top of all the roofs. Coupled with the handcuffs on our hands, escape became absolutely impossible. This gave me a good reason for peace of mind. The exquisite tranquility of that state of mind was something I had never experienced before and never would again. If there were books, I believe there would have been no better learning environment than that. To pass the time, during the day in the cell, we tried every way to entertain ourselves. We made chess pieces out of paper. Despite the handcuffs, we even played arm wrestling. After getting tired, we boasted about the food and drinks we had enjoyed or heard of.

The Detention Center of Doumen had a strange rule: detainees could receive packages from their families. This rule allowed us to have cigarettes mailed to us by our families, which was the most humane act. On the Mid-Autumn Festival Day in 1974, not only did we have meat for supper, many of us, including myself, also received mooncakes sent from home. Through those cylindrical pillars, we were able to enjoy the bright full moon. The cellmate Aji, who was jabbed by the guard, was an excellent storyteller. Even the simple phrase "the sun rises from the east" became highly entertaining when spoken by him. He claimed he could recite the entire novel "The Count of Monte Cristo" by Alexandre Dumas and recounted it for two nights. Waving his handcuffed hands, Aji added dramatic gestures, making the story even more captivating. On the third day, he procrastinated, saying he was too tired to continue, which annoyed everyone in the cell. While everyone knew what he was up to, no one had the courage to confront him. I, on the other hand, am always good at finding solutions to problems. I suggested that we each offer a spoonful of our food to him at every meal so he would continue the story. He pretended to be shy but eventually agreed.

My suggestion was met with approval from most of the cellmates, although some objected, claiming they had already heard the story and didn't care to sacrifice a portion of their meal. During mealtime, most of the cellmates voluntarily shared their food, while a few deliberately avoided the situation, hoping to save that spoonful of rice. During mealtime, I guided Aji and walked around the cell, making sure Aji gets that extra spoonful of rice from those who wanted the story to continue. There is a saying: "With great rewards come great heroes." With the 15 additional spoonfuls of rice at each meal, Aji's spirits were uplifted, and his storytelling with handcuffed hands became even more mesmerizing, lasting over two months.

The guards soon caught on to our activities, and from then on, some of them would come up, leaning against the door's round logs, spending good times with us. Aji was good at adjusting his storytelling based on his audience, and he particularly enhanced scenes involving food and feasts. For instance, when he described Edmund Dantes escaping from Château d'If and being rescued by a pirate ship, he deliberately elaborated on the food provided by the pirates. Since we all had escaped before, to a certain extent, we could relate. When he talked about the food, many of us felt as if we were Edmund Dantes at that moment, and the descriptions made us salivate. I later read the Chinese and English versions of the novel, Aji's storytelling in prison was about 98% accurate.

## 10. Released from Detention, Rest and Recuperation

It was November of 1974 when Wang Qiang and I were finally allowed to be transferred back to our county detention center. We spent two more weeks there and was sent back to our commune. Then we had our hands tied together by a rope and escorted back to the production brigade by a militiaman carrying a rifle on his back. Wang Qiang used to be the secretary of the brigade's Communist Youth League, and was well liked. The militiaman escorting us happened to be from the same production team as Wang Qiang. He liked Wang and even idolized him. But now he was in an awkward situation. Holding one end of the rope, he escorted us from the commune, walking five kilometers, absurdly guiding us into the village while carrying his gun and leading us like cows. After my first failed attempt, it was like crossing of the Rubicon — there was no return. There was no need for me to hide my intention anymore. Strangely enough, my relationships with the villagers became even better. The head of the production team, who used to be authoritative and stern with me, now spoke to me humbly and even asked me a few times with a smile if I was interested in doing any work of my choice. I politely declined his offers. I figured he might recon that this smuggler in front of him might become successful one day or even become wealthy, so it was better to flatter him now. The newly appointed secretary of Youth League was either trying to salvage me or to utilize my neat handwriting, convincing me several times to transcribe a few articles criticizing Lin Biao and Confucius onto the brigade's bulletin board, a privilege I had never dreamed of before. It was hugely better than performing hard labor and sweating in the field. While I enjoyed practicing my chalk calligraphy, I actually felt sick of the endless and senseless political movements one after another. Seeing all this only strengthened my determination to escape from this place. Each time when I thought of my hands bound behind my back, and my shaven head, I indeed was frustrated at my repeated failures. Every time when I entered the detention center, I felt a special sadness thinking of my father. Since I was sent to the countryside, for seven years, my father had sent me ten yuan each month from his meager income, never uttering a harsh word. I felt deep pain knowing that I, his firstborn son, had not been able to bring him any joy or peace of mind, but only worry and shame. I only wished to stand on my own feet and ease my parents' worries. I hoped to escape from this place, find a decently paying job, support myself comfortably, maybe even start a family.

In the late autumn of 1974, it was a low season period, it was too cold to swim in the ocean. We had to adapt and recuperate. I can't recall how it started, perhaps out of a kind of carefree attitude, I began reciting "The Count of Monte Cristo" in the evenings in Wang Qiang's dormitory. Every night, the EYs, local villagers, including my production team leader, about twenty people, would gather punctually at Wang Qiang's room to listen to my storytelling. What surprised me was that I remembered every detail of what Aji had recounted in prison. I imitated his demeanor, tone, and words effortlessly, even pausing exactly at the same spot each night as Aji did, replicating his performance flawlessly. For over two months, with no written text at hand, the story flowed naturally without any preparation during the day. When evening came, what had to be told that night naturally flowed from my mouth. I believed this was a result of the inner calmness I experienced during detention, combined with Aji's outstanding storytelling. Though I could speak rural slang fluently, as Aji spoke pure Cantonese, I chose to narrate the story in authentic Cantonese. When I spoke, it felt as if Aji was inside my head, narrating through me. Listening to such a long story in a rural village in 1974 was undoubtedly a top-class luxury.

After finishing the story, it was 1975. By this time, my aspirations had surpassed simple materialistic survival. Privately, I even worried that the brigade was too kind and might make arrangements for me to return to the city for a city job. If I were sent back to the city, attempting to escape again would not be as justifiable. At that moment, I was totally disgusted with what was going on in China. And I saw no future for myself, at all. Despite being caught three times, I found solace in the path I had chosen for myself. Even if one might gain and become a Party cadre, what was the point? Working in such a place entailed disguising one's true self, stifling one's desires, distorting one's soul, and lying. Even with official titles and monetary rewards, what was the worth of such a life? I daydreamed about a strong wind carrying me across borders to foreign lands. In my mind, I could vaguely envision the rolling green hills of England or Scotland, a distant church spire amidst a few cottages. I closed my eyes and imagined navigating my descent to an English-speaking country, living freely and independently. I always had a tendency of idolizing western cultures, and I understood the importance of English, a global language, viewing it as a channel to the understanding of advanced civilization.

I was resolute in my pursuit to escape. With my mind set on daring adventures, I firmly upheld two principles. 1) Wasting no time with those who were not committed to escape; 2) Caring about nothing "unrelated to escaping." Nevertheless at the beginning of 1975, an incident seemed unrelated to my pursuit but left a lasting impression on me. By then, I had befriended Aji, who narrated "The Count of Monte Cristo." He was between homes in Guangzhou, often staying with his friend Chen Jinrong. One evening, I went to Jinrong's home to look for Aji, but unfortunately, they were holding a funeral for Jinrong's elderly aunt. Before her passing, the elderly lady had a will against cremation. However, in those days in Guangzhou, one couldn't simply choose not to be cremated, as burial was illegal. After midnight, Aji, Jinrong and I, and a few other friends used a tricycle to secretly transport the coffin to the banks of the Pearl River, where we loaded it onto a small boat and carried it out of Guangzhou, eventually reaching a pre-arranged cemetery near the Guangzhou Sugar Factory. Despite the rain and late hours, everyone urged Aji and me to stay and keep vigil. In the cold wind and rain, the cemetery was dotted with pale soul paper flags and joss money, occasionally lifted by the wind and floating above the graveyards, as if souls were wandering in the night. The plastic covering the coffin rustled all night from the wind and rain. As expected, Aji and I, each wrapped in a quilt and holding an umbrella, sat on the cemetery grounds, guarding the coffin of Jinrong's aunt, sleeping soundly through the night. The next day, during the burial ceremony, I prayed with my hands clasped together, seeking Aunt Jinrong's blessing for a smooth journey to Tsim Sha Tsui (the most vibrant district in Kowloon). In my memories, I seemed to have no acquaintance with Aunt Jinrong; but somehow, my act of guarding her vigil moved her, and she might have helped me in strange ways later on.

## 11. The Fourth Attempt

Sure enough, several months later, I encountered a benefactor. In 1975, after two failed attempts with me, Wang Qiang faced significant social and family pressure and decided to give up. But I would not quit. If I couldn't find a partner, I would go solo. I vowed: I would crawl to Hong Kong even if my legs were cut off. In July, by chance, an upper schoolmate and I ran into each other and started chatting. During the school years in our teens, students of different grades normally didn't hang out together. I was a sophomore and Lin Jun a senior. Thanks to my being a star on the school soccer team and Lin Jun also active in sports, especially skilled in basketball. We became and remained friends and he knew about my experiences. When the conversation turned to my then inactivity, he told me that his younger brother Wen Biao had EY friends in some good locations for the Macao route, and his brother, Wen Biao, was looking for a partner. He suggested that I talk to his brother.

Wasting no time, I got on a bike and rushed to the Lin's home the very same evening. After Wen Biao explained the situation, I recounted my own past experiences. When I asked what kind of partner he was looking for, Wen Biao responded, "I'm just looking for someone like you." That was it, we hit it off immediately. He later introduced another friend named Hong Yichang. Hong's advantage was that his father had a business in Hong Kong, and he had friends in Macao. I suggested a departure different from my past approaches: this time, we would leave on the 15th day of the luna month of July, which was a full moon night. The advantage of a full moon night was that the water flowed swiftly, increasing our speed; the militia patrols were lax; and we could gauge the time by the position of the moon in the sky. Of course, the downside was that we could be spotted easier. Our solution was to wear transparent plastic hats on our heads so that the moonlight would reflect off them, preventing our heads from appearing as dark spots on the shimmering water surface. My experience and strong analysis won their trust, and they accepted my suggestion.

On August 20, 1975, the 14th day of the lunar July, early in the morning Wang Qiang took me on a bicycle to the bus station for Doumen. By noon, we arrived at Jing'an, the county seat of Doumen. We passed the station checkpoint with forged documents. Local EYs Zhang Jianhua and others met us at a restaurant in Jing'an. After lunch, we took a ferry across to Baijiao. Previously, Wang Qiang and I had disembarked about ten kilometers north of Baijiao and headed east. This time, we started ten kilometers south, aiming southeast. It was clear our point of entry was more advanced than in the past. Reaching such a place required local connections. Zhang Jianhua and the others led us through several hours of perilous paths to a thatched hut where provisions were prepared for us in advance. The journey was perilous because we encountered militiamen armed with rifles midway. If they had been more alert or inquisitive, our cover could have been easily blown. After a late supper around eleven o'clock that night, we swiftly made our way to the waterfront.

After midnight, under the bright moon, the ebbing tide water flowed swiftly outward. It was my first time swimming so far south; we were all excited. To avoid making noises when communicating the three of us held onto a thin rope stringing us together. Whenever necessary to talk we gently tugged the rope to bring the others closer, whispering in hushed tones. The current was strong, and the scenery along the shore moved quickly backward. We reached Modao Estuary shortly. We turned slightly left to the east, and entered the main channel towards Macao. At that point, we were about one to two kilometers from the shore, with waves approximately one to two feet high. Hong Yichang pulled the rope. He was somewhat scared and whispered that with such rough waves, we should consider approaching the shore to reconsider. I bluntly dismissed his suggestion, crushing any ideas of surrender. We braved the waves, and soon, from a distance we saw the lights of the Grand Lisboa Hotel and the Ponte Governador Nobre de Carvalho bridge in Macao. As we swam forward, we saw more bridges and brighter lights. The capitalist world and freedom were right before our eyes. With each stroke and kick, we drew closer. It was incredibly uplifting, and our excitement turned swimming into enjoyment, without traces of fatigue. Once we were out of the estuary, the waves calmed down. In the distance, the magnificent Ponte Governador Nobre de Carvalho bridge and the shimmering sea water reflected each other, presenting a picturesque scene. Around four o'clock in the morning, I felt something solid under my feet. My goodness had we reached the western end of Hengqin Island? Sure enough, we were there! Macao consists of three islands: Macao, Taipa, and Coloane. We didn't know the size of Hengqin, but its eastern end was just a stone's throw from one of the islands - Taipa. Hengqin was just our destination for the first night. We continued east, intending to swim a bit more before dawn, getting closer to the eastern end of the island so that the second night would be easier. Thus, we swam for another hour eastward.

Suddenly, a loud shout like thunder tore through the quiet night sky, followed by the sound of guns being cocked, which sent shivers down our spines. Damn it! It was only now that we encountered these ominous gatekeepers! Realizing immediately what was happening. I instantly submerged my head into the water, broke the thin rope connecting us, discarded the backpack containing our provisions, and swam shallowly towards the shore against the current. I didn't know how long I swam, but when the water became too shallow to conceal me, I stood up and saw that it was already dawn. There was a public security boat not far away, and Hong Yichang was less than ten meters away from me. Luck was on our side! Without a word, both of us desperately ran towards the island. I later thought that the public security must have mistaken our floating backpacks for our heads and chased after them instead. Honestly, given the circumstances at the time, I found it hard to believe that we managed to shake off those border guards with little effort. If not for some supernatural intervention, we would have been caught again.

Hong Yichang and I ran uphill towards the mountain, diving into the bushes. Of course, our ordeal was far from over, and hunger awaited us. Besides the shorts I was wearing, the only thing I had was a small bundle of tobacco shreds wrapped in several layers of plastic film in my back pocket, secured by a safety pin. Hong didn't smoke, so those hand-rolls were the only things that touched my lips that day. In those years, unable to afford factory-made cigarettes I smoked hand-rolled ones. I had about ten of those, and from then on, I enjoyed one approximately every hour. At that critical moment, they were my emotional sustenance. Though those ten cigarettes couldn't fill my stomach, a few puffs surely helped stabilizing my nerves, restoring my wits, and keeping calm, which played a crucial role. It was August 21. We hid in a secluded trench on the mountainside without a drop of water to drink. Despite his stout figure, Hong shivered several times from the cold, his teeth chattering. Perhaps smoking helped, I felt alright. I held him tightly to warm him up whenever he was chilled.

Finally, the sun went down and the moon rose in the east. Around nine o'clock, we descended from the mountain and resumed our journey on foot. The August water was not cold, but after swimming for about an hour, maybe due to exhaustion and hunger, even I shivered. So, we decided to walk along the shore. Just as we reached the tree grove by the water's edge, OMG, a small boat silently glided over the route we had left just half a minute earlier. There were five or six shadowy figures with guns on board. Thank God! How could I not believe that divine intervention was secretly watching over us! Along the way, we found rice paddies. But, the rice shoots of August hadn't yet earred or grained, otherwise we could have at least gotten a few calories into our mouths. Around 2:30, we arrived at the eastern end of Hengqin Island. There was a bunker by the water, and under the moonlight, we saw a figure inside, armed with a rifle. We carefully avoided the bunker and silently slipped into the water, swimming towards Taipa, where the whole Macao appeared before us. My goodness, only then did I see there were at least three or four gunboats on the surface. Their machine guns on board were uncovered. Just as I was stunned by this sight, I suddenly realized that Hong Yichang was nowhere to be seen. Looking up, I saw his head rapidly drifting towards the opposite shore, leaving me behind by a good twenty meters. I wanted to catch up with him, but then I abruptly found that my limbs wouldn't obey me. Despite being a much better swimmer than Hong, all this time I had been supporting him physically. Who would have thought that in this crucial moment, I would become the weaker? His bigger body must have stored enough energy to help him now. Sadly, I was so exhausted that I could barely move through the water, just managing slight movements of my forearms and palms to guide my direction. It was the first time in my life that I felt so helpless in terms of physical strength. Knowing the gunboats were so close by, I dared not even utter a sound to call for help. If either of us made any noise, I knew we would be caught for sure. I had no choice but to muster every last ounce of strength to weakly paddle towards the opposite shore, carried by the current at an angle. By this time, we had already swum thirty kilometers, spending eight or nine hours in the water, without anything in our stomachs for twenty-eight hours.

## 12. Narrow Escape

At about 3 am(I was able to tell time by the moon's position in the sky, and I had tested it—my margin of error was less than ten minutes), I finally swam to the opposite shore. By then, I was completely exhausted and I allowed myself to collapse onto a bed of gravel, falling asleep instantly. A quarter of an hour later, I woke up, feeling restored, I landed myself on the land of Macao. There happened to be a tunnel, with a propaganda poster on the brick wall beside it that read "Please cast your sacred vote," written in traditional Chinese characters. I heaved a long sigh of relief: I had finally made it out! It was about 3:30 am, , August 22, 1975.

I ran across the road, and climbed a small hill. Since it was still early, I lay down on a large slab of bluestone to rest for a while. But I couldn't settle my mind because I had to find someone to shelter me before daybreak; otherwise, if caught by Macao police, I would be repatriated to mainland China. So, I groped my way towards the village at the foot of the hill. Just as I reached the village entrance, a frenzy of barking dogs filled the air, scaring me from approaching. I had no choice but to retreat back up the hill. Around 4:30, I stumbled upon what seemed to be a vacant shed at the end of a bridge. As I pondered what to do next, footsteps suddenly approached. Before I could react, a flashlight beam shone on my face. My heart sank, thinking trouble was brewing. To my surprise, the person moved the flashlight beam away, apologizing profusely, and turning around to leave. This scene reminded me of the bunker on the hill over a year ago. Anticipating his next move, I took a step forward, grabbed his hand, comforted him gently, and pulled him into the shed. He told me his surname was Xiao, a native of Zhongshan, who had also come from mainland China to Macao, in his forties, keeping watch over a quarry. Without much ado, the night watchman took me in. At this crucial moment, besides safety, the second most important task was filling my stomach. He took out a large bag of biscuits, letting me eat voraciously. He then directed me to jump into a clear pond on the mountainside for a thorough wash. Next, he obtained information about my contacts in Hong Kong and instructed a fellow townsperson to find my connections there. During those days, he locked me in his small warehouse, treating me to two meals of delicious white rice and a can of "Five-Spice Anchovies." Though every meal was the same, to me, it was like a feast. After eight anxious days, one evening I heard voices outside. I lay on the ground, peering through the door crack, and saw my cousin whom I hadn't seen for over four years! My excitement was indescribable! I waited calmly for them to open the door. My cousin brought me a stylish Hong Kong shirt and a pair of pants, and paid nine hundred Hong Kong dollars to ransom me from the night watchman. In 1975, that was about two months' earnings for an ordinary garment factory worker. My cousin cautioned me: "You're still only at fifty-fifty odds," meaning a 50% chance of success, so I needed to be careful. Because in 1975, young people in Hong Kong and Macao wore long hair, while I still had mainland-style short hair. No matter how modern I dressed, I could still look suspicious, and there was still a possibility of being recognized and questioned by Macao police. My cousin also handed me a semi-X rated magazine, then we took an inner-city bus to a restaurant in downtown Macau. My cousin treated me to a very delicious and sumptuous dinner that night. We drank German "Blue Girl" beer and I ate fifteen bowls of rice.

    My cousin had made contact with Hung Yichang's father in Hong Kong and he had learned of the address of where Hung was. After dinner, my cousin took me there. It was a small business that collected local fishermen's catches and distributed them to Hong Kong restaurants. There I reunited with Hung, whom I had been separated from for eight days. We stayed together in Macao for ten more days. Upstairs above the fish shop was an English school, where young men and women diligently attended English classes every evening with books under their arms. How envious I was of those young people! About a month later in Hong Kong, I also attended an English school. Over two years of night school, I skipped a grade once, and in every exam, I ranked either the first or second in the class, without exception. Ten days later, arranged by Hung's father, who had considerable social connections, we took a late-night sail on a Chinese Junk to Hong Kong. Two weeks later, we re-united with Wen Biao in San Po Kong, Hong Kong. He did something similar to us and evaded pursuit by the militiamen.

## 13. Days in Hong Kong

Upon arriving in Hong Kong, I truly experienced the precious freedom, a sweetness that was almost indescribable in words. I remember waking up in the middle of the night and asking myself: Is this really Hong Kong? Am I not dreaming? When I touched the cold steel frame of the iron bed, I knew for sure I wasn't dreaming, and I felt a deep satisfaction from within. Within clear legal frameworks, I had the freedom to choose to do anything or nothing. As for making a living I chose to work as a laborer because the hours weren't too long and the pay was good. Relying on the skills I honed in the countryside, I made a name for myself in the hard labor sector of Kowloon. Every day after work, I diligently spent 5 nights a week attending English school. I was determined to learn English grammar well, and I succeeded. Even after several decades in the U.S., I am still learning today. Once the grammar foundation is laid, it's like the main trunk and branches of a large tree that grow fuller with each additional twig and leaf.

Two weeks after my arrival in Hong Kong, my childhood friend Michael left Hong Kong for the United States as a refugee immigrant. In 1976, many other friends applied and eventually all immigrated to the

United States. I had long dreamed of living in an English-speaking country, settling in the U.S. suited me perfectly. So, I followed suit immediately and turned in my application at the International Social Service Center in Causeway Bay. At that time, the requirements for obtaining immigration status were that we needed an American to provide us with financial sponsorship and job guarantees. I had no acquaintance in the U.S. except Michael, who was just a new arrival. Nevertheless, I decided to submit the application first and figure out the rest later.

By 1977, the Hong Kong subway was in the excavation stage, and the wages for laborers were twice that of hard labor. I gave up hard labor and switched to subway construction as a miner.

At about the same time, the International Social Service Center had repeatedly urged me to provide refugee sponsorship documents. Michael had been in the States for only two years so he did not qualify for naturalization as an American citizen, and I could not find anyone else to sponsor me. At that time, I thought I should try to integrate myself into the circles of English and American people to see if I could find an opportunity to make American connections and thus solve the problem of sponsorship. I even day-dreamed about meeting a blue-eyed, attractive blonde American girl like those I had seen in movies.

I had a knack for identifying outstanding individuals in any situation and befriending them. Thanks to Michael, I promptly made friends with some smart people from Guangzhou. At that time, there was a University Service Center on Prince Edward Road that helped Western scholars conduct research. Bob Lau, a new friend I met, was a standout in our group of friends, and he worked at the center. I told Bob that I wanted to find a Westerner to share an apartment with. Bob promised to keep an eye out for me.

In early 1978, Bob and his wife also left for the United States. Before leaving, he entrusted my request to Miss Chen, his successor.

One day in April 1978, Miss Chen called me and said she had found a Westerner for me. I was to go immediately to the service center on

Prince Edward Road to meet him. His name was Mark, an Englishman of Australian nationality. I had hoped to find an American. Encountering an Englishman was somewhat disappointing, but I decided to make do.

Mark was a freelance journalist. Though not American, through him, I could integrate into Western circles and perhaps have the opportunity to make American friends. On weekends, I often went out with Mark and his Western friends. Just a few weeks later, I had several new friends in my social circle, all of them British, American or South Africans.

## 14. Meeting and Getting Help from My Benefactor

At the end of 1978, one evening, Mark returned home and asked me if I wanted to join him for dinner at a friend's home over the weekend. How could I refuse? Of course, I agreed! Mark then informed me that this friend was Jonathan Basset, who had been expelled from mainland China earlier that year. Oh, it was him! I knew about this; I had read about it in a column in Ming Pao, where the journalist expressed outrage on behalf of a Canadian reporter expelled from mainland China for the Globe and Mail.

On Saturday evening, as agreed, we went to Jonathan's residence on the Mid-Levels of Hong Kong Island. Jonathan was the Hong Kong bureau chief for Time magazine. Jonathan wasn't American but Canadian. After learning about my intentions and the difficulty of not having a sponsor, he contacted his friend Roland Green in Santa Barbara, California, to vouch for me. Through a series of efforts, including Jonathan personally writing a letter to the U.S. Consul General in Hong Kong, I finally achieved my wish and immigrated to the United States in May 1979. Because Roland Green was the owner of a computer communications company, I realized during my time there that my only two years of middle school education was too lacking. When I found out that American community colleges were open to anyone of any age, I chose to resign and attend community college in 1980, when I was 29 years old.

In middle school in 1966, we had just finished algebra functions and factorization. 14 years later in a new environment, I started with algebra again, while also studying trigonometry. After three semesters of physics and chemistry. I finally had the opportunity to study calculus, which I had always felt unattainable, and studied it for three semesters. After spending three years and getting the prerequisites taken care of, I transferred to San Diego State University in 1983. In 1986, I finally earned a bachelor's degree in electrical engineering, realizing the dream of a college degree. Since my first job in the United States was related to computer communications, I entered the computer communications engineering industry and earned myself a Cisco Certified Network Professional certificate, CCNP.

More than 50 years ago, Mao Zedong waved his hand and issued a call to "send educated youth to the countryside for re-education by the poor and lower-middle peasants, which was very necessary." He sent millions of young people who were in their teens and twenties to the countryside. Adverse environment indeed tempered and cultivated some and even turned them to hers, it also ruined the future of millions, and even destroyed their lives. As for myself, I have to thank that member of the Revolutionary Committee who refused to allow me to continue high school . If I did continue high school, I definitely would not have been put on a dire situation which woke me up and caused me to leave that autocratic state. Looking back, I have millions of reasons to be thankful for the path that was chosen, and to God who help me all along.

## 15. Memories and Reflections

Looking back over the past few decades, despite the hardships, those years in the countryside truly tempered me, enhancing my resilience and shaping me into a physically and mentally tough individual. During my years in Hong Kong, I was able to excel as a laborer, thanks to the hardships endured in the countryside. Meeting Jonathan Basset in Hong Kong and later working at Roland Green's computer communications company brought me into the high-tech field. Eventually, I entered the computer networking industry and became a Cisco-certified CCNP, transforming from a laborer to a technical professional.

Of more significance was to live and be part of the great nation founded by the great statesmen like: George Washington, Thomas Jefferson, and many others. In this country and as I travel freely around the world, I have the firsthand experience that Americans and Westerners, whom billions of people in China still curse today, are not what they are construed to be. In the 1970's Hong Kong, white western people were respected as superior in the social hierarchy. Jonathan Basset was white and bureau chief of an international major magazine, our social status was hugely different. I would've never dreamed of such a friendship. He took the initiative to befriend me and offered me his help without expecting anything in return. If our roles were reversed, I know I couldn't have done the same. As a Chinese grew up in China, I had been brainwashed with racial discrimination for decades that the western white people, by nature, discriminate against Chinese. Upon arriving in the United States, I was mentally prepared to face some discrimination as an Asian newcomer entering a high-tech company in an English-speaking, predominantly white environment. To my surprise, not only did I encounter no discrimination, but I also felt the respect that I had never experienced among fellow Asians in China or Hong Kong.

Growing up in a state-owned factory environment, due to my father's humble position, my encounters with children of high-ranking officials or senior engineers always stirred up my sense of inferiority. They naturally exuded an air of superiority that made me feel inadequate. This was the real discrimination I experienced in that society from a young age. In the countryside, farmers were already considered social outcasts; yet they always found opportunities and reasons to discriminate against and ridicule groups in even worse situations than themselves, such as those categorized as "four categories" or impoverished farmers in remote areas. After rolling around in American society for a year, I deeply realized what equality for everyone feels like. I no longer need to wear a disguise and for the first time feel equal to those around me. Having the opportunity to get to know and understand Western society up close, I feel fortunate.

In recent years, due to the rapid economic advancement of mainland China, many of my peers who fled to Hong Kong or eventually moved to the United States would ask a question: Life in mainland China seems to have improved quite a lot now. Did we make a wrong move back then? They cast doubt on the wisdom of our risky decision. Over these years, I have also traveled back to mainland China several times to visit friends. Development there has indeed progressed by leaps and bounds, and some of my former classmates and friends have achieved considerable success, with a few even entering the ranks of the super-rich. Some of them also advise me: China is still better. Look at what we have achieved here?

What's hard to articulate is what they don't have—the spiritual freedom we enjoy in the Western world. Perhaps they are satisfied with materialistic extravagance, fine clothes, delicious food, and the glittering material life. Yet, after our basic needs for clothing and food are met, we value and cherish spiritual freedom more.

For over forty years, I have been constantly grateful, feeling a deep satisfaction from the depths of my soul. This satisfaction cannot be measured by wealth; it stems from the awakening back then and the successful escape to the free world. It is the greatness of a country like the United States, the humanistic ideas of the West that provided me the opportunity to transform myself.

The Cultural Revolution and my exile to the countryside—whether regrettable or not—are things of the past. The Guangdong EYs were wise, intelligent, optimistic, and audacious. They adapted to the circumstances, turned the tide, escaped dictatorship and fled to freedom. They took control of their own destinies. Their bravery, refusing to be fooled and suppressed, showcased the brilliance of human nature. Their spirit of refusing to succumb to fate, persevering tenaciously, and fighting stubbornly already made a mark in human history.

# The Braves Have No Fears

*By Wong Zichang*

October 15, 1972, was Chinese people's Double Ninth Festival, but in the "New China," the traditional holidays held less importance, besides Chinese New Year, and even some characteristic national holidays with thousand-year traditions were criticized as belonging to the "Four Olds" ("destroy the Four Olds" ...the campaign of the Cultural Revolution) and being feudalistic. Especially during the Cultural Revolution, nearly all of China's 5000 years of fine, traditional culture was seen as "rubbish." For example, the Qingming Festival, the Dragon Boat Festival, the Mid-Autumn Festival, the Double Ninth Festival, and other traditional Han festivals of elegant, legendary character, passed down through history, were replaced by such so-called "Revolutionary" days as "Five-One," "Seven-One," and "Ten-One."

Wu Junpei was born in Guangzhou to an aristocratic family of literary excellence. His parents were both teachers, and as for traditional culture, he'd known since he was small that Double Ninth Festival and Qingming Festival were days of remembering ancestors. Junpei chose that day to leave and seek freedom because he knew that fleeing would be gambling with his life, that he'd face fierce dangers on the way, and he hoped his ancestors would protect him and bless him with a safe and smooth trip. By that day, it was already the second week since Mid-Autumn Festival, and only one week until *Shuangjiang*, and the weather in South China was already getting cooler; some nights, the temperature would drop below 20 degrees Celsius.

Wu Junpei and two educated-youth-peasant friends rode their two shabby bicycles from Boluo to the south side of Huizhou, by the side of South Mountain, and left their bicycles hidden in the trees, and loaded their rations (fried rice flour mixed with sugar, sesame seeds, peanut oil, and kneaded into a ball), a canteen, rope, a small knife, materials to help them cross the bay onto their backpack and take advantage of the hazy moonlight to climb up the mountain.

This was the same spot he'd been on his first attempt back in July, so he was familiar with it. Because Junpei's efforts had been crudely executed on the last journey, and his companion had been too weak, they'd walked for eight challenging days, their provisions were insufficient, and they'd finished them by the sixth day, forcing them to rely on the wild fruits to get their fill. Scorched and drenched by the strong sun and the rain, the rainstorms at time too, and they became extremely exhausted and Junpei's companion did get sick also, with his extremely weak body, he eventually propped up till they reached the water front, consciously, he knew that he/they lacked the strength to cross the billowing waves of Dapeng Bay, and they were forced to give up. By the time the People's Militia spotted them and arrested him, his companion was just lying paralyzed on the ground. Two weeks later, they were repatriated back to Boluo, and the two suffered greatly in the detention center before being returned to the production team near Boluo and publicly denounced again. Soon after, Junpei secretly returned to his family home in Guangzhou to recuperate for over a month.

This time, Wu Junpei's companion was swapped for two young people just one village away, also from Guangzhou, a boy and a girl, who were boyfriend and girlfriend. The boy was named Ni Zhugang and the girl was named Chang Weizhen, and they were barefoot doctors in their village, and were passionately in love. Zhugang was an older high school schoolmate of Junpei's, and they were already fairly close back then; they'd visit each other often. Zhugang. knowing that Junpei had just returned from a failed attempt to reach Hong Kong, wanted to connect with him, to ask that the next time he planned to try again, he'd let them come along. He said to Junpei, "We were just like you. From the day we were sent to the countryside, we knew we would have no future here, the fact that we were born into the Black Five families, We had been pushed into the lowest rung of the society in Guangzhou, and we too had been looking for the right way to flee to Hong Kong, and now that we knew how brave you had been, on one hand we admired your being brave, and on the other, we hoped that we could venture with you."

At first, Junpei was concerned that because Weizhen was a girl, she couldn't be taken care of on the route, and he advised Zhugang of this, but Zhugang's love was stronger than gold, and he brought Weizhen to Junpei's house several times trying to persuade Junpei, who at time thought to himself, Zhugang already had been so up front and persistent with the issue, how could I be so evasive with it? And according to Junpei's observations, Weizhen was a rather strong lady, not tall, and very robust, who'd borne the hardships of toiling in the field. After days of intensive discussion, he agreed. And Weizhen later proved not only to not become a burden, but even to have helped the two boys on some occasions, especially when they were discussing equipment for crossing the bay, and she came up with an unexpectedly good plan.

Because, in that era, everyone who fled universally used equipment to help cross the bay, like basketball bladders or plastic children's flotation devices, the government, in order to crack down on the wave of illegal escape, had prohibited their sale in public, and they became hard to come by among the people. Junpei had, with great difficulty, got ahold of only one basketball bladder, and they were all worrying about it's not being enough, Weizhen intelligently came up with a very clever idea: she made a sack out of bedsheets, about three feet square, sewing the sides together, leaving an opening on one side, which she fastened a button over. She then took some latex surgery gloves, that would be relatively easy to come by as a barefoot doctor, and blew them up, tying them with string, and putting them inside the sack. When put in the water, they were able to hold the weight of an adult, The practicality and creativity of it left the two boys in adulation of her. They secretly tested them many times, which proved their practicality and feasibility.

On the first night, they climbed a mountain from a remote section of a highway far from the village. Because it was nearly dark, desolate, and there was no one that would find them, they easily climbed Huizhou

South Mountain and the mountain range northeast of Chenjiang Village, which can be classified as part of the Huizhou South Mountain region. That evening was the ninth day of the month on the lunar calendar, and the half full-moon was obscured by clouds, but the moonlight managed to shine through enough to illuminate their path up the mountain. Because Junpei was climbing up the mountain in the same place, on the same path, as he did in July, plus he had now adequate strength, crossing the first mountain proved very easy. Four or five hours later, when the sky was getting lighter, they finally arrived at the woods on the western shore of Huangsha Reservoir, found a secluded spot, and rested there.

Because, on the first day, they were so nervous and excited, even though they were tired, they were still awake and chatting when it was getting lighter. Junpei took advantage of the lack of sleepiness and carefully gave an account of his experiences earned back in July, on one hand recalling the route he'd walked not long before, and on the other hand calling attention to the multifarious difficulties and dangers that his two companions might run into on the route ahead, to prepare them. At dawn, they felt sleepy, and went to sleep on the ground. Because they were on top of a mountain, the temperature was low, so they all slept together.

Around noon on the second day, the three of them got up one by one, and washed their faces and bodies at the edge of the reservoir and discussed whether or not to continue forward. It was quiet at this time between the mountains, but the sun shining down was like a stove in the middle of the sky, and even though it was late autumn, it still could burn painfully. After Junpei and Zhugang talked it over, they agreed that under those never-ending mountain peaks, most of the farmers would be rushing to reap their harvests, and relatively few would be working in the mountains, so they decided to continue walking in the daytime.

Unexpectedly, the three of them didn't meet anyone as they continued walking until four o'clock.

After four or five hours of mountain hiking, they were feeling tired because of their walking in the nighttime, and Junpei suggested they rest, saying to Zhugang: "Last time we tried to go as fast as possible, and ended up using up our energy, with the result that we got to the sea and had no energy to swim. Also, we must conserve food well, and as much as we can, find things from the fields and fruit from fruit trees to eat if we could.

That way if we got to the sea and would need to rest or wait, we would still have food to eat.

When he finished speaking, he pointed to a place not far from the foothill of the mountain with a sugarcane field and he proposed that he and Zhugang go cut some down and bring it back to eat. Zhugang said yes and told Weizhen to wait where she was. The two of them ran down to the sugarcane field and used the knife to cut down a few thick stalks of sugarcane and carried them on their shoulders. Seeing there was no one around, Junpei seized the opportunity and dug up some sweet potatoes that had been planted there by the sugar field. When they got back up to the mountain, Weizhen had smoothed out places for them to rest, and they rested there comfortably for a while. They gnawed on the fresh sugarcane, ate some sweet potatoes, and then slept for about three or four hours. When they got up, the snow-white moon was already high in the sky, and they packed up and continued walking with the moonlight.

Because he'd walked that route three months before, Junpei relied on his startling ability to memorizing things around him, and never made a wrong turn. But they were crossing mountains in the dark, and even with some moonlight, they didn't actually have a "path." They staggeringly felt their way forward, ascending and descending, until it got to daybreak, all three of them with wounds all over their bodies, scared and bruised all over their hands and feet.

The three of them started out from Huizhou. They heard from others who had followed the Eastern route that it was longer. The most often chosen starting point was to the south of Huizhou, in a secluded mountainous area near Danshui. This route was approximately five days at the least, six or seven days at the most. "*Maidui*" (gathering & prepare to escape) from near Huizhou would at least require spending seven or eight days, and possibly ten. If they took a wrong turn, it would be more than ten days before they reached the sea. Escapees found themselves in danger if they made a wrong turn in the mountains, and many escapees never found their way out, falling off cliffs or starving deep in the mountains. But in the part of Huizhou from which they left, it was relatively safe, because it was in the interior far enough from the sea that the monitoring was relatively relaxed. Like Danshui, classified as a so-called Frontier Defense Area, if they saw strangers, the locals with "Revolutionary Consciousness" would stare at you. (Because of political and economic factors in Guangdong Province since 1949, a continuous stream of common people fled to Hong Kong and Macau, and, in an effort to stop them, the authorities had inculcated in the common people of the neighboring areas the notion that escapees were treasonous defecting class enemies, wicked beyond redemption, and encouraged the people to report them and capture them, and not let them slip by.)

By now, Junpei and the two others had climbed for three days and had only arrived at the south of Xinwei Village, on a mountain beside Changliukeng Reservoir. To the south of Changliukeng Reservoir, the topography was somewhat milder. But with the planes around Pingshan Village in front of them, how could they continue without being seen? Junpei, Zhugang, and Weizhen discussed it, and decided to go around the mountains to the southwest once it was dark, so as to be able to walk over ten kilometers of the winding route; to be safe, that was the way they had to do it.

That night, the three of them walked as fast as they could to gain time, hoping to reach the mountains south of Pingshan Village before dawn. But they estimated wrong; and those small mountains south of Pingshan were more than ten kilometers from the main range. By morning, they'd only covered half the distance, and they had to hide in a rocky crevice on a densely tree-covered hill. That day was extremely hard. They could hear farmers below doing their work, and were too scared to run for it, so they stayed crammed in the crevice the whole day, not budging, only moving about to a limited extent at noon, when the farmers were eating lunch. They waited until nightfall to hurry onward. When they reached the towering mountains and precipitous ridges south of Pingshan, it was already getting brighter.

Looking up from the foothills, Zhugang and Weizhen were a little frightened: these mountains were at least 700 or 800 meters above sea level and continued as far as the eye could see. Junpei saw their concern and consoled his two companions: don't worry, we can cross it. Last time, we started climbing from near here, and just over these mountains is Dapeng Bay; we only need two more days to get there.

Junpei's estimate was indeed not wrong: within two days and two nights of clambering over mountains, they saw the end of their suffering. Zhugang and Weizhen both fell into a mountain stream, but luckily, they were stopped by a pine tree and didn't suffer injuries which were too bad. Junpei, trying to reach the last mountain quickly, lost his footing and fell into a crevice, and Zhugang and Weizhen spent two hours getting him out, but his shoulder and knees were gashed open, and one of his pant legs was torn off. Even like this, the three of them relied on their conviction and bravery, inspiring each other, supporting each other, surrounded by the howls of wild animals, under the downpour of torrential rains, finally crossing innumerable towering mountains to arrive at the summit by the sea.

Looking south to the distant Hong Kong at nighttime, you could faintly see, behind a chain of mountains, rays of light shining through the cloud layer to the horizon. Upon first seeing this beautiful sight, everyone's hearts skipped a beat, and they all felt in an unusally good mood. But looking down below their feet at the vast, billowing Dapeng Bay, their warm feelings immediately cooled, knowing they still had a severe trip in front of them.

They rested for a short while at the peak, before hurrying down the mountain, striving to reach the sea before eight or nine o'clock.

Inside a shrubbery next to the seashore, Junpei found a suitable hiding spot and called Zhugang and Weizhen to come over, saying, "The sea is not too far from here, but not too close either; it it was too close, it would be too easy for the border guards to find us. Let's throw away the things we don't need to use to swim across the bay at once, leave behind some food, take the canteen with us, prepare in as little time as possible, and descend to the sea in front of us!" Weizhen quickly took some things out of the backpack, and Junpei solemnly urged them to be quick, that any delay would endanger them to border guards, and or the para millitia. So, all three of them took out the inflated latex gloves and put them in the bedsheets as fast as possible, and Weizhen carefully fastened each of the buttons. Junbei blew up a ball bladder, and, so as not to be undone by the waves, tied two nylon cords to his body, then slowly left the shrubbery, walking toward the sea with the greatest care. At that moment, Junpei saw a fire sparkling in the distance, and assumed it was people lighting cigarette, but that it could be border guards or People's Militiamen coming towards them from the west while smoking, so Junpei quietly told everyone to speed up, and they quickly crossed a road by the sea unobstructed, and Junpei then took the lead and started to run, and Weizhen, though she was a lady, was running faster than Zhugang, who had the bedsheets on his back. Everyone restrained their panting, barely thinking of their fear, only concerned with desperately reaching the sea.

At that point in time, they had undergone eight days of resting by day and walking by night, crossing mountain after mountain, and had used up most of their energy, at that moment both hungry and tired, and any other day, they'd be unable to move. But with explosive energy that came from who-knows-where, they sprinted at lightning speed, and not even five minutes later, they reached the shore and plunged headlong into the sea water. Fortunately, the thick clouds that night didn't let in the moonlight, and from 50 meters away, they couldn't be seen. Later, he would say that the Heavens had protected them that night.

Looking back as they were crossing the bay, they saw through the moonlight several ghost-like shadows on the path they had followed, who could have been soldiers on patrol, but it appeared like they hadn't discovered them, the black masses in the water. The sea was perfectly calm, with only the sound of waves lapping up onto the shore.

The three of them sprinted through the water for over ten minutes, and then started to feel tired, and simultaneously slowed down, panting.

Junpei saw that the waves were not too big, and took out the two nylon cords from his waist, and tied one end of one to himself, and gave the other end to Zhugang to tie to himself, and then he gave Weizhen the other cord and told her to tie herself to Zhugang; that way the three of them wouldn't be pushed apart by a wave. Junpei held his ball bladder, and Zhugang and Weizhen held on to the "inflated" bedsheets and swam towards the shining islands to the southwest. At that point, the wind began blowing down from the north, and Junpei shivered, feeling the chilling cold, because the water temperature was already very low! He estimated that it would be in the teens or twenty degrees Celsius. Zhugang and Weizhen also felt the cold at the same time, and they all agreed they needed to speed up the pace a little to warm up and withstand the low temperature.

As the three of them slowly moved across Dapeng Bay, Junpei felt extremely excited, and he told Zhugang and Weizhen that three months before, when they reached the shore, they didn't have the energy to go down to the water and were arrested; but the dispirited feeling from that time at the vastness of the ocean had finally, and suddenly, been washed clean off of him. Looking at the endless rays of light shooting out from the direction of Hong Kong on the horizon, though Hong Kong still far off, nonetheless, he could now rely on himself, and his freedom was surely within his grasp, his success clearly visible. They hoped that to achieve a new frame of mind and warmth enough to counteract the cold. Zhugang and Weizhen became infected with Junpei's optimistic mood, and everyone, brimming with expectation, paddled with all their strength.

For the first hour or two, their strength was relatively abundant, and the sea had no wind or waves, so they moved very quickly. Seeing the shadow of the mountains of Hong Kong growing closer and closer, they became very excited. But they'd soon be put to the test: the three young people who had never before swum in the open sea, floating amid the dangerous Dapeng Bay, didn't realize death could be just before their eyes... Wind soon began to blow ever harder, clouds rolled over the sky, and two-to-three feet high waves surged up, followed by a torrential downpour. The three of them were tossed back and forth by the waves like toys. Zhugang and Weizhen were choking on the water, coughing and unable to breathe, when suddenly a huge wave hit them and broke loose from them the Weizhen's secret weapon, the 'bed sheet' which was tossed ten feet away from them. Weizhen said, "Oh no, that was our lifesaver, we must go get it!" The three of them swam as fast as they could toward the inflated bedsheet, and Zhugang had just grabbed ahold of a corner when other waves ripped it apart. They fought the waves for a while longer before the three of them finally had a firm hold onto it. At that point the rain abruptly stopped, and the wind and the waves somewhat subsided a little. Weizhen held the bedsheets tight, crying with rage, and said to the two boys, "This is our lifeblood! Without it, we would be toast for sure; we wouldn't let it get away again!" Zhugang quickly moved close to Weizhen, brushed aside the hair covering her face, and consoled her: "Don't cry, don't cry, we'll do everything we can to hold on to it." Junpei looked her in the eyes and felt sad. He thought, on this boundless sea, not counting wind and waves, only with the route onward, it looked like without five or six hours more, they wouldn't be able to cross it, and he could'nt help but feel a chill through his chest. Moreover, at this juncture, they absolutely could not let go! He shouted to them: "The wind and waves would soon be past, the Heavens would certainly watch over us; and, many people had swum across the bay before us, we could surely make it ourselves too! We've already gone halfway; we're doing great!"

With Junpei's encouragement, Weizhen calmed down a little bit, and braved the waves swimming forward for another half hour as the sea gradually pacified. Everyone was extremely tired, and Zhugang suggested that they stop for a bit and eat something to make up some strength. They each took a drink from the canteen and then took the dough out of the plastic bag and ate their fill of it, resting on the inflated bed sheet, and letting it float.

After a while, just as they were about to start swimming again, they noticed that the lights were getting farther and farther away. "Why are we straying to the east?" asked Junpei. "We should swim toward southwest!"

Everyone strived to swim southwest, but after about an hour, it looked like as if they hadn't made any progress at all. Junpei started to get scared. He'd heard that there were strong countercurrents here. He told Zhugang and Weizhen this; what could they do? They agreed that their only option was to continue to fight and see if they could break through the current. They had already used up a lot of energy, but supported by their hunger to survive, they continued to struggle for over an hour, in spirit-weary condition, without making it through. All three gave up, seeing faint light in the sky, and started to feel despair, letting the current push them along for the time being. Weizhen unexpectedly started comforting the two boys, saying: "We would just rest a little bit, then eat something and drink some water, and then we would see how we feel."

Junpei quickly agreed, saying: "Never give up hope. The Heavens will watch over us."

After they ate, there was only a little bit of dough and potable water remaining, and they kept the empty canteen as a floatation device and lied down, as before, to rest on the inflated bedsheet. They floated for a while as the sky got lighter, and though they could now see the distant, undulating mountain range in the direction of Hong Kong, they had no way of approaching it, and were even gradually getting farther away as the strong current was still pushing them eastward; the Chinese mainland to the north was still obscured by the morning mist and couldn't be clearly seen. Zhugang suddenly saw a few fishing boats coming towards them that would pass right by them very soon. The three of them were stupefied suddenly and thought they would really be done with this time, that they'd come so close and yet failed, that they could do nothing but simply wait to be caught with their hands tied! Just as they were despairing, however, they faintly heard a voice from the ship: "hey, you young people, don't swim toward the direction to Hong Kong! It's way too far; instead, on your right is an island, and that's considered part of Hong Kong! It's much closer!"

Voices were coming to us twice from the fishing boat, as the two boats rumbled over. Still recovering from the shock, they turned east and saw that there really was a strip of island lying flat not far away.

They half-believed, half-doubted the words the fisherman had just shouted at them. Should they trust them? Then Junpei said: it would be beyond our control; we would never get to Hong Kong with the strength we had left with; to seek survival, to try our luck, we would have no choice. Weizhen took the lead in agreeing, and Zhugang agreed. Junpei went on to say, since everyone agrees, we should try to fight for time, so as to avoid any possibility of coming across any patrol boats from the mainland.

They soon after obeyed the tides and exerted all their strength to swim to the island in front of them. When there was about a kilometer or so off from the island to which they were heading, Zhugang suddenly said to Weizhen, "My foot hit something," followed by a scream and letting go of the bedsheet, shouting: "I had been bitten! Aiyaya!" Junpei knew that this was far from good—he could have been bitten by a shark—so he immediately reached out and grabbed Zhugang and took a piece of bright orange cloth out of the backpack and shook it out in the water (After it was over, Junpei would tell the two of them that when he was in the prison in Boluo after his first failed attempt at fleeing, one of the inmates had told him, Dapeng Bay had sharks, and the brutes were afraid of the color orange, so it was best to carry some orange cloth with you, which Junpei did.) Weizhen also instantly reached across the inflated bedsheet and grabbed ahold of Zhugang. The water around had turned red by the blood of Zhugang's wounded leg. Weizhen knew that sharks were blood-thirsty-creatures and quickly jumped in the water and, with Junpei, pulled Zhugang on to the top of the inflated-bedsheet, and quickly fished out a handkerchief with which to wrap up the shark bite on Zhugang's leg, then wrapped it up with the plastic bag they'd used to keep the dough. Fortunately, the wound was not too big, and it wouldn't be letting out any more blood for the time being.

Junpei quickly told Weizhen to push the floating device out of the area dyed with blood, and they'd just done so when the same fellow came back. Seeing that brute's terrifying dorsal fin swimming straight toward them, Junpei and Weizhen were utterly petrified, but on the edge of life and death, they had no use for being scared, so Junpei had Weizhen shake the plastic cloth in the water, and he took out his small knife, and waited for the instant when the shark approached them, its body concealed under the water, then prepared to firmly stab it in the head with the knife, but unfortunately it turned sideways a little, and he end up just punched it in the nose with his fist. Weizhen summoned her courage and swayed the plastic cloth in the water near it with all her might, Zhugang shouted from the top again and again: "You bastard, go away!" Fortunately, this time, it didn't bite anyone, and when Junpei hit it again on the bridge of its nose, the shark was hurt, and it swam away. But the shark's wake almost knocked Zhugang into the water, and Junpei and Weizhen had to quickly help him up.

Junpei and Weizhen both knew that they had to accept that the shark could come back at any time, and they intensified their efforts to push Zhugang forward. Zhugang was still in a panicked state, his legs still oozing blood unceasingly, his face turned pale, enduring severe pain, incessantly shivering, his eyes half-closed. Weizhen was constantly consoling him: "We're almost to shore; you have to make it! With the two of us, nothing will happen." As she spoke, tears fell continuously from her eyes, and Junpei echoed her encouragement from the side. Actually, at that moment, to speak honestly, Junpei and Weizhen were completely drained, they were powerless to defend themselves, and the cold October seawater had chilled them to the bone and left them shivering.

And yet, because of the condition of Zhugang's injury, Junpei and Weizhen exerted all their energy, vigorously paddling with their hands and feet. Because of the push of the current, they approached the island quickly, and they could clearly see the buildings on the island. Weizhen turned the now-unconscious Zhugang around, and at first there was no reaction, and when she pulled him some more there was still no reaction. Weizhen started to get worried, and, with beads of tears falling down, yelled: "Zhugang, what's wrong? Wake up, we've arrived, wake up…" Zhugang's eyes opened a crack, and slowly he spoke: "We're in Hong Kong… Am I okay?" Weizhen quickly answered: "Yes, yes, of course yes, you have to stay up! We're about to arrive in Hong Kong!" She gently caressed his face as she comforted him. Junpei also encouraged him: "You must stand your ground, we'll be in Hong Kong soon, and didn't you say you wanted to study in America? We're just these few steps short, look, that's it in front of us." Zhugang opened his eyes with supreme effort, and followed Junpei's gesture to the island close by, forced a smile, and then lost consciousness again. Weizhen tried hard to suppress her grief and urged Junpei onward. At that point, the waves suddenly rushed forth, and several times nearly knocked Zhugang into the water, and Weizhen and Junpei went all out to keep him afloat.

Although the waves were adding problems to the steadiness of the waterbed, they managed to reach the shore quickly. Junpei could dimly see shadows moving on the beach, and he told Weizhen, and Weizhen stared at the shore, then said: "Yes! Yes!" And shouted to the shore: "Help us! Save us!" Junpei couldn't take it and began to shout with Weizhen.

The screeching pierced through the tranquility of the early morning, covering the billowing of the waves, and reached onto the shore. After a while, several Gurkha soldiers with South Asian faces ran over and pointed their guns at the three people coming ashore. Weizhen felt no fear and took a big stride forward and fell to her knees, pointing to Zhugang and saying: "Save my friend! He won't last much longer! I'm begging you…" One of the Gurkhas said to his companion in Cantonese: "Help him, quickly, he may be in bad condition." Two of them quickly carried Zhugang into a building, leaving one behind to point his gun at their backs. Junpei seized an opportunity en route and asked the ethnic Chinese soldier: "Is this Hong Kongese territory?" The soldier nodded: you are free now.

Junpei and Weizhen couldn't believe their ears, and asked again: "Hong Kong really isn't on the other side? How can it be here, too?" The soldier responded, analytically, this is the easternmost of Hong Kong's outlying islands. You are very fortunate that the current didn't push you back to the mainland. Upon hearing that, Junpei and Weizhen simultaneously pulled each other into a tight embrace and cried. Weizhen relaxed and suddenly was unsteady and slumped onto Junpei. Junpei comforted her and asked a soldier to help him with Weizhen. The soldier was very good and said to Junpei: "From the looks of it, you won't be walking either pretty soon, so you just let me carry her!" With that, he put Weizhen on his back and took big strides forward as Junpei hobbled behind.

As it turned out, this island was called Tung Ping Chau, and it was an outlying island at the edge of Hong Kong's domain. It had residents, and Hong Kongese British troops stationed as defense. It was said that the British troops here had received many mainland fugitives.

Zhugang's leg had lost a significant amount of blood, and the wound had been soaked in saltwater. If he didn't receive medical treatment promptly, his life would be in danger. Under the rescue of the island's British army medical treatment station, he would wake up not long after and be sent with Junpei and Weizhen to be treated at the hospital near Yuen Long police office in Hong Kong.

Nearly a month later, the three of them finally got together at Junpei's family's house in Cheung Sha Wan, Kowloon, and celebrated their rebirth.

# My Path is Not Walked Alone  Part I

## *By Wong Zichang*

From the moment we landed on the shore of Hong Kong—the moment we escaped from the clutches of Death—we thought ourselves simply the fortunate ones that the gods of Luck had taken special care of. Already excited and nervous, with this pain-sticking survival frame of mind and our fresh-experience of the escape journey, we wouldn't expect that the next day we'd bump into someone we knew, and or that this person would be Yang Zhong.

The odds of the happy encounter wouldn't be high; yet classmates from the same city and the same school, without communicating at all in the planning to escape to Hong Kong, nevertheless came by chance, starting from different places along different routes, all almost lost their lives, at almost the same time, arrived at almost the same spot at Hong Kong's New Territory, and even met together at the same Yuan Long Police Station of Hong Kong…; it cannot be said to be anything but a fortuitous coincidence.

But seeing Yang Zhong while being introduced to the same jail cell in Yuen Long police station, and seeing that prison being filled with all the other young "traitors" from the "motherland", there we were, behind the "fortuitous coincidence," indeed an in-depth meaning of ours as well: my path is not walked alone.

Through a long talk with Yang Zhong, I found out the endurance of his "treasonous journey" was another magnificent feat. The difficulties, the narrow escapes of his, together with death of one of his companions, the rugged distances of the land route, the tragic course of events weren't in the least inferior to ours.

Yang Zhong was our school classmate, and of the two friends with whom he had traveled, one he had lost contact with, and one had been bitten by border-guard-dogs and caught before they swam out from the coast of Shekou. Only he was fortunate enough to arrive in Hong Kong. They had all been sent to Dalang Township, Dongguan Prefecture, Guangdong Province, as middle/high school "educated youth." Qi An, who Yang Zhong had lost contact with, was an honnor graduate of the Guangzhou Experimental Hight School, and Tao Ming, who had been caught, was a junior at the Guangzhou #21 Middle School.

Yang Zhong and Tao Ming were with Dalang Commune's Standard Production Brigade Number One Production Team, and Qi An was settle at the Number Seven Production Team. Their residences were only a stone's throw apart, and because they were all educated youth and that the village life was rather lonely, with only a few friends around, they'd see each other frequently with communal meals, playing chess, hunting uphill, and with the time-killing games, and thereby got to know each other like brothers. Furthermore, they all somehow grew in time and harbored resentment at being sent to the countryside against their wills, knowing that having arrived in the countryside they'd have no prospect for the future, especially Qi An, who in school had been an especially gifted and ambitious student. If not for the Cultural Revolution, he'd have gone to university with high hopes of a bright future. Now they came to realize that only in the land of freedom—Hong Kong—could they achieve their dreams.

Before 1949, Yang Zhong's family was a prosperous aristocratic family in Xinhui, Guangdong. Yang Zhong's father had studied in Japan in his adolescence, then returned to China to repay his home-country as a well- known agricultural expert. After the Communist Party established its government, he was labeled a reactionary academic; in that era of class divisions, his home had been dragged deeply into every political movement.

No one in the younger generation of the family could receive a higher education, and Yang Zhong was, of course, no exception. Following the Cultural Revolution, he and his younger brother Yang Da, who had only a middle school education, were sent together to Dalang, Dongguan to work the land, to be reeducated by the peasant. Dongguan and Bao'an neighbored with Hong Kong, because of its unique location, the youths from there fleeing to Hong Kong were numerous, the atmosphere of escape was flourishing, and almost everyone would be, if not already so, thinking about fleeing. Yang Da left for Hong Kong with a local-farmer-friend a few months earlier. Not long after Yang Da left, the three of them began to plan for their own escape.

On a cool autumn night at the beginning of September, Qi An, Tao Ming, and Yang Zhong started out from Yang Zhong's house, groping about in the dark through the rice paddies which had been harvested not long before, hurriedly sneaking into the mountains, with it the thick darken forests, and began the course of their thrilling and dangerous escape journey.

The three all carried backpacks, inside which they'd prepared food rations, old military-use aluminum canteens, rope, small knives, and other goods, and of course, the inner bladder of a basketball. (Speaking of basketball bladders, in that era, when the fleeing to Hong Kong and Macau was "common and trendy", it could be said that in Guangzhou, those were the one of the items in high demand. The government, as a result, disallowed their private sale, and work units and schools needed to show approval from the authorities to buy them. In large part because youth were using them as life-saving tool to swim across the open waters, as the violent waves and sharks of Dapeng Bay, Houhai Bay, and Macau's territorial waters could wreak havoc at any time on the youths who, after having already endured a week or more of the trials and tribulations of walking by night and hiding by day, now had to, with weary bodies, swim a further six to eight hours, wrestling the sea waves, and so, without the aid of basketball bladders or other floatation devices, it would be almost impossible to succeed, and or end up being death amid). The three also carried a compass and a rough sketch of the route. Yang Zhong already had the experience of one failed attempt, so it was up to him to lead the way. On that day, the 22$^{nd}$ of the month by the lunar calendar, the weather was not bad, the moon shining down across the foresteded mountains.

On his first night leading his teammates, Yang Zhong quickly found the path and marched over two small mountain ridges to Luotian Reservoir. The second night they continued the same way, and the third day they began to suffer the consequences of their haste: the foot-soles blistered, the leg-joints became inflamed, their hands and feet were scared from cuts by rocks and the bushes & the tree branches. Awake after daylight sleep, they were unable to move a single step, their bodies like piles of mud. Especially Tao Ming, who was relatively young, and had never made a long trek, was already weary and in pain on the second day, almost ready to beat the return drum. Luckily, Qi An gave him a morale boost, helping him physically and emotionally along the route, which enabled him to persevere. During the day, the three helped each other, massaging each other's shoulders, backs, legs, and feet, puncturing blisters and wrapping them up, and finding herbal medicine to apply to their wounds so as to avoid inflammation, and that night they could only walk slowly, could only cover half of the distance traveled the night before, striving as much as possible to rest. Going like this, their bodies slowly adapted over the third and fourth days......

They say the storm puts the strong grass to the test, that distance tests the horse's stamina. Who'd have guessed that the ordinarily bashful, soft-spoken Qi An would make such a big contribution, devise so many schemes, and work so exceptionally hard? Even though it was Yang Zhong who was relatively familiar with the route, it was Qi An who, whether selecting the better route, coping with pursuit by the People's Militia, or taking care of his companions, showed extreme wisdom and care.

The first night, the three of them crossed Daling Mountain; the second night they passed through the fields of Gongming and arrived at Shiyan; the third night they hurried to Yangtai mountain and arrived as dawn approaching. That night was the most difficult one, plus the occurrence of an incident. With three days of walking by night and resting by day had left them weary and drained, their backs sore and legs numb. The blisters on the soles of our feet had been rubbed raw, our inflamed & swollen knees hurt a frightening amount. The three of them all agreed as one: the next day they had to stay on the mountain to rest; so, they found a concealed cavern at the top of the mountain and slept soundly hidden inside, around noon, a middle-aged, local farmer climbed the mountain looking for herbal medical plantation appeared at the cave entrance, meeting face to face with Yang Zhong who was just awake , by then as a shocked and scared one, Yang Zhong was about to turn and wake his companions to escape, the man slowly waved his hand and said to Yang Zhong: "Don't worry, young man, I'm not here to arrest you, I'm only here to collect medicine. Are you trying to flee the country?" "No, we only came here for fun, and got lost," Yang Zhong stammered back, unable to conceal his confused expression.

The man smiled and said: "Young man, there's no use hiding it from me. I saw right away you were escapees, but it's no matter, I'm not a para-militia, and I have no interest in arresting you…just keep up with your good marching forward, you nevertheless seemed to have taken a circuitous route. Straight ahead is the Xili Reservoir; you should go around the west side of the reservoir, but now you're headed for the east side; if you continue like this, you'll have to add at least a day's time. Therefore, you should take this path here down the mountain and continue straight through the fields on the right side, and you might be able to make up some time. Nevertheless, you'll have to walk at night. In the day there are too many villagers and para-militiamen." Having said that, this man with his face full of sorrow & hardship simply fished out a few lumps of fried rice he had and gave them to Yang Zhong, and then went on and added to his statement,  when walking through the fields at night,  on the right side of the reservoir, there was a field of guava tree, and they should take fruit from it to allay their hunger. He then continued his way ascending the mountain in big strides.

The three of them quickly thanked the man, and watched his healthy silhouette disappear into the woods, rejoicing for having met such a noble person.

On the fourth night, the three of them continued along the route pointed out by that kind man, going around the reservoir by the west side, and sure enough, they did arrive there sooner. Looking back, if they had continued according to their original path, it would have added at least another day's distance. They talked all day about that matter, and how grateful they were.

However, on the fifth day, Yang Zhong's party met its most severe challenge. That day, they arrived on the north side of Tanglang mountain, and the morning's weather was exceptionally nasty, with the dark & heavy clouds rolling overhead and the torrential rain pouring down in bursts. The three of them, with nowhere to hide on the mountain, were thoroughly drenched. They couldn't find a suitable cave, were all hungry and tired, and they had to sit under a thick banyan tree and rest for a while and ate some yams. By this time, the rations they'd been carrying on with them had been nearly exhausted, but Qi An suggested that everyone take some grain products (like biscuits and fried rice) and eat them before descending down to the sea, because wrestling waves for a few hours as they swam would take some energy; those two days they spent as much time as possible picking fruits, digging up yams, gnawing on sugar cane, and so on to allay their hunger and replenish their stamina, and storing as many as possible in their knapsack. In the afternoon they took advantage of the sun's showing its face to dry their clothes a little, and before night fell, they anxiously started out, descending the mountain early.

They didn't expect that because of their early departure; they would be more likely to be caught in dangerous circumstances. Just as they arrived at the foot of the mountain, two militiamen suddenly appeared right in front of them, and from between them a tall, solid figure raised a rifle at them and shouted: "Stop! Don't move! What are you people doing here? Thinking of fleeing? Son of a bitch…" At that moment Yang Zhong and his companions were scared stiff. When they couldn't muster a reaction, they had to simply raise both hands. But because the three were still more than 20 meters away from them, Qi An gave Yang Zhong a look and said in a low voice: "let's run in different directions! We would meet up in Shekou, but first we must draw them apart. Saying this, Qi An suddenly took off up the mountain. At that moment, the militiamen for some reason all started chasing after Qi An, and Yang Zhong just stood next to Tao Ming and watched them suddenly running away, were in shock and decided to run away quickly, pulling Tao Ming along onto the opposite direction with all his might. They squeezed themselves into a pile of dense undergrowth, and, still panting, they heard gunshots coming from far away: bang, bang, bang! The muffled gunshots pierced the vast sky, echoing in the complete vacuum of the valley. It was a while before the sound ceased, but in Yang Zhong's head the buzz was still echoing.

An ominous thought came in vain into Yang Zhong's head: could it be that Qi An who had fallen to their evil scheme, been shot to death? With this thought, Yang Zhong suddenly half-collapsed onto the ground, voiceless for quite a while, Tao Ming pushed him a little, saying "Brother Zhong, what's it, could something bad had happened to Qi An?" At that moment, Tao Ming couldn't control himself anymore and started crying with his hands on his cheeks. It was a long time before Yang Zhong replied, in a trembling voice: "Probably... probably no, nothing's wrong. Heaven helps the worthy. We should move on so they couldn't find us!" He wiped dry his tears with his sleeve. Tao Ming, too, now, had the ominous thought in his mind, his eyes filled with tears. As he hurriedly followed Yang Zhong, he turned his head back to the direction QiAn had run, praying that by some miracle, he would reappear...

That night, as they walked, Yang Zhong and Tao Ming were extremely gloomy, walking without saying even one word the whole way. Unfortunately, at midnight thunder suddenly erupted, a torrential rain poured down, and the frightening lightning looked as if it wanted to rip apart the sky. Yang Zhong and Tao Ming hid in a cave and watched the mountain flash flood roaring by, feeling indescribable grief and indignation throughout that sleepless night, staring blankly as the thunder and lightning slowly abated, the torrential rains grew softer. As the sky lightened, they gradually calmed down, and a long time later, the two exhausted people fell asleep.

When they awoke, the sky had cleared up. It was already midday, the fierce sun made it difficult for them to keep their eyes open, Yang Zhong walked out of the cave and found that there was a dragon eye fruit tree

(Longan Tree) not far away, with plump & juicy fruit ready for harvest. At that point, they hadn't eaten anything all night, and their stomachs were rumbling with hunger. Yang Zhong called over Tao Ming at once, and they grabbed a whole bunch and wolfed it down.

Just as they were eating enthusiastically, Tao Ming stared fixedly behind Yang Zhong, pointed above Yang Zhong's head, and there recoiled a snake as he said to Yang Zhong: "A vi—a viper! M—move away!" Yang Zhong being suddenly terrified and afraid to move, turned his eyes up and caught a glimpse of a black-and-white striped viper rolled up in the tree branch above his head. Yang Zhong looked up momentarily, and in lightning speed, swatted it down with a dried-up tree branch, which hit the snake in the head with a bang, Yang Zhong quickly rolled himself over and, looking at the snake's limp body dripping blood from the head, said: "Close call! This guy's highly toxic; one bite would be all it needs to kill! all would be gone by then! Fortunately, that you saw it in time; today's not the day we die!" Saying this, he thrashed at the snake's head again, to make sure it was no longer breathing. The two of them quickly threw the remnants of the fruit down into the underbrush, picked a few more and put them in their bags, and continued down the mountain.

It was around two in the afternoon then, and in the daytime, they didn't dare walk down the official path, instead having to wind through the undergrowth, blazing a new trail forward. They spent over half the day on that little distance, bruised and scared by branches, thorns, rocks, their clothes considerably torn, and with their wild hair and beards, they looked like beggars. But Yang Zhong knew that after he descended this mountain, he'd have crossed the Tanglang mountains, and then after that came Shekou and Houhai Bay…across which would be the place called Hong Kong.

So, he didn't think about it too much and just kept walking.

Yang Zhong had always been a strong person, and Tao Ming was also, but Tao Ming was, after all, much younger, and clearly didn't match Yang Zhong in endurance. Having spent five- or six-days crossing mountains and severely using up his physical strength, he often fell far behind Yang Zhong, and many times Yang Zhong needed to care for and help him.

As the ancients said:

"Ninety miles would merely be one half of a one-hundred-mile journey."

Yang Zhong knew that this last section would be hugely difficult, and would require even more perseverance, and furthermore the last section required exceptional caution. With that in mind, he pulled Tao Ming aside and told him: "*A* Ming, let's rest a while; you're too tired. We must save strength. Because we'll arrive at the waterfront soon, what's ahead of us is Tanglang Mountain; and behind that is Houhai Bay."

Even though he was very tired, Tao Ming resolutely replied, brother, you didn't need to worry about me. I could support myself, it's okay. Yang Zhong relaxed a lot at these words. In the afternoon, they rested for a full three hours, so they'd be ready to climb the mountain in front of them when it got dark.

As a result, they were lucky that evening, and met no obstacles, spending only half the night climbing Tanglang Mountain. They found a safe spot to stop for a while on the mountaintop, and as they rested, looked out past Shekou and Houhai to Hong Kong. There was no moon that night, but there were also no clouds, and the visibility was very high, and behind the shadows of the endless mountains on the opposite side of the bay, you could see the spectacular magnificence launching itself straight up into the clouds. Laying eyes on the destination they'd soon arrive at; it was impossible not to be excited. But turning their eyes downward, they saw the vast expanse spanning Houhai Bay, in the billowing of the waves of the sea, and in the darkness, they could hear the heavy sound of a tsunami and felt a sudden chilliness in the air. They asked themselves: "Could we really swim to the other side safe and sound?"

Yang Zhong and Tao Ming hid in a mound behind a large tree and found a level place to lie down. Tao Ming actually had been extremely tired and fell asleep quickly. But Yang Zhong was unable to sleep with all the thoughts flashing back in his mind, of all he'd experienced these past few years; one by one, he turned over everything in his mind…

When he was young, with his parents working and teaching in other parts of the country, he and his brothers lived with their paternal grandfather. The Yang family was a distinguished one in its home village, Yang Zhong's father was a well-known agricultural expert, and the brothers lived a life of luxury, a life of plenty, and a life of being well taken care of. Afterward, his father was painted as a landlord-class counterrevolutionary and cruelly suppressed and made out to be a right-wing reactionary academic authority and sent away to the outer provinces for Reeducation Through Labor. With all that, the illustrious family Yang was ruined, its former days of splendor vanished; the family scattered, and people died. The survival Yang's brothers moved in all different directions, and Yang Zhong was left with nowhere to stay, suffering all kinds of humiliation, until he was finally adopted by his paternal aunt. In school, he still carried the social status of a landlord counterrevolutionary, but fortunately, with the help of a classmate of his father's, he was accepted into Guangzhou Peiying Secondary School (Guangzhou Number Eight Secondary School). In school, the view of the Dictatorship of the Proletariat was in vogue. As a child of one of the Black Five, he could only nod his head at what others said. And he certainly would not be able to take the college entrance exam; he prepared early for his "*shangshanxiaxiang*"(a movement of sending the young students to the countryside to be reeducated by the poor peasants). He remembered that once, during the Cultural Revolution, there was a group of sons of the high honored cadres (party members) that directed a "struggle-session", and when it was time for Yang Zhong's self- denouncement, Yang Zhong falsely said: "I was born into a family of counterrevolutionaries, and the apple does not fall far from the tree. I was by nature a successor to reactionaries; I would be a son of a bitch! Through the teachings of the party and the proletariat, I had profoundly recognized my and my family's crimes, and from today onward, I would set myself clearly apart from my staunchly criminal family and reactionary parents! Long live Chairman

Mao! Long live the Great Proletarian Cultural Revolution!"

Thinking of all this, Yang Zhong couldn't contain his sadness, and tears began trickling down his face: he never thought that to the family that gave him such a good life and a good childhood, his dear parents, he would go so far as to dishonor them so…

Then he looked at the sleeping Tao Ming and thought: how could his life experience not be even more miserable? His father had been suppressed immediately after Liberation, as he had been an officer in the Nationalist military (a low level one), and his beautiful mother had been forced to remarry a chief-cook in the Southern People's Liberation Army. Yang Zhong thought, then, in a daze, dozing over and started to try to get some sleep. He'd wake up when it was already at day break.

At dawn, still on top of the mountain, they found some fruit to stave off hunger, and the remaining provisions they kept for the last moment, reducing as much as possible what they were carrying, to prepare for the nighttime when they'd make their last sprint.

That day the time seemed to be the hardest to endure; the sun seemed to Cross the sky exasperatingly slowly, finally disappearing below the horizon with great difficulty. Yang Zhong and Tao Ming seized the moment, hurriedly descending from the middle of the mountain. From the base of the mountain to the open sea, it was still another hour's distance, and, furthermore, it was the most dangerous part. At any time, they might meet border guards on patrol with loaded rifles ready to excute, and the border guards at Shekou, Bao'an would kill fugitives without a second thought, with no mercy.

Yang Zhong led Tao Ming in an S-shape through the trees, after every short interval checking their surroundings before continuing. They continued this walking and waiting-and-see for about half an hour, until Yang Zhong and Tao Ming stopped in some low bushes along the side of the road by the sea. From there, the water was still maybe 100 meters away. Separating them from it was the so-called National Defense Highway. You could already hear the sound of the waves throwing themselves at the shore. They couldn't help but feel a little nervous, in the darkness they exchanged ideas, and both thought they'd fully prepared, when, at the very moment they were about to set off, they heard the sound of panting and the sound of very fast running. The shadow of a huge monster had suddenly reached them, and Tao Ming had just been where the shadow now was. Yang Zhong, thinking it was the dog of a border guard, secretly thought it was all lost. By the time he thought to pull Tao Ming and flee, that shadow had already pounced on Tao Ming. In a moment of desperation, Yang Zhong picked up the rocks around him and flung them at the dog.

But the rock missed it, and Tao Ming had already been knocked down by that big dog, screaming into the night: "Brother, save me .." When Yang Zhong picked up a bigger rock intending to fling it again, he suddenly noticed that they had been joined by several shadows on the road not far away, sprinting toward them, shining flashlights as they came, Yang Zhong was now even more alarmed, and Tao Ming, pounced upon by the ferocious beast, blood pouring from his open-leg-wound, already knew after several rounds of wrestling with his hands that he could never free himself from that animal with his strength alone, and hastily told Yang Zhong with a painful look on his face: "Run brother! The armed border guards are coming! Forget me, just run…"

Saying this, he fell onto the ground and stopped struggling. Yang Zhong saw the shadows of two border guards getting closer and closer, and he felt there was no way he could bear it; his heart torn with grief and indignation, tears forced their way out of his eyes, and he threw the rock at the dog with all his might, hitting the dog's rear leg. The senseless animal was, after all, a trained army dog, still unwaveringly biting onto Tao Ming's leg, a pair of claws in his body, and its claws were incomparably sharp, tearing apart Tao Ming's clothing in several places during the struggle, with dark red blood dripping out (his legs and torso were already badly mangled).

Yang Zhong knew he couldn't save Tao Ming with the bullets shooting all around them at an alarming speed. Using the body-height bushes by the sea as a shield, Yang Zhong rushed forward to the ocean.

Of the two border guards, one had already reached Tao Ming and taken control of him, and the other one was chasing after Yang Zhong, shouting "Treasonous thief, stop!" with the popping sound of the shooting of an automatic rifle. The bullets were flying around him; the crack of gunshot pierced through the heavy night sky. Yang Zhong knew he was trapped in a risky spot, but he also knew that in this critical moment, he could not hesitate, and so he ignored the bullets screaming past his ears, summing up all of his strength sprinting himself toward the waterfront. He tripped and fell on a rock but still kept madly sprinting forward with all his might, occasionally turning his head to see behind him. By now, several other border guards had rushed over as reinforcements, their flashlights making doodles in the sky, their shouts to catch the treasonous thief growing louder and louder, piercing through the quite sky… But Yang Zhong's will to live, his faith in liberty, and his determination to escape these severe politics would ultimately triumph over their lawless pursuit. In a flash, he arrived at the shore of Houhai Bay, dashed himself right into the water, and began swimming as fast as he could.

By the time the frantic soldiers arrived shouting at the shore, Yang Zhong had already swum out to the center, out of their firing range.

Yang Zhong let out a sigh and relaxed his swimming speed slightly to turn his head and look back at the shore.

The soldiers' silhouettes were already fuzzy, and all that was visible from afar were the shines of flashlights, and Yang Zhong knew that he was out of danger of being shot at and had passed into the limits of safety. He relaxed a little, but thinking of the sight of Tao Ming's bloody leg, he felt ineffable grief and indignation. But now, what he would soon face with was a fierce fight against the black expanse of the bay, it's rough waves at time and he would be forced to calmly respond to the predicament he now faced: How could he swim across? Did he have sufficient. Yang Zhong raised his head and took a deep breath, then took the basketball bladder out of his drenched backpack and blew it up and tied a small rope around the mouthpiece, and floated for a little while, letting his body rest.

He opened endurance. Right now, the sea was relatively calm, without many big waves his eyes wide and looking at the twinkling stars on the black horizon. Yang Zhong thought of Tao Ming, just attacked by the dog, and Qi An, just lost to the gunfire, and worried about their whereabouts and situations. Could Qi An really have been shot dead? What cruelty could the injured Tao Ming have been met with? Thinking of these pessimistic thoughts, sadness welled up within him and two trickles of warm tears dripped from his eyes. But Yang Zhong soon found strength in his sorrow, knowing that then was not the time for grieving: his current situation still a nasty one: his strength had been worn down by the long trek, the wind and waves could pick up at any time, he truly didn't know what would be the environment lying ahead, and he had no clue how long he would have to keep swimming. He straightened out his state of mind, felt around for the almost-gone rations—the fried rice that man had given him, stuffed some in his mouth, and drank a mouthful of water, but immediately choked on the saltiness. He'd swallowed the food, but Yang Zhong knew he wouldn't have any potable fresh water that night. Fortunately, the water near the Pearl River Delta was relatively mild, and now in the last part of the journey, unbearably hungry and thirsty, Yang Zhong must drink to survive.

Yang Zhong swam south at an average speed, and perhaps half an hour later, wind suddenly began blowing across the water, and the waves gradually grew larger, which Yang Zhong strenuously fought. The countercurrent in the bay started pushing him north, and Yang Zhong panicked, fearing he'd be pulled back to the north shore, and did his utmost to work against the stream. He swam like that for around one and a half of an hour, until the wind and waves gradually pacified. Yang Zhong had used up his energy and slowly began to rest again. He could dimly see the south shore, and a little hope rose up in his chest. But one lone person floating in the sea was still helpless and drifted and added to that spirit-weary and unbearably hungry and thirsty. Yang Zhong thought of his father and brothers, and he vaguely heard his father encouraging him, and Yang Da on the opposite shore beckoning him on… Yang

Zhong said to himself, if my brother can do this, why can't I? I'm fighting for my life now; I can't give up! With this thought, he regained strength and continued swimming, as the horizon began getting brighter.

He suddenly saw the south shore, and Yang Zhong couldn't contain his excitement. He sped up more, and suddenly his foot hit something, and he felt a stabbing pain. When he put his foot down again, he found it was solid ground! But he quickly realized that this wasn't regular solid ground, but an oyster farm. Yang Zhong was both excited and concerned. Excited to have finally reached Hong Kong but concerned because he'd flung off his shoes when he reached the water on the other side, and now that he'd reached this oyster stack, how could he walk across it! Yang Zhong couldn't take it for very long, so he took advantage of when the water was still up to his chest by cautiously swimming for another stretch, and when he had to walk a few steps, his feet were gashed open in several places, dark red blood trickling out and dying the water red. Yang Zhong had to stop, resisting the pain at his core, and took off his clothing and used a small knife to cut off the sleeves, which he tied around his feet, and then he slowly dragged his weary body out of the oyster farm and onto the shore land, even though he only added to the scars on his legs this way.

By the time Yang Zhong was pulling himself up onto the shore from the water, the sky was lighter, and the eastern sun had already quickly risen above the horizon. Yang Zhong knew he'd reached his freedom, but even though he was excited, after a night of persecution, he was utterly exhausted, and couldn't hold himself up, and after taking a few steps into the forest, fell over, collapsed…

He stayed there for he didn't know how long, until he heard a thickly Hakka-accented man say in his ear: "Hey, get up, young man, you're in Hong Kong!" Yang Zhong slowly opened his eyes and saw an old man standing by his side, laughing to himself and saying: "Congratulations, wake up, get up! Let's get to my house and I'll make you something to eat!" With that, he helped Yang Zhong up and pulled him slowly along to a stone house nearby. When they entered the house, the man made a place for him and sat him down on an old sofa and then went into the kitchen and made a bowl of warm sweet potato porridge for Yang Zhong to eat. The warmth of the porridge restored some of Yang Zhong's strength, and he got up at once off the sofa and kneeled in front of the old man, bowing with his hands in front, wanted to thank the old man for his gracious help. The wrinkled old man hurried to say: "There's no need. It's enough that you made it to the safety, and that's your own good luck, and add to that your own great effort and courage, your fate! I've seen I don't know how many corpses had floated onto this shore from the north side! The lucky ones aren't many, young man, so treasure your future! You just rest here a little while, then I'll tell you to turn yourself in at the Lau Fau Shan police station. They don't repatriate people now; they grant amnesty to the crowds of escapees from the mainland."

Yang Zhong slept at the old man's house for perhaps two hours, then followed the path the old man had directed him on, to turn himself in at the Lau Fau Shan police station, and would in turn be sent to the Yuen Long police station, where he waited for Yang Da to pick him up.

After meeting us in the police station and until we left Hong Kong, everyone kept in continual contact. When we were first starting our new lives, because none of us had relatives or societal connections, nor specialized skills in Hong Kong, nor record of higher education, everyone had to look for work in the "Three Professions" (the construction industry, the food industry, and dock work). But we all knew that from now on, our fate was in our own hands, so we never found the work bitter, and we supported each other, helped each other, and worked very diligently. Some of us toiled away in our free time to continue our studies. Yang Zhong always missed his two friends, and many years later, learned that Qi An really had been shot dead by those two cruel, inhumane militiamen. His sister was heartbroken when she heard the news, and didn't dare to tell their elderly mother, who nevertheless knew by other means the news of her son's death. Qi An's mother would think of her son all day long, without any news of him. She went mad thinking of her son. In the end, with the tear washing her face, it wasn't too long before she suffered from schizophrenia. Mother Qi muttered to herself all day and all night: "An, son, come home quickly, Mama's made you your favorite *tangyuan*, *tangyuan*, *tangyuan*, a mother-son reunion. Be a good son and come see your mother, okay?" Her family members all cried when they heard this. Every Qingming Festival, Qi An's sister and father would secretly prepare an offering for the family shrine to pay their respects to Qi An.

After Tao Ming was captured, he was held in a camphorwood detention center and suffered a month of torment before being sent back to the supervision of his production team. Because the dog bite wounds had not been taken care of timely, they became inflamed and festered, and it was nearly a year before they recovered completely and left behind permanent scars. Afterward, Tao Ming underwent several more attempts, and after much difficulty, finally successfully arrived in Hong Kong in 1975. Not long after, he became a counterrevolutionary and was sent by Taiwan's general mobilization efforts to study at a university in Taiwan. By then, Yang Zhong had already immigrated from Hong Kong to New York. They would never see each other again.

# My Path is Not Walked Alone  Part II

## By Wong Zichang

Time passes quickly. One day, many years later, HuQi was entertaining guests at his son's wedding in Los Angeles, at a big banquet in Atlantic Seafood Restaurant in Monterrey Park, Southern California. At around seven o'clock, nearly all of the *laosanjie* (high school senior class of the year 1966) schoolmates who were living in Los Angeles was present, with many of them I hadn't seen in many decades. All were entering their old age and, after having seen many great changes in the world, being able to reunion with old classmates, old schoolmates and old friends of many years ago, in a foreign land, made us feel a sense of regret, and yet thankful, even more wistful, and we talked unceasingly with endless topics.

Sitting by my side was Zhong Jia, who I'd known for many years, but had rarely meet-up. He worked at Jinlan Company, in the same profession as me. Because Hu Qi had excitedly introduced us (me, Zhiyou, and himself) to his guests as his "Same Boat" companions, the topic of our fleeing from Guangdong to Hong Kong came up between us. As it turns out, Zhong Jia was by then also one of the youths who'd fled to Hong Kong in those years; just like me, he'd failed one time, but after unremitting efforts, proving his perseverance and courage, he succeeded in reaching Hong Kong on his second attempt.

After he graduated from GuangXi High School in Guangzhou, he was sent to countryside, to Houjie, in Dongguan Prefecture, Guangdong Province. After around three years of working in the field(farmland), on a day in June of 1972, he and a local farmer companion rode their bicycles in the direction of Humen, bypassing numerous People's Militia lookout posts along the highway, finally arriving at Songgang in Bao'an County in the evening, near the house of a friend who promised that she would help them, but then that friend didn't show. They were very worried, because all of the prepared backup food and articles, they'd stockpiled in her house! With no other way around, they found themselves a place to hide and waited there till around 10:00pm, then felt around in the dark and somehow got into her house, and took the provisions they'd hidden in her house, then tiptoed out of the village before climbing the mountain to the south, keep running and walking till about midnight, they found a patch of pine trees in the dark in which they could rest, because they were so exhausted, they fell asleep as soon as they sat down. When he opened his eyes in the morning, feeling the uncontrollable itch all over his body, and when he looked down, he saw caterpillars crawling all over him. He hurriedly took off the clothes and knocked off the caterpillars, ran out of the pine trees, found another concealed spot on a neighboring peak and stayed hiding again, till it got dark.

They, subsequently underwent five arduous days of the hardships of travel before arriving at the peak of the mountain(Tanglang Shan)by the National Defense highway in Shekou, and Zhong Jia and his companion had, over the course of their journey, met many like-minded people on the same route, and all decided to continue the journey together, helping each other along the way, by the time they reached Tanglang Shan, there were more than 11 people in their group! They crossed mountains and waded rivers, resting by day and walking by night, cutting their way through thistles and thorns, their bodies unbearably weary, both hungry and tired. The rations they had were nearly used up, they were forced to pick wild fruits along the way to stave off hunger, with their clothes being so badly torn, they looked like beggars.

They could already clearly see Hong Kong from across the bay, and everyone was visibly moved and boosting each other's morale, all thinking that after another day and night, they'd be breathing the air of freedom. Everyone was preparing to cross the National Defense Highway, when, unbeknownst to them, they'd already been surrounded by border guards, like a turtle trapped in a jar. (Perhaps there were too many of them in the group, became too big of a target; sometimes people speaking too loudly... being the root of the trouble.)

At around six or seven in the evening, with the sky growing dark, they heard dog barking from all around, and the border guards shouted coarse and ear-piercing: "Hands up! Don't move...!" Everyone frenetically got up at once, knowing they had lost, staring at each other blankly in absolute silence. But by then, they'd already arrived at the water's edge, and they'd seen their destination... How could they just sit with their hands tied, waiting to be captured? They passed along in a low voice a solemn and stirring "order": We must run away from each other! And everyone obeyed the order and rapidly dispersed. Zhong Jia picked a direction in a panic, tripped over his feet, falling ten meters down the hill, and was immediately knocked down by a ferocious military dog released by the border guards, and was arrested. Fortunately, besides a few bites from the dog, he had only some superficial wounds, but those border guards immediately tied up the "class enemies" with their arms behind their backs, lecturing them orally and corporally, howling about "You treasonous defecting sons of bitches, how dare you?! Firmly suppress the counterrevolutionaries! Long live the Dictatorship of the Proletariat!" and such slogans. The border guards hit them with fists and the butts of their guns until they became unable to resist the violent strikes; Zhong Jia lost consciousness because of that, when he woke up, he was lying on the ground in a detention center.

Later he learned that most of his companions had been captured, some had been simply killed injured by the gunfire, but there were also a few of them in the group who'd been fortunate enough to safely escape to Hong Kong.

He also said that prior to arriving at Tanglang Shan, he'd had an unique-encounter on the journey that had boosted his morale, and that that was having met some "true Chinese people": The third day after they'd set out, they were seized by four local Para-militia(People's Militiamen), not expecting that his farmer companion would suddenly kneel down and plead, imploring the 4 men to let them loose , and did his utmost to pull Zhong Jia into his pleading. At first, he thought how could these four para-militias possibly all agree to let them go?! But after begging and begging with them, the unexpected happened, and the militiamen looked at each other and actually agreed, kindly communicating their decision: not only did they let them go, but they also gave them the *zongzi* (粽子, Rice-wrap)hey had with them, and gave them directions for the route ahead, reminding them to be careful of the border guard-camp ahead! He thought to himself, "Compared to those diabolical border guards, these common people still had empathy for us. Even in that era of a tyrannical government that had been fiercer than a tiger, somehow, in heaven and earth righteousness still existed, consciences had not vanished, and our path was truly not walked alone…"

After he was caught, Zhong Jia stayed more than a month in a prison. When he recalled the inhumane treatment of the detention center, Zhong Jia became extremely indignant, giving this example: in the prison, there were two inmates from Hainan Island, who were classified as "Hainan Construction Corps Farmers." (The so-called Construction Corps involved the forcible concentration of high school and college students from every part of Guangdong Province being sent onto Hainan Island for the hard labor of land reclamation for the designated farming and rubber plantations.) In the prison, they were handcuffed to the metal bars and forced to stand for 24 hours straight, where they had to urinate and defecate on the spot, and at night, they even had to sleep standing up! This was reportedly defined as an applicable martial law punishment. The food that was served to the prisoners was often mixed with sand, the disciplinarians would use the slightest pretext to beat up and mistreat the "illegal defectors," and at mealtimes, the prisoners only received about two *liang* (about-3oz) of coarse grains filled with tripe. Knowing that there existed his constitutionally ensured basic human rights to freely migrate and freely leave the country and still being treated as cruelty and inhumanly as such in return, how could one not be indignant?!

After Zhong Jia returned to the commune, something happened that he thought very unexpectedly: their local People's Militia commander had learned of their unsuccessful attempt to cross the border and asked that when Zhong Jia made the next attempt, to take him along! Zhong Jia was stupefied and, thinking that it was a trap, ended up telling him that he didn't currently have any plans and should tactfully decline.

Despite all this, with the militia commander having the thought of escape could be a real possibility, especially during the Cultural Revolution, too much information about the government's scandals had been laid bare in the public, many bright and admirable goals concealed with wretched scandals that ordinary people now saw very clearly, with loincloths removed, beneath the heartstring-pulling government slogans was the raw violence that ruled the country. The Communist Party's so-called Pinxiazhongnong Policy was nothing more than empty words. Added to that many years of administrative lapse, and the populous and once rich and affluent Pearl River Delta was suddenly starving! Our Xiani, in Lingshan commune, Panyu prefecture, had a born-poor production team leader who once said: First they take the taxes, then they take the surplus, but we're starving, what "surplus," those swindlers!

It was in that environment that the news proliferated of a better life for those who went to Hong Kong, and many Down-to-the-Countryside young people, one after another, risked one's life to escape to Hong Kong… It would be hard not to be swept up into the powerful atmosphere and undercurrent…i.e., to team up the right people and do the right thing.

Secretly, Jia Zhong had been intensifying his preparations, and one month later, he began his second attempt, bringing with him a robust, like- minded fellow villager. This time you could say that Jia Zhong came with himself a set mind of no retreat, "break the axe and sink the boat", He prepared as well as he could and diligently practiced his swimming. Sure enough, this time it was another six days of hiding and six nights of walking in one direction. They crossed mountains and rivers, cut through thistles and thorns, ate wild fruits once they ran out of provisions, fell down, then got right up and kept charging forward, wrestled off wild beasts and vipers, quarreled with each other, then pulled together again and braved rainstorms…finally reached at a different section of the same National Defense Highway. They still met the pursuit of the armed border guards, but this time they were able to take advantage of the darkness of the night to break away from them, and pounce into the waters of Shenzhen Bay.

After almost eight hours of swimming & fighting, fighting the rough waves at times throughout the way;  fought really hard several times against the odd-currents, almost give up at times, they eventually  broke free of the well-known formidable countercurrent in Shenzhen Bay; and midway across the  bay while Zhong Jia's companion was struggling to swim and had lost his basketball bladder, so Zhong Jia selflessly helped him (they shared his own equipment, with pushing and pulling it in the water…), and they finally reached the beach at Lau Fau Shan in Hong Kong's New Territories at dawn, he simply collapsed Just as he was barely ashore and was being carried by his companion to look for an enthusiastic local for help and be woken up then.

# Old Soldiers Never Die

*By A Ho*

Cantonese is one of the most vivid and humorous languages in the world. Half a century ago, "卒" was a synonym for escapee. In Chinese chess, "卒" is the piece with the lowest value and function, much like the lowly common people. The character "督" in Cantonese means "to push forward the chess piece." When the escapee "卒" crosses the river, its value multiplies instantly! The "卒" almost becomes like a "chariot," transforming from a sparrow into a phoenix, with a fortune change rising suddenly. People aspire to higher places, water flows downward, and those seeking a better life and freedom ventured into risky journeys. In this world, it is always "the brave who win"! Therefore, "督卒" became a semi-public adventurous fashion and the greatest gamble of life. Crossing the Shenzhen River and the natural barrier of the Pearl River estuary was like entering paradise on earth. Of course, the adventure was akin to crossing a ghost gate and was by no means an easy task. The success of an escapee's "卒運" was always an unknown, with success relying more than half on the favor of the heavens. When someone lives a life without hope or a sense of value, risking a "zero" value life for the dawn of rebirth is a great stimulation of personal initiative, allowing them to disregard life and death. With the completion of the "Escape to Hong Kong Memorial Monument" in the Barstow Desert, memories of half a century ago ripple like water, filled with gratitude for the mercy of the heavens and remembrance of those who lost their lives and their unfulfilled aspirations. Their bodies have left us, but the "spirit of the 卒" remains. The vibrant murals on the monument depict the tragic separation of life and death and the cold-bloodedness of armed guards. The inscription—"Old Soldiers Never Die"—though simple, is profound, comforting the souls of the unfortunate escapees, and evoking the survivors' contemplation and gratitude. As a surviving old soldier, I offer a bit of historical witness here. With no political motives, I only wish to describe that piece of history a little. The river of history leaves traces, and I am just a speck of sand in its trace, light in intention. But grains of sand form a tower, and years later, our generation of old soldiers will become rare creatures like World War II veterans, as our limited lives draw to a close. Though we lack the writing prowess of Sima Qian, we have the heart of elders telling stories, which can serve as a small reminder and warning to the world.

## Three Years of Sharpening the Sword

In the late autumn of 1968, following a decree stating, "It is very necessary for educated youth to go to the countryside and receive re-education from the poor and lower-middle peasants," over 17 million middle school students across China, having completed the so-called mission of "seizing power from the capitalists in power," suddenly became "dispatched soldiers" or sent-down educated youth. At that time, I was only 17 years old. Because of my family's background as "industrial and commercial landlords," our home was repeatedly raided from the start of the Cultural Revolution, and we faced political attacks, making going to the countryside my only option. With the pain of losing my education and the feeling of being exiled, I reluctantly joined a production team in Shunde County, located in the Pearl River Delta.

Shunde County is a water town crisscrossed by rivers. Small boats and ships are the main means of transportation. From the production team where I was sent, it was about a day's journey by water to Wanqingsha in Panyu, and the sea facing Wanqingsha led to the open waters towards Hong Kong. At that time, the trend of sneaking into Hong Kong and Macau was growing stronger along the coastal areas, and Wanqingsha became one of the best departure points for such escapes.

The harsh life of a farmer and the meager work points that barely sustained my livelihood became increasingly unbearable. Worse still, my frequent weekly correspondence with my father in Hong Kong began to be intercepted, opened, and inspected, fueling my anger. My father had fled to Hong Kong in 1952, narrowly escaping becoming a victim of the land reform movement. Labeled as a "fugitive landlord," my father left my mother to raise us siblings under difficult circumstances. At the age of 13, when my mother was critically ill, my father risked his life to visit us in Guangzhou, but he could only stay for a brief day. Back then, customs did not have computer systems, and fortunately, he left early; otherwise, he would have been arrested. Deprived of a mother's love, my father's letters became my sole source of faith and love from my teenage years through middle school. Now, even this little bit of emotional support was being taken away, leaving me in deep sorrow and anger. I secretly told myself: Escaping to Hong Kong was my only way out. I had to find a way to sneak into Hong Kong and reunite with my father, even if it meant risking my life and being buried at sea if I failed!

From then on, I began earnest preparations for my escape. A strong physique was a necessary condition for sneaking across. To build my strength, I persisted in winter swimming and took on the heaviest tasks in the production team, especially rowing boats and cutting water grass. Each outing lasted from three to seven days, and I had to manage food, clothing, and shelter on the small boat. I remember one trip when I was caught in a sudden storm. The small boat's canopy was no match for the wind and rain. To make matters worse, a giant wave from an approaching large ship capsized my small boat before I could react, sending my cooking pot, stove, and other belongings into the water, where they sank instantly. My quilt, the most valuable possession I owned, was swept away, but I fought desperately and was lucky enough to retrieve it.

Another unforgettable experience on the boat was when there was a severe shortage of fertilizer. Somehow, a resourceful member of the production team managed to secure a rare deal with the Guangzhou sanitation department to trade white sugar for yellow human waste As if it were a treasure, the production team arranged for people to transport the "gold" from Guangzhou weekly. Despite knowing it was a tough job, I volunteered for the special mission of transporting the "gold" to train my boating skills and familiarize myself with the river conditions and currents.

Since the wooden boat was not motorized, we relied on bamboo poles for propulsion and pulled the boat along the riverbank like traditional trackers. It took three days to travel one way from Shunde to Guangzhou. The journey with an empty boat was relatively easy, but the most daunting part was loading the cargo in Guangzhou. The large boat docked by the Pearl River, where the sanitation department's trucks pumped the yellow, thick sludge into the boat's hold like a raging torrent. The yellowish thick juice splattered everywhere. The wooden boat had no cover, and under the scorching sun, the stench intensified. Worse yet, the boat's cramped space offered no escape, so we ate and slept surrounded by the human excrement. A single misstep could lead to a disastrous fall, covering oneself in the foul substance.

Despite the stench, my stubborn nature meant I wouldn't back down from a task I had chosen myself. It was midsummer, and strangely, after two days of sun exposure, the surface of the sludge formed a hard, black crust, seemingly covering the smell. However, upon scientific reflection, I realized it wasn't that the crust wasn't smelly; it was a phenomenon akin to "becoming accustomed to the smell."

The return journey with a fully loaded boat presented another challenge. As the boat rocked with the waves, the sludge danced along, occasionally splashing onto the deck. For a city youth unversed in agriculture, this was revolting. In the river's upstream section, we had to rely on manpower to pull the boat. Among the five boatmen, I was the youngest and least experienced, so the most arduous job naturally fell to me. With a hundred-foot-long hemp rope on my shoulder, I dragged thousands of pounds of waste, trudging step by step along the riverbank and muddy shoals. My heart bled: how did I fall to such a state? Taking orders from the poorest and most uncouth people, doing the hardest, most primitive labor, and risking my life to transport the dirtiest, most unbearably foul human waste! Lost in painful contemplation, I was at a loss. Suddenly, a shout snapped me out of my daze, "Use your strength!" It turned out that in my silence, I had slowed down, loosened the tow rope, and the boat had stopped moving forward and started to drift back! The man at the front of the boat, holding the bamboo pole, shouted in panic, which immediately woke me up. That night, the boat docked by the riverbank. As I lay on the deck, gazing at the starry sky, my mind was racing with thoughts. Tossing and turning, unable to sleep, I glanced over at the man's face in the dim night. Seeing his weathered features and sun-worn, half-bald head sent a shiver down my spine, as if I saw my future self! I gritted my teeth silently: I would fight with all my might to escape this cage, or else I would end up like this man, spending my life with human excrement as my companion.

## The belief in escaping was as solid as iron in my heart

Day by day, I endured the life of working the land, secretly investigating and pondering ways to escape. I concluded that there were three key conditions for a successful escape: First, there must be a group of five people who can absolutely trust each other and share life and death together. We needed a grass boat about 20 feet long, divided into five compartments, each with one person. Too many people would overload the boat, while too few would lack strength. Second, we had to familiarize ourselves with the water route from the production team to Wanqingsha. Coastal defense areas were restricted zones, and without a special permit, we could be detained by local militias. Third, we needed five small grass boats. The 20 feet sea-going boat would be our main vessel and had to be particularly sturdy to withstand the Pacific's waves. Before setting out to sea, the five of us would split up into five small boats to divert the attention of the militia and border posts.

At that time, many people along the coast wanted to escape, but finding partners who were both brave and resourceful was rare. Through extensive networking and long-term observation, I selected four friends who shared my ambition. Over the decades, we became close friends and sworn brothers. The eldest was the son of a wealthy farmer who had previously failed in an escape attempt and was subsequently imprisoned and publicly humiliated in town. The second was from a waterborne family of three generations of poor farmers and had served as a militia platoon leader. His family was very close to mine. The third and fifth were also sons of poor farmers, but their fathers had escaped to Hong Kong years ago, so they had the "heroic genes" of "a hero father's son is a hero." I was the fourth in rank. Age wise, I ranked the third. For easy reference, I'll call them: OldOne, OldTwo, OldFourth and OldFive from now on.

After years of exploring routes, we used the excuse of going out to cut grass and gradually ventured further south with our grass boats, becoming bolder until we reached the vicinity of the last outpost of the thirteenth inlet of Wanqingsha. The militias considered it unlikely for a small grass boat to attempt a sea escape, so they relaxed their vigilance toward us. Finally, everything was ready except for the wind—the selection of the "set sail" date.

Due to the wind conditions, winter was typically the peak season for escape attempts, but it was also when border defenses were the strictest. In summer, the southeast winds created headwinds, and the combination of headwinds and favorable currents produced huge waves, making it a life-threatening gamble for escapees. Therefore, summer was considered an off-season for escaping. However, driven by reverse thinking, we decided to set sail in the off-season summer, using the disadvantage of high-risk sailing to exchange for the advantage of relaxed coastal defenses. This was a decision made at the cost of our lives, a do-or-die move where failure meant being buried in the belly of the sea.

## Fleeing to the Furious Sea

July 1, 1972, was the 51st anniversary of the Communist Party. After our research, we found that the weather forecast and tidal cycle were favorable that day. Thus, the Party's birthday became our auspicious date to flee to the sea. An old, expired village travel permit was cleverly modified by removing the ink with bleach and resealing it with rice water, creating a flawless valid document. (This historical document with commemorative value is still preserved with me today.) I also crafted a highly magnetic semiconductor radio to listen to Hong Kong radio stations and determine direction based on signal strength. Additionally, I obtained a compass and prepared a 1930s Hong Kong HSBC-issued 20-

dollar bill, moldy and worm-eaten, for emergencies upon reaching Hong Kong. OldFive, a devout Buddhist, and I made a special trip to the ancestral temple in Zen City, Foshan, to pray to the Water Emperor "Beidi Gong" for blessings. Strangely, when I tossed a coin in practice, it landed precisely on the head of a stone turtle in the wishing pool. We were delighted and filled with hope.

The night of July 1 was pitch dark. After meeting with OldTwo, we quietly left the village with paddles in hand. Two small grass boats moored in a nearby fish pond had been under our watch for days. We felt a bit nervous along the way, as stealing boats was the start of our escape and a treasonable act. Avoiding main roads, we chose small paths. Suddenly, we saw five little field mice, each biting the other's tail, crawling slowly in a line ahead of us. This was a sign of mice moving house, considered a bad omen by the superstitious. Later, we encountered a few-foot-long banded krait blocking our way. I have always feared snakes, and a snake blocking the path was not a good sign. Indeed, upon reaching the pond, we found the two grass boats had been moved and filled with mud by farmers during the day. We quickly stripped off our clothes, jumped into the water, and worked together to overturn the boats and dump the mud back into the pond, taking quite some time to clear the boats.

When we tried to lift the small boats over the embankment to the other side of the small river, we found the embankment too high to manage. Despite using all our strength for nearly half an hour, we couldn't succeed. We were very anxious. Failure to get the boats out would ruin the entire plan since OldOne, OldTwo, and OldFive were each heading to the first meeting point. As the saying goes, "A cornered dog will jump over a wall," and it was no exaggeration. In our desperation, a surge of wild strength erupted from within us. Using the inertia from pulling and dragging the grass boat and the momentum from our bodies pushing through the mud, we managed to heave it over the embankment in one go. And we got the second one over the embankment the similar way.

A few hours later, our five small boats finally met at the predetermined first meeting point. Four of the boats were stolen, and

OldFive's boat was the one usually assigned to him for outings by the production team. This boat was 20 feet long, sturdy, and streamlined, with less resistance. We relied on this main vessel of OldFive to break through to the open sea. Among the five of us, the OldFive had the best rowing skills, so he was the natural choice for steering. OldOne had excellent endurance and composure in emergencies, so he was placed at the front of the boat to help the helmsman correct any directional deviations. The second and third brothers were designated as the "center-forward" and "rear-guard," respectively. As for me, the "center," in addition to rowing, I was responsible for watching the compass, checking the radio for directional positioning, and bailing out any seawater that entered the boat. I also played a central role in maintaining morale. We knew that the five of us had become a single entity, bound by fate. To escape the patrol's line of sight and fire, once the small boat set off, we had to row with all our might, reaching the highest speed achievable with our combined strength. Upon entering the Pacific, with strong winds and high waves, any misalignment in effort, loss of balance, mishandling of the rudder, or incorrect course correction could cause the small boat to capsize instantly, leading to destruction and death. This was not only a sailing principle but also a gamble with fate for the five of us. By dawn on July 2, our boat had reached the mouth of the Pearl River. To distract the militia, we split into two groups: OldFive and I each took one of our small boats south along the eastern side of the river, while OldOne, OldTwo, and OldF proceeded in a staggered formation along the western side. We agreed to meet at Wanqingsha, and at nightfall, the five boats would simultaneously head into the river and then board Ol'dFive's "main vessel" to venture into the furious sea.

Around 4 PM, OldFive and I arrived at the foremost outpost near the thirteenth inlet of Wanqingsha with our two boats. We immediately started a fire on the boat to cook a meal, both to have a hearty meal before the 'battle' and to create a false impression to deceive the patrolling militia, making it seem as if we were just ordinary grass-cutting farmers. Just as expected, two armed militiamen approached us along the riverbank. Before they could ask any questions, OldFive took the initiative and loudly invited them to join us on the boat for a cup of sugarcane wine. Seeing this, the two militiamen responded with a thankful gesture and continued their patrol elsewhere. Watching them walk away, we breathed a sigh of relief. Looking across the river, we saw that the three boats of OldOne, OldTwo, and OldFour were already moored at not-too-distant locations.

We observed and waited. As we didn't have watches, we were used to judging the time by the position of the sun. Around 6 PM, the tide began to ebb, indicating the time to head out to sea had arrived. However, the sun hadn't fully set yet, and the situation on the river could still be seen clearly from the outposts. The time for the ebb tide was limited. We anxiously watched as time ticked away. Suddenly, we saw OldOne and his group taking action, with their three grass boats darting rapidly towards the center of the river. The OldFive and I were inwardly concerned: the sun hadn't completely set yet! Perhaps they were worried about missing the tide window or maybe something had happened at the outpost across the river. We had no choice but to act quickly. We steeled ourselves and decided to follow the group. The two of us rowed with all our might, and our two small boats shot like arrows to the center of the river. In the blink of an eye, the five small boats met at the center, which was our starting point. We then swiftly and agilely boarded OldFive's main vessel. At that moment, each of us was filled with passion, using every ounce of strength to row, shouting "Go!" with each stroke. It was a perfect harmony of mind and movement, a volcanic eruption of desire suppressed for many years. Each person's oar was synchronized with OldOne's, rising and falling in unison, with each stroke piercing the water almost vertically. With five powerful strokes, five deep, swift whirlpools appeared in the water. We knew that quickly escaping the militia's view was crucial to our success. The strength generated by the human body at a life-and-death moment is incredible. Our small boat, following the current and against the wind, shot like an arrow towards the open sea.

The sun rises and sets quickly at sea. Within half an hour, night had already fallen. At this point, I realized that the compass and radio had been soaked in seawater in the boat's cabin, rendering them useless. In the distance, a series of rapid drumbeats could be heard. It was definitely the militia's warning drums. Perhaps they had just discovered the four small boats we abandoned, or maybe they had witnessed our departure through far-off binoculars. Either way, we had managed to get through the first hurdle of our escape to sea.

Before we could savor the joy of overcoming the first challenge, we faintly heard the intermittent "thud, thud, thud" of an engine. Alarmed, we turned to look behind us and saw the faint silhouette of a motorboat with a swinging searchlight. After a short while, the motorboat and searchlight became increasingly clear. It was undoubtedly related to the drums onshore; they must have realized someone was attempting to escape and were coming after us.

We rowed with all our might, and although the small boat was moving at full speed, it was still powered by manpower. Could we really escape from the motorboat's pursuit? Suddenly, about 300 meters ahead, we saw what seemed to be the shadow of a large ship. Gradually, we saw it clearly—it was indeed a fairly large ship anchored at sea, facing us, with faint lights on board, likely indicating that the crew were already resting. United in thought and effort, without a moment's delay, we approached the large ship. Remarkably, without any verbal communication, we maneuvered our small boat under the cover of the large ship's shadow on the starboard side. Fearing that the people on the ship might hear us, we didn't dare speak, held our breath, and stopped rowing to hide in the shadow. At this point, the "thud, thud" sound of the motorboat engine slowed down as it approached the port side of the large ship, using a strong searchlight to scan the ship and the sea. Hidden in the darkness of the starboard side, we heard someone on the large ship shout: "What's the matter?" Someone on the motorboat responded loudly: "We're chasing escapees. Did you see a small boat?" The person on the large ship answered: "No, we didn't." The person on the motorboat exclaimed: "Damn it, we clearly saw them, where could they have gone?" The person on the large ship joked: "Maybe you've been seeing ghosts?"

The "thud, thud" sound of the motor continued to linger on the port side of the large ship, seemingly in the same spot. I thought it was over; if the motorboat circled the large ship with its strong searchlight, we would have nowhere to hide and no chance of escape.

Time seemed to freeze for about three minutes. In my heart, I kept silently praying, "Bodhisattva, please bless us," over and over. Suddenly, the motorboat's engine started to go "thud, thud, thud," accelerating gradually, then faster and faster. To my surprise, it turned around and headed back from where it came.

Oh my, the weight on my heart finally lifted. We continued to hide in the shadows, not daring to move. Only when the sound of the motorboat's engine faded into the distance, almost inaudible, did we quietly steer our main vessel away from the large ship. Thank you, Bodhisattva! Thank you, crew of the large ship!

After rowing vigorously for about an hour, we once again heard the rumbling sound of an engine approaching from behind. We were immediately filled with dread—could it really be that misfortune never comes alone? Within minutes, a People's Liberation Army Navy gunboat suddenly appeared on our right side. My heavens, could it be that the motorboat, unable to catch us, had called for reinforcements, and the navy was now after us? Suddenly, there was a loud explosion, and the sea was bathed in a blinding light. It was a flare fired from the gunboat. Everyone was petrified, and we quickly ducked down. Amidst the glare, I turned my head slightly and saw a sailor standing by the gunboat's railing. The two ribbons fluttering in the wind behind his cap are still vividly etched in my mind. At that moment, the five of us barely breathed, and our oars were still, with only OldFive gripping the rudder tightly. The fear of being caught or shot at any moment pounded in each of our hearts. In my terror, I prayed to my mother's spirit for protection. Since my mother's passing when I was thirteen, I had always believed that she, who loved me, was by my side and would forever be my guardian angel. A person's faith and belief can often provide infinite courage and composure in the most critical moments. I also heard OldFour and OldFive muttering, "Bless us, Beidi Gong," repeatedly. The flare quickly extinguished, and besides the "thud, thud" of the engine mingling with the waves, nothing else happened. About two minutes later, the engine noise gradually increased, and the gunboat sailed away on its own. Wow, we were both shocked and overjoyed, barely able to believe it was true. We imagined several possible explanations: one was that although the rough sea made the gunboat clearly visible to us due to its size, it might have been hard for the gunboat to spot our small boat; another possibility was that the sailors on the gunboat sympathized with us and intentionally let us go; a more mystical explanation was that the heavens took pity on us five youngsters, allowing Beidi Gong to intervene and shield us from the sailors' eyes. The undeniable fact is: we had narrowly escaped failure.

Suddenly, I felt a chill in my feet. Looking down, I saw that during the brief pause in rowing, the small boat had been tossed by the fierce wind and high waves, allowing seawater to flood into the central compartment. I quickly grabbed a wooden scoop and frantically bailed the water out of the boat. Once our nerves had calmed a bit, we regrouped and continued to row forward with determination. After about forty to fifty minutes, another gunboat appeared ahead, though it's uncertain if it was the same one from before. This time, however, the gunboat was much farther away. Although it also fired a flare, we were not as frightened as before, thanks to our earlier experience. With my call of "Bless us, Beidi Gong!" everyone seemed to gain a bit of proud courage. Whether they pursued us or fired upon us, there was no turning back for us now; we decided to gamble everything on this escape!

The second gunboat circled the sea twice and then left. The wind grew stronger, and waves four to five feet high crashed down on us with overwhelming force. OldOne, worthy of his reputation as an extraordinarily composed leader, stood firm against each oncoming wave without wavering; OldFive proved to be a "great helmsman," averting several near-capsize and out-of-control situations. Our only concern was whether the wind and waves would intensify further. One massive wave after another struck the boat heavily. Could it withstand the impact? Would it break apart? I kept bailing water out continuously, telling myself that I must not lose grip of the wooden scoop, or the small boat would surely sink.

The seawater splashing on our faces tasted increasingly salty, indicating that we had ventured deep into the Pacific Ocean. Gradually, in the southeast corner of the pitch-black sea, some lights began to appear. Those were likely the lights of Hong Kong, the "Pearl of the Orient." Our small boat, like a moth drawn to a flame, pursued those faint lights.

After encountering the gunboat, we also crossed paths with several cargo ships traveling at night. It was common for escapees to be captured by mainland cargo ships in international waters and sent back, so we remained vigilant. After some time, the lights from Hong Kong began to fade, but to the east, not far away, rows of mercury lamps along the riverbank came into view, brightly lit. Based on the information we had, we judged that this was likely a place called "Shekou" (now an industrial area and the site of the Daya Bay Nuclear Power Plant), deliberately set up by mainland border authorities as a "fake Hong Kong" to mislead escapees into surrendering themselves. I promptly issued a warning not to approach! It was better to maintain our southern course, continuing into the vast sea, than to mistakenly enter a trap. (We later learned that my decision was somewhat overly cautious at the time because we were not far from Shekou, and heading directly southeast would have brought us into Hong Kong waters.)

After passing Shekou, each of us was utterly exhausted. From the moment we stole the boats, we had been fighting continuously for over thirty hours. At this point, the sea breeze slowed down, and we suddenly and fearfully realized that our boat seemed to be stationary. As we puzzled over this, a shiny, one-foot-long fish suddenly leapt into the boat's cabin, startling us. The superstitious OldTwo shouted, "Quick, put it back in the sea!" I quickly grabbed the wooden scoop and gently flipped the fish back into the sea. This seemed to be a warning, making us realize that the fish was chasing a reverse current lifted by the waves, indicating that the sea had started to rise. This was bad news; the incoming tide's reverse current would push us back toward the Pearl River estuary, nullifying all our efforts! We immediately turned the boat towards a faintly visible small island to the east and rowed with all our might, regardless of anything else. We truly experienced the difficulty of rowing against the current. Our dry food had long been drenched, and, more critically, we had run out of fresh water. We were both hungry and thirsty. The reverse current, combined with the headwind, added insult to injury, turning what seemed like an hour-long journey into a two-hour struggle. Finally reaching the shore, unsure of our exact location and fearing the need to continue escaping, we used our last bit of strength to lift the small boat ashore. Then, the five of us collapsed on the beach like dead pigs, completely exhausted. After half an hour of catching our breath, not daring to delay, we anxiously began searching the coastal grass for any clues about our location. Suddenly, I couldn't help but cry out in surprise when a Coca-Cola bottle and a tattered Hong Kong newspaper appeared before my eyes. It was the most brilliant moment; we jumped and shouted for joy, hugging each other tightly. The long-pursued dream had finally come true! OldTwo suggested we become sworn brothers on the spot. The five of us immediately knelt to the world, with our hands over our hearts, swearing an oath amid the colorful dawn breaking over the horizon. The scene was deeply moving and unforgettable for a lifetime. From then on, our life-and-death brotherhood has continued to this day, 52 years later.

It was the morning of July 3, 1972. An hour later, as dawn began to break in the east, we found ourselves on a large island. It seemed to be British territory, but we were unsure of our exact location. In the distance, there appeared to be signs of habitation near the mountains. For safety, each of us held our oars as weapons and walked toward the distant mountains. My father in Hong Kong had once sent a message through someone: the first thing to do upon arriving in Hong Kong was to surrender and report to the police station to obtain protection and notify the family. At that time, there were many "leftist fishermen" or local thugs in Hong Kong who would ambush and extort those they captured, with the most terrifying scenario being that they would escort them back to the mainland for a reward. It was said that the reward for each snakehead was a hundred pounds of fish. The safest approach was to surrender and report to the Royal Marine Police station, then be bailed out by family.

Those without family to bail them out might face the misfortune of repatriation. Shortly afterward, two villagers approached us, and we were a bit nervous. However, we all understood that if they meant harm, five skilled men with five oars would be enough to turn them into mincemeat. Despite our heightened alertness, I decided to be polite first. Among the five of us, four were farmers from Shunde speaking the local dialect, so the diplomatic task fell to me, the city dweller speaking authentic Cantonese. I put on a friendly expression and politely asked for directions. The two villagers informed me that we were in Tai O on Lantau Island, and the Tai O police station was just half an hour's walk into the village. After thanking them, we headed straight for the small village. At the village entrance, there was a small shop selling snacks. I took out the soaked 20 Hong Kong dollar bill from my pocket and bought five sodas from the shopkeeper. It was obvious to anyone that we were newly-arrived escapees, but the shopkeeper was kind and handed us five bottles of Hong Kong-produced Yuquan orange juice without taking my money. Who says the humanity of capitalist Hong Kong is as thin as paper?! This small encounter truly moved me! Having not had a drop of water for over ten hours, the first sip of Yuquan orange juice was like sweet nectar, soothing my insides, an indescribable sensation and enjoyment.

In those days, Tai O was just a small fishing village, and the marine police station was located in a house by the mountainside, with its doors shut tight. I went up and rang the doorbell, and a sleepy-eyed middle-aged policeman opened the door, jokingly saying, "Ha, another five snakes!" He went on to say that five more escapees had arrived the day before. It turned out that he was the only person at this small village police station. He then led us into a living room, which surprisingly didn't resemble a police station at all, except for a portrait of the Queen of England hanging on the wall. I felt a strange sensation, perhaps because we were used to the omnipresent image of Chairman Mao. Being in a place with a portrait of the Queen, wasn't this what we had risked our lives dreaming of? Looking at the Queen's kindly face, I was delighted to finally be under Her Majesty's protection. Knowing we were hungry, the policeman took out a loaf of bread from the fridge. Even though it was just a square loaf of white bread, it was the best food in the world for which we had traded our lives!

The middle-aged officer made a call to the Tsim Sha Tsui marine police headquarters in our presence. The headquarters issued an order—for each illegal immigrant to receive a vaccination.

Half an hour later, two young and attractive nurses with a friendly demeanor arrived at the station with a medical kit. They asked us to lean over the desk to receive our injections with our pants half down. Faced with these beautiful nurses, I felt a bit shy and didn't know where to look. Unconsciously, I suddenly noticed that OldFour's buttocks were so red they were nearly bleeding, with a large area of skin abraded. Perhaps it was a reflex, but I immediately felt a burning sensation on my own backside. I quickly realized that after over thirty hours of rowing, the friction between our buttocks and the boat's floor, combined with the effects of seawater, had taken a toll on us. We were so focused at the time that we hadn't noticed. But now, in front of the beautiful nurses, the saltwater-soaked skin on our butts began to sting painfully.

About an hour later, a high-speed marine police boat from the Hong Kong Royal Police Headquarters arrived at Tai O to take the five of us away. We saw for the first time the towering skyscrapers on both sides of Victoria Harbour. We, a bunch of country bumpkins, were left dumbfounded by the bustling and magnificent sight before us. It was unimaginable that just two days ago we were floundering around in the rural fish ponds, and only a few hours earlier, our fate was uncertain on the high seas. Now, we were standing on the deck of a British Royal Marine police boat traveling at over 30 miles per hour, entering a completely unfamiliar yet undoubtedly safe and hopeful new world. Such a stark contrast! Standing on the speeding police boat, with the Union Jack flapping loudly in the wind at the bow, I took several deep breaths of the refreshing air of freedom. The thought of soon seeing my father, familiar yet distant, filled me with immense excitement. Yet, I also realized that I might never set foot again on the land of my birth and be separated from my siblings, which overwhelmed me with mixed emotions, leaving my mind suddenly blank.

The police boat took us to the Tsim Sha Tsui police station, where I held a sign with my Chinese and English names and date of birth to take a photo. That photo later became my identity card photo.

The first dinner in Hong Kong was even more unforgettable. In those days, there were no takeaway meal boxes, so a prison guard handed five transparent plastic bags filled with food and five cans of soda into the cell. Inside, I saw rice, vegetables, and white rolls that looked like modern hair rollers used by women. As I ate, I didn't know what it was, only that it was incredibly delicious. Out of curiosity, I asked, and found out it was fresh squid. It was the first time I had eaten squid. I chewed it thoroughly, reluctant to swallow it too quickly. The five cans of soda also puzzled us, as we didn't know how to open the lids of the aluminum cans. We were like country bumpkins in a grand mansion. OldTwo contentedly said, "If we could eat such delicious food every day, I'd be willing to spend my life in a Hong Kong prison."

At night, the constant sound of traffic came from the sleepless city outside, especially from the brightly lit Tsim Sha Tsui, which was bustling all night. Although I was very tired, my excitement kept me awake for a long time. In a daze, I suddenly heard terrible screams from the cell across from mine. I stood up and quietly moved to the iron bars, seeing several policemen taking turns kicking a prisoner curled up on the floor in the opposite cell, cursing him with foul language. I lay on the floor, not daring to make a sound, secretly worried: would we five new prisoners be the next to receive a "welcome beating"?

Fortunately, the night passed peacefully without disturbance. At breakfast time, a prison guard, holding a cup of coffee in one hand and a cigarette in the other, opened the cell door and walked over to OldTwo with a smile. He flicked some cigarette ash into the coffee cup and handed it to OldTwo with a sinister grin, telling him to drink it. OldTwo was the tallest and most rustic-looking among us. He was so frightened that he didn't know whether to take it or not. Then, the guard suddenly punched him in the chest, half-jokingly saying, "Behave yourself here!" and then walked away coolly. I thought this might be a customary way of intimidating new prisoners in the cell.

By evening, my elder sister came to visit me at the prison, but she wasn't allowed to see me. She left 100 Hong Kong dollars with the prison guard, ostensibly for buying me snacks. In 1972, the monthly salary of a garment worker in Hong Kong was about three to four hundred dollars. A hundred dollars was roughly a third of a typical garment factory worker's monthly salary. Subsequently, the prison guard brought me a loaf of bread and said, "The rule in prison is to share the wealth." The bread only cost two dollars, so the rest naturally became a benefit for the guard. The Hong Kong ICAC (Independent Commission Against Corruption) was established in February 1974, and after its creation, corruption within the Hong Kong government and its disciplinary forces significantly declined.

From then on, the guards were much more polite to us. It turned out that OldFive's uncle was also a police officer. Naturally, family members would receive extra care. My elder sister also sent money to the prison once more.

### Father and Son Reunion

I experienced four days behind bars in the cells of the marine police headquarters. On the evening of the fourth day, a prison guard opened the cell door with a smile and told me I was being released. The others, however, were not yet free to leave. I looked at the four companions I had lived and died with, filled with doubt and reluctance. I was worried about OldTwo, who had no relatives or friends in Hong Kong. Back then, those escapees without family in Hong Kong were sometimes sent back to the mainland by the Hong Kong government. I later learned that my brother-in-law knew an influential detective, which is why I was granted special permission to leave. The prison guard also told me that they had arranged for a police car to take me directly to my father's herbal medicine shop in Mong Kok. I was absolutely astonished by the special treatment. In contrast, I was even more worried about the four brothers still in custody. However, at that moment, I was helpless and full of resignation.

I stepped out of the police station and boarded the waiting police car. With sirens blaring and lights flashing, the car sped towards Mong Kok. The contrast was stark—from being pursued by military police just days ago to being treated and protected as a guest by the authorities on Her Majesty's territory. I witnessed the vibrant world of the Pearl of the Orient for the first time, dazzled by the neon lights and signs. The main road, Nathan Road, from Tsim Sha Tsui to Mong Kok was bustling with traffic, and the police car weaved through the streets like it owned them. I felt a slight thrill of vicarious power. Suddenly, the police car stopped at a bustling intersection, and the officer next to me gestured towards some young women in mini-skirts crossing the street, jokingly saying, "Hey, look closely, young man, Hong Kong girls don't wear underwear!" The two policemen in the car burst into lewd laughter. I was embarrassed and blushed at their blatant joke. At that time, young people from the mainland were quite ignorant and conservative about "sex," never having encountered such explicit and vulgar jokes. 1972 was the era of hippies, and naturally, Hong Kong kept pace with global trends, with mini-skirts being all the rage. As school rules didn't allow skirts to be too short, girls wearing short school uniforms would pin up their skirts as soon as they left school to follow the fashion of "short." As we neared Mong Kok, one of the policemen sternly told me, "You're lucky to be in our police car today, but you'd better stay on the right path in the future. If you ever break the law and end up in our car again, we won't be so nice." I understood their warning. Back then, some of those who fled to Hong Kong took reckless shortcuts, getting involved in vices like gambling, drugs, and even bank robberies. The brief police car journey and the officer's words left an indelible memory on this naive young man, just stepping into the colorful world of Hong Kong.

The police car drove into the bustling streets of Mong Kok and stopped in front of a herbal medicine shop I had seen in countless photos. The shop was distinctive, with fresh and dried herbs hanging inside and out. The shop, less than a hundred square feet, was unexpectedly tiny, highlighting the scarcity of space in Hong Kong. Amid the array of herbs,

I saw a very old man, but full of vigor. That was my 82-year-old father. He must have been standing at the shop front for some time, eagerly awaiting the son he had only seen for a brief night. (As I mentioned earlier, when I was thirteen, my father hurriedly returned to Guangzhou for one night to see my critically ill mother. That was eight years ago, the only time I saw my father after becoming aware of things.) Amid the blaring sirens, I thanked the police officers and then, under the dazzling police lights, quickly jumped out of the car. With a swift step, I ran to my father and, with trembling hands, tightly grasped the hands of this strange yet familiar old man—my dad. He was a stranger because we had only seen each other for one night; familiar because our years of correspondence had long connected us in spirit. My father's handwriting was excellent, and he had a high level of literary attainment. Often, I used his letters as copybooks to practice my calligraphy. The deep connection between father and son was evident.

The arrival of the police car attracted neighboring shopkeepers and residents to come and see the commotion. My father, beaming with joy, clasped his hands together and told the neighbors that his youngest son—I—had just arrived in Hong Kong by sneaking across the border. The onlookers whispered among themselves, surprised that this 82-year-old man had a son in his early twenties. The astonishment was due to my youthful and slender appearance, which often led people to mistake me for a high school student, making me look more like my father's grandson. Before the mainland changed hands, my father was wealthy and had three wives. My mother was his youngest wife, and I am my father's fifteenth son! When I was born, my father was already sixty-one years old, and I often joked about being my father's "Fifteenth Prince." My father took good care of himself and looked young; he was still seeing patients at the age of 86. Naturally curious and eager to learn, my father studied traditional Chinese medicine and pulse diagnosis in his spare time while running a business in his youth. With the changes of fate, his medical knowledge unexpectedly became his livelihood in his later years in Hong Kong. This might have been a reward from heaven for a diligent and studious person.

Successfully arriving in Hong Kong was the most crucial turning point in my life, bar none. Like a bird flying out of a cage, I cherished the freedom I gained even more. In a free society, those with abilities rise to the top, and personal skills and talents are indispensable assets. My primary focus was compensating for my education. For someone who had just completed the second year of middle school, intensive study in both Chinese and English was imperative, and working by day and studying by night was the only feasible path. In a society rife with "pornography, gambling, and drugs," maintaining integrity and integrating into society were constant reminders for myself. Outside of work, attending night school, reading newspapers, and visiting bookstores were my only hobbies. Like a sponge thrown into the water, I desperately soaked up knowledge. My father's dual-purpose shop and residence was cramped, and my bed had to be dismantled and stored each morning after use. In the hot summer, I simply set up a canvas bed under the shop's eaves and hung a nylon sheet diagonally for privacy. Mong Kok's streets were quite dirty at the time, with piles of garbage everywhere, and fat, well-fed rats would come out to forage in the quiet of the night. Initially, I was often startled awake by rats moving under the bed, which was quite frightening. Gradually, I got used to it; I slept, and they foraged, without interfering with each other. I figured it was better than sharing a bed with human waste.

In the mysterious ways of fate, heaven had its plans. Three years later, on a bus after evening classes, I happened to meet a former classmate of my elder sister from Foshan First Middle School. "Fellow travelers in life's journey," she told me, excitedly, that she was going to the United States in a week. It turned out she was going as a refugee. Hearing this, I was very excited and, after clarifying the application process, immediately proceeded with my application. A month later, I bid a reluctant farewell to my father and embarked on my journey abroad.

## Afterword

The day after my release, the four sworn brothers were also released.

Knowing that OldTwo had no relatives to bail him out, my brother-in- law contacted the police, vouched for him, and arranged a job for him at a construction company in the New Territories. The brothers quickly found their footing in their careers, and each later achieved remarkable success in various commercial fields.

A month later, word came from fellow villagers in Hong Kong that the production team cadres and members were furious over the loss of the grass boat, which was our main vessel. This was understandable since it was the best grass boat of our production team and a vital tool for their livelihood. The production team cadres declared that the group of escapees must compensate the production team with four hundred yuan. If their families obediently paid, that would be fine, but if not, there would be consequences. On hearing this, we quickly gathered five hundred yuan and sent it back to the production team. As for the other four smaller and older grass boats, which we had stolen from different places, there was no clear owner to compensate, so we let it go.

OldFive had large, bright eyes and was nicknamed "Big Eyes." In 1979, he visited Shunde and brought back a 27-inch Japanese color TV to give to the Longyan production team. A 27-inch color TV in 1979 Shunde was no small matter. The team decorated the headquarters with lights and ribbons, and the whole village, from the elderly to the young, from young girls to young wives, spread the word: Big Eyes had returned from Hong Kong and brought back a 27-inch color TV! The elderly, in their eighties and nineties, grinned widely with their toothless mouths: this was the biggest event in Longyan in years! As the saying goes... if you achieve success and wealth but don't return home, it's like "wearing a brocade robe at night"... unnoticed by anyone.

For someone like me who was forged in hardship from a young age, especially during those difficult years as an educated youth sent to the countryside to farm, my survival skills are like those of a cactus in the desert. I can proudly say—I can take root anywhere I'm thrown! Moreover, America is a fertile land, with the free air and bright sunshine being the sources of life, providing every new immigrant with superior conditions for life. "Work hard and don't worry about the harvest' has been my motto for many years in America. Those who have worked in farming know the habit of working hard and diligently, and when combined with working smart, it allows one to take shortcuts and achieve twice the results with half the effort. At the age of 55, after working for 26 years in a power company, I suddenly had the urge to retire... I felt like I had spent my whole life working hard and that my life's work seemed to be the equivalent of two lifetimes of work for others. I thought: it's time to give myself a chance—to retire early! There were many things I wanted to do when I was young but never had the chance to because I was too busy, leaving many unfinished tasks, such as traveling, calligraphy, painting, reading, repairing and trading houses... or even dabbling on Wall Street. When I first came to America, I admired Americans for their Do It Yourself lifestyle, being versatile and skilled in both the literary and martial arts, and they pursue the enjoyment of a "sense of achievement," which aligns perfectly with my own personality! Similarly, I thoroughly enjoy the "sense of achievement" that comes after putting in effort. This "sense of achievement" is a brief pleasure easily attainable each day. Keeping active in retirement, doing work yet not quite working, has allowed my retirement to reach a state of "life lies in motion" while still retaining the essence of retirement. Fifteen years have passed like this, and I still relish it! My father, in his youth, studied medicine in addition to doing business; perhaps I was somewhat influenced by him, preparing myself, copying his model. As early as the 1980s, I obtained building, electrical, and real estate licenses in California. Just like my father, whether intentionally laying the groundwork or unintentionally indulging, I too felt a compulsion to buy good tools whenever I stepped into Home Depot. Having a few spare tools in life's toolbox feels reassuring, and in reality, I have over ten power drills at home. The desire for possession is human nature. In this free country, with open skies and wide seas, a few years ago at the start of the pandemic, unable to go out, I took my renovation tools and flew to the volcanic island of Hawaii to renovate my two guesthouses. Being willful is an inherent trait of "graduates"; otherwise, there wouldn't be the daring "crossing the Chu River and Han border."

Every immigrant "graduate" who crossed the ocean to America is a second-time "crossing graduate," still carrying the courage and stubbornness of those days, full of hope for a bright future. One must know, a pawn on the chessboard can only move forward, never backward—old soldiers never die!

Time flies, and the five sworn brothers each went their separate ways. OldOne worked as a textile machine apprentice in Hong Kong for a few years and, taking advantage of the mainland's reform and opening up in the mid-1990s, started with a small business and expanded significantly in Guangdong. He set up numerous factories, running a production line from cotton yarn to fabric weaving, dyeing, and garment export. However, with changing geopolitical economics, he eventually closed down and retired early. OldTwo, once a militia platoon leader, was tall and strong, working on construction sites installing cement molds. He contributed significantly to Hong Kong's concrete jungle and owned two properties as a reward for his hard work. OldFour was dedicated to his trade, working for decades in the vegetable market as a butcher, wielding a cleaver to sell pork. We often joked with him, calling him the market butcher. Sadly, he passed away from illness a few years ago. OldFive naturally optimistic and adaptable, made a name for himself as a site foreman in Hong Kong. Seven years after I came to the U.S., he followed in my footsteps and came to America. With perseverance, he opened a restaurant in a Western neighborhood in Los Angeles, which did exceptionally well. Influenced by me, he continuously invested in real estate at the right times, becoming something of a landlord in America. After running a Chinese restaurant for 25 years, he retired decisively just before the pandemic, enjoying the good life of retirement, unlike me, OldFour, who believes in "life lies in motion" and is always active. I often think that fate may be a divine will, but one must carve out their own path to the unknown, just as those who crossed mountains and rivers in pursuit of Hong Kong's lights, moving forward like moths to a flame, each choosing their own path forward.

In 2004, I took my two sons back to Hong Kong to tell them my Hong Kong story. We revisited old places and showed them the former site of their grandfather's herbal medicine shop. The shop had been converted into a dried seafood store, but my father's Chinese medicine practitioner sign still hung high there. Although the sign, over half a century old, had rusted and faded from years of exposure to the elements, the writing "He ×× Chinese Medicine Practitioner" remained familiar and robust. It was my father's own handwriting, and gazing at the sign brought back many poignant memories. Two years after I left Hong Kong, my father had an unfortunate fall and broke his femur. Complications from surgery ultimately claimed him. I had promised to visit him as soon as I obtained a green card, but the delay in processing it meant I could not return, a source of lifelong guilt and regret. During the two years we were separated by the ocean, we resumed our frequent correspondence, almost a weekly exchange of letters, maintaining the deep father-son bond. The letters covered everything from daily life to poetry and social topics. My father had a special fondness for his "fifteenth son," perhaps due to the joy of having a child in his later years. To him, I was always his little boy who hadn't grown up. After he passed, I tearfully organized over 80 letters between us, noting how in the last few, his handwriting showed uncharacteristic shakiness. At that time, no one could afford expensive long-distance calls... It was already 10 PM, and the market was quiet. As I took photos and shared stories of coexisting with mice with my sons, two large, fat market rats leisurely ambled in front of us, swaying side to side like little dwarves, struggling with their weight. My wife and two ABCs (American Born Chinese) exclaimed in surprise: Dad's stories were true! I muttered to myself, perhaps these two fat rats were descendants of the one I encountered under the eaves over 30 years ago... its many offspring? Nice to meet you again! What a coincidence! The end.

# The Fiery Dragon on the Road to Freedom

*A Qiang (narrator), Zhao Jineng*

## My father blessed me with a new birth

At the beginning of December 1979, when my father's severe emphysema had reached a critical stage, my neighbor gave my family a new four-centimeter-thick fir plank advised me to be prepared. I asked a carpenter to make a coffin out of these cedar planks and found a cemetery in Heng-sha on the outskirts of the city, and I wanted to wait and be by the bedside when my father pass-away, until then I can go on with my venture, to escape to Hong Kong. On the 15th. December, just 15 days before the end of the year, my partner urged me to get going with the trip immediately because of the much fanfare being advertised about the new criminal code, which stated that from 1 January 1980, illegal border crossing would result in a two-year prison sentence. The situation was precarious, and I was in a dilemma, and my spirit almost collapsed. At this time, my mother said to me: son, you should leave quickly, the future of your life is important, and it wouldn't be of much help for you to stay around! I was grateful for my mother's understanding and forgiveness, and I gave my father one last affectionate look and walked out of the house with tears in my eyes. Later, I heard from my mother that on the 16th, my father woke up and asked of me, and my mother told him that our son had already set off, and my mother asked my father to bless me for a safe journey to Hong Kong. My father closed his eyes peacefully, he must have prayed for me at the last moment, he died on the 17th. I arrived in Hong Kong on the 25th of the same month (Christmas Day), and after five failures, and with the sixth attempt, I finally managed to reach the place of my rebirth with the blessing of my father's sprit.

My partner and I were still following the route of "fire dragon" this time, and the so-called "fire dragon" was to stowaway in the freight train with Hong Kong being the final destination. There were many ways to get there, such as "with clogs" (by rowing a wooden boat), "netting" (by climbing over barbed wire), "grass" (by crossing mountains and rugged terrain, forest), "old oak board" (rubber boat), "soaking" (soaking, floating tools in Cantonese, inflated pillows, ball-bladder, etc.) nonetheless, with any of these ways and means there always came with many heartbroken stories of countless injuries and deaths when these escapees risked their lives for freedom.

This time, my friend and I went to Chen-zhou, Hunan Province trying to board the freight train, although Chen-zhou Station was only a small station, but the train with cargo-car(compartment) bounded for Hong Kong would aways stop here. This was the fifth time that I have tried by riding the "fire dragon" (freight train), and although I failed in the previous four times, but unlike many escapees I was never caught and had not suffered being prisoner, yet this time around it's a big deal for us all, because the cost of failure with the "new criminal law" already in place would be much greater.

When the train whistle started, my colleagues and Sanmao, the "Railway boy", jumped into the wagon, and were surprised to see that there were as many as ten of us jumping onto the train at the same time, nine men and one woman, who did not know each other except us three. Too many people in one car were not good due to the limited space, but who can drive who away? End up we all jumped on the roof of the car, from car to car, looking for the one with the Hong Kong cargo tag, and we worked together to pry open the window, slide down the ladder on the side of the car from the roof one by one, and then get in through the window. (The details of the stowaway in the train car would be explained later). The cargo car found this time was full of nylon socks, commonly known as "atomic socks".

We came prepared this time, and there was a Hunan "railway boy" Jiancai, who once used the method of "nailing the mezzanine" to arrive in Hong Kong smoothly, but he was just unlucky, end up being detained and returned to his hometown by the Hong Kong police shortly after landing.

The so-called "nail sandwich" method is as follows: at that time, many truck compartments were iron sheets on the outside, and three horizontal wooden fangs were attached to the iron sheets inside, and the inside of the wooden fangs was two groups of wooden liners. "Nail mezzanine" is to remove the wooden fang and wood lining board at one end of the carriage, move forty or fifty centimeters to the middle of the carriage, first nail three horizontal wooden fangs to make the skeleton, and then nail back according to the order of the wooden board (the wooden board is divided into two groups, vertical splicing, there is a convex groove structure between the board and the board on the opposite side, and the order between the board and the board on the opposite side cannot be confused and cannot be wrong, otherwise the board wall cannot be restored to the way it was ), and the person is hidden between the lining plate and the iron sheet of the car shell. In this way, even if they encounter an inspection, the inspectors would not be able to find anything suspicious at a glance, unless they actually came in the train-car and carefully measured the length of the carriage and compared, they would not be able to find out if anyone had done anything to it. Of course, doing all of these requires that we had to have the appropriate tools: hammers, nails, wrenches, saw blades, and one or two wooden planks, etc., and we brought conspicuous tools such as crowbars to the Chenzhou Station through our acquaintances (they were train attendants) of the "railway boys".

Naturally, before "nailing the mezzanine", it is necessary to move the goods to the compartment gap one by one, to make room for the working face, and then pry down the wooden planks and wooden fangs of the mezzanine one by one, and move the wooden fangs and wooden liners forward, so that the space so created can squat down a person But we have as many as 10 people this time, and the width of the truck is barely enough to accommodate 10 people standing, if all the people having to stand all the way, obviously it wouldn't be the best way, since we didn't know when the train would arrive in Hong Kong? So, we nailed two horizontal beams in the middle of the mezzanine, and let the two shorter fellow sit on them, ending as if they were riding right on top of the heads of the others, and still the rest of the position still couldn't sit the eight of us, only seven people could sit and one person takes turns standing.

While we were working nervously, the train came to a full stop at Shao-guan Station, the middle door of the carriage opened with a "horn", and we exclaimed: Oops! we thought the inspector were going to come up for an inspection, Unexpectedly, it turned out to be four more escapees(the Canton boys), who cut open the lead seal of the car door and climbed up. After these four Canton boys got on the carriage and asked to enter our mezzanine, we said: We were already ten people here, besides, didn't you just cutoff the door seal which was like telling the inspector that someone had broken into the train, how can we accommodate you? But what's the use of being angry? And we couldn't just drive them away…. I ended up warning them: if you all were being found/caught at the Sun-gang checkpoint, you would not want to expose us to the inspector, or we would definitely go after you!

After we finished nailing up the Mezzanine, we stacked the cartons back to the original position against the newly built Mezzanine wall, and then we all 10 of us, one after the other, stepped on the cardboard boxes pushing up the ceiling and slipped into the sandwich wall one by one. The four Cantonese boys watched us doing it, I believed that they by then had learned the critical part of the "Fire Dragan way" and if they didn't succeed this time, they would be able to do it again themself, and they hid themselves on the other side.

When the train arrived at the Sengang checkpoint, which was five kilometers away from Shenzhen, several soldiers opened the door and came up to check, and the lights were so bright outside, it penetrated through the cracks in the ceiling. We heard the Mandarin speaker asked, "hey, you, were there anyone else, turn them out now or I'll kill you", and heard Canton Tsai reply, "no, there were just two of us in the car in Shaoguan." They didn't betray us, we could still hear people talking outside, and it was probable that the railroad personnel were discussing with the soldiers whether to detain the carriages for a throughout search, and we were extremely nervous by then, trying to be ready for something bad to happen. After a while, the lights went out, and about an hour later the train started moving again, and after a short while, the train stopped again, presumably in Shenzhen station already. Till next afternoon, about two o'clock, the train moved again, it should have been that the train being pushed across the Shenzhen Bridge, then the train started moving again, faster and faster, suddenly we all managed to jumped up and down with joy, climbing out of the Mezzanine one by one, opened the window a crack, watching the scenery which were definitely different from that of mainland, and even saw the Hong Kong police at the station, crossing the border and being finally in Hong Kong by then, we knew the final success would depends on the next step - jumping out of the car.

In the midst of the excitement and hectic, I did not forget to look at my watch, and it took 32 hours to get on the Fire Dragon from Chen-Zhou to the border!

*Picture illustrates the stowaway about to jumps out of the train*

Success and failure in one fell swoop, in the rumbling sound of collision of the steel-joins/couplings, we slipped out of the window one by one, through the iron ladder next to the window, and then climbed/crawled to the two ends of the carriage, distributed ourselves at the junction/space between the two carriages, the carriage on both sides of each has an iron pass, we hold the top of the iron pass while standing on the bottom of the other iron pass, nervously waiting for the opportunity, but "When"? It should be the time when the train turns, when the speed of the train slows down, and if the train turns to the right, we must jump on the left; If the train turns left, we must jump on the right. Why? Because there would always be the Hong Kong policeman at the rear of the train watching, they were there to monitor the whole process from the border crossing to the final station, and once they found that someone jumping out of the train, they would notify the driver to stop the train and arrest the person or notify the police along the way to arrest that person, the stowaway.

At a coming big/sharp turn, the speed of the train would slow down as expected, moving towards for a big right curve, we climbed to the ladder by the window on the left, facing forward, standing on the ladder with our right foot and jumping down with our left foot as high as possible. upon landing, I found that I only had a slight abrasion, and I was rejoicing, but soon as I looked up, I was shocked with chill through my spine realizing that my landing spot was right in front of the tunnel, and I would have become another Yang Zaixing (introduced later) if I jumped just one second slower. I was separated from the others after jumping out of the train, and I knew that it was not quite yet to say that it had been a successful journey, because at the time, Hong Kong is implementing a "barrage policy", and escapee must reach the urban area to receive the "street paper" and the ID certificate subsequently, and those who are caught in the New Territories would all be detained and returned to mainland immediately.

I saw a Hong Kong gentleman walking by, and I said sir, I just arrived in Hong Kong, can you help made a phone call for me, but he ignored me. After I walked a little further, I saw a few young men and women picnicking on the grass, and after I made a request to them, one of the young women took me into the nearby telephone booth in the cafeteria of the Hong Kong Chinese University and called my eldest younger brother, who arrived in Hong Kong earlier, and somehow his friend came to pick me up and take me into the city instead. (Later I learned that my eldest younger brother went back to Guangzhou to help with our father's funeral arrangement when I was calling him upon my arrival his home in Hong Kong.)

Sanmao and the two Hunan boy, with the address I gave them, also had met up with my eldest younger brother, and the two Hunan boys were later picked up by their own brothers who also had arrived in Hong Kong earlier, but unfortunately when the four of them were waiting outside for a taxi , the police patrolling by saw that they did not look like local Hongkonger /Cantonese , and took them back to the police station for questioning, end up the two Hunan boys were deported back to mainland while their two brothers were released since they already received their Hong Kong Identification card.

A few days later, when the Christmas holidays ended and the government offices resumed, my friend took a taxi with me to the "Hong

Kong People's Immigration Department" in Queensway, Hong Kong Island, to apply for my identity certificate. The office area was way overcrowded, with hundreds of people lining up along the iron railing that had turned around several times in the open space in front of the building. Waiting patiently for my term, I filled out the form, taking the fingerprint with my right thumb, then I was given almost instantly the identity certificate commonly known as the "street paper", and with this legal residence permit, I carefully stepped out of the office, looking up to the sky and roar, I did it!!

After five attempts, overcoming so many hardships and obstacles, I finally succeeded!!

And shortly after, I sent home a telegram with the wording: "no worry, I am not coming home", just wanted to tell my mother that I had arrived safely!

Later I learned that my mother was crying with husband's passing away and with son being still out somewhere in a dangerous journey…. she turned into smiling upon receiving my telegram!

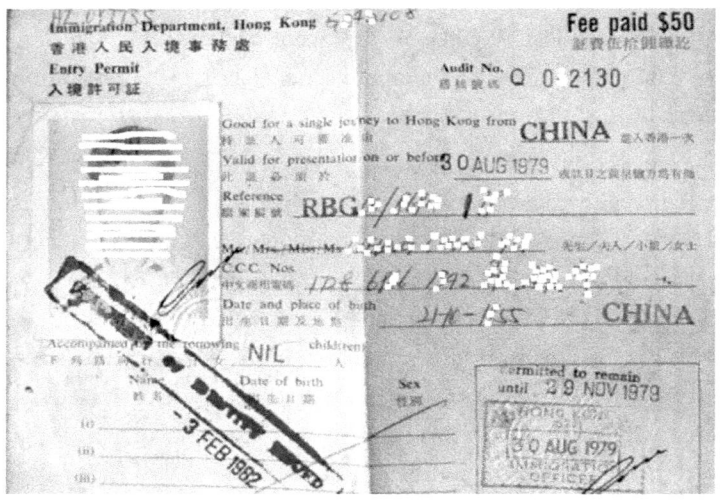

*For reference, the "street paper" issued in the period*

*January 7,1980,13 days after my arrival in Hong Kong, photographed at the Wong Tai Sin Temple Hong Kong*

## Thrilling, the so-called "Fire Dragon"

Why did I choose the route the "Fire Dragon"? It all started with my first escape:

The first attempt was in May 1979, I remember that it's on May 11, the five of us used 250 yuan to charter a taxi and set off for Zhuhai, Zhongshan. Our destination at that time was Macao, we put all of the emergency items, the compass, the live-buoy, food and water all in the car trunk and dressing up like the Hongkongers, somehow at the Zhongshan County border checkpoint, the para-militia flagged us to stop for inspection, we, instead ordered the driver to speed up, and rushed through, driving even faster for quite a while, and when we reached the mountainside, we got out of the car and ran straight up the mountain. After walking through the mountains for three nights (hiding during the day), on the fourth day we were captured by the para-militia patrolling the mountains.

Being escorted to the "Admiralty" detention center in Zhongshan

County, where we were detained for more than 10 days, and was then transferred to the provincial detention center in Shahe, Guangzhou, and then again transferred to Paitan Farm(more like a Labor Camp) in Zengcheng County to do hard labor, carrying out the manure of the highway health center and the pig manure of the pig farm every day. After two months of hard labor, the factory people came to bail me out, with my family agreeing to pay them back with the pork tickets, oil tickets, food stamps, and four cents a day (12 yuan a month for food) to Paitan Farm to redeem myself. Facing with Humiliation is common in detention and during the transfer, and I actually witnessed a Canton boy biting his finger over a cigarette, and when he tried pulling it out, it was only revealed with his bloody finger bones. When the factory people picked me up, I was warned that if I went for the escape again, I would be sent to "re-education hard labor camp" for at least two years.

When he was doing hard labor in Zengcheng Paitan Farm, he got acquainted with the railway boy "Sanmao", and he told me that next time around, he could take me with him going for the "Fire Dragon", because he had acquaintances at Chen-Zhou rail Station, and he could have access to the manifest, and would be able to identify the Freight train with a tagged freight car bounded for Hong Kong, and also the detail information about the freight car..

Ever since then, we had always been accompanied with each other in our next few escaping trips by the "railway boys" who were familiar with the things on the railroad and the freight trains, and knew how to avoid dangers, such as: keeping an eye on the situation ahead of the train, and warning us to try to lie down as low as possible every time before passing the tunnel, because the ceiling of the tunnel would simply sweep you off the train, I remembered one time the front of the car whined in the tunnel, and we felt all over the soot and became "blacken". The most important thing would be that the railway boy had the means to find out the situation of the tagged car going to Hong Kong, which would be an extremely important part, together with the above-mentioned, for the "fire dragon" to be a viable route to the escapee. These "railway boys" had no relatives in Hong Kong and did not speak Cantonese, and they in turn relied on us in Guangzhou and Hong Kong once we got there, so, we really wanted to and could help with each other, and cooperated with each other sincerely, and successfully.

One of the "grand occasion" of the "fire dragon" at that time: there were more than 100 young men and women cruising around near the Chen-Zhou Station at the same time, and their eyes were wandering, and you could see immediately why they came. Some station personnel jumped to their feet and scolded: Fuck you the escapees, wait till I make a phone call to Shenzhen Station and arrest you all! We were all so frightened that we simply gave up on that train.

As mentioned earlier, among the risks involved, the most dangerous part of the "fire dragon" routing would be that the escapee being scraped off when the train passing through the tunnel by the ceiling of the tunnel and the corpse will be broken into thousands of pieces; When hiding in the gap of the truck's cargo, they would possibly be crushed by the cargo moving violently, and they would starve to death, died of thirst, and would be caught.

A week after I arrived in Hong Kong, I read the newspaper: the porter found two dead escapees under the sacks while unloading the dried chili peppers.

There was an even more terrifying thing: at the "Sungang checkpoint" in front of Shenzhen, military police came up to inspect and search for stowaways, and they directly inserted the iron crowbar randomly into the pile of goods in order to force the smugglers out Even finally arrived at the Hong Kong section, in order to avoid being caught by the police, you had to jump off the train before it arrived at the final station, and if you didn't grasp the essentials, you would end up in pieces. While it would be easier for the Railroad boys to do so since they all grew up by the railway, and it was much more difficult and dangerous for us to jump on and off the train, I'll talk about my neighbor Yang Zaixing later, who almost died instantly jumping off the train in front of the Mong Kok Tunnel in Hong Kong. I, eventually was led to believe that climbing the "fire dragon" comes with a higher injury/disability and mortality rate than that using other means and routes fleeing to Hong Kong for freedom.

There was a Suxian Ridge in Chenzhou, and there was a Suxian Temple on the mountain, and every time we arrived in Chen-Zhou, we had to go to worship and prayed for the gods, hoping that someone up there would watch over us throughout the dangerous journey. In the early days of the Cultural Revolution, the entire Suxian Temple was destroyed by the Red Guards to the point that only the walls remained, the roof tiles were all full of holes and cracks, the Bodhisattvas were all broken into pieces and scattered in the backyard, and the gate of the temple was gone.

After arriving in Chenzhou, Hunan, the "railway boy" Sanmao found out the train car number and time-schedule set to Hong Kong, and we hid near the station that night. The last car of the train was generally an open-top coal truck, the location is already out of the station, the whistle would be generally sounded before the train started moving, with the whistle blowing we immediately rushed out to climb onto the open-air coal truck, lying on the pulverized coal, after the train leaves the station, we would start jumping/moving forward car by car, looking for the tagged car bounded for Hong Kong, each time we would need to jump-over about 20 cars to locate the correct one.

Of course, we also must bring plastic bags to pack the urine and poops, and tie it with a rubber band after we were through with it, because once we enter the "pile" (smuggling term, which means hiding well), everything is left to your fate, you wouldn't know when the train would start moving and when it would stop, when it would eventually arrive at Hong Kong, and you wouldn't know what kind of accidents you would encounter.

*40 years ago, the car/compartment was different from the picture when the windows were opened horizontally*

Once we find that the car with the right tag, we had to try to open the window with a special tool, a spudger, which would be made of spring steel, and we must bring it with us every time. At that time, the train car had a window at the higher end of the car, and the window door was open horizontally. With the 1st person lying down on the roof of the car, stretches out his head and hands, and tried pried open the window door with a spudger/crowbar, while the other person also lying down on the roof and pulls the 1st person's feet with both hands, so that the 1st person's hands can exert force. At the time, the train is speeding, swaying left and right, and there is a fierce wind, and you have to pay attention to whether there would be a tunnel ahead. If you're not careful, you'll die with body parts flying all over the place.

So why not just pry open the car door, someone asked? The doors were sealed with lead seals, and the doors with a broken seal would easily be identified by the inspectors along the way with multiple stops/stations, and there would be also multiple border checkpoints in Sun Gang, Bao'an

County Shenzhen.

From the end of July to the end of December 1979, I picked up the "Fire Dragon" a total of five times, and the last one was successful. I can't remember exactly which time and on what day, but the process is unforgettable.

Once, one of my classmates and Sanmao and his friend and I got on a tagged car full of pears headed to Hong Kong. We first "dug pile" (smuggling term, that is, to carry goods to hide), at one end we would move the boxes of pear to make room for shelter, after hiding ourselves, Sanmao's friend helped to build five layers of the pear boxes above our heads, then jumped out of the car and left. The train "stop & go" and turned "left & right" numerous times along the way, we ate pears when we were thirsty, and we still ate pears when we were hungry, and after 84 hours, the train simply stopped on an idle track in the wilderness, and did not move. We had been rolled up and bend down ourselves while hiding in the limited space that we created on the ground for all these times under the pear boxes, my classmate just couldn't stand it anymore... .. and wanted to give up, I sadly said to him, we all knew that the day before the departure I sent my mother to the hospital for her Kidney surgery, and my father was so sick that he would pass away at any time, this time we were able to join the "pile" (Escapee's group-up, ready to go), and finally found someone to help capped it, after fighting against all the odds and here we are, I would rather die here than giving up now. He said: I have been classmates with you for many years, whatever you plan to do please don't leave me out, he then asked me for the Ren-dan( an energy pill) that I brought with me, I turned on the flashlight to search for it, noticing that he was crying, my heart was so sadden, mummering softly, let's just forget it, I took out the electrician's knife ytterbium to open the top five layers of cardboard boxes, the pears were rolling down…were all over us, we climbed to the top of the goods. The space was only about 50 centimeters high, and it was around 2 p.m., with the sun shining directly on the roof top of the car, it was hot as an oven inside the train car, and we were simply drenched in sweat, by then, I had to agree with my classmate we indeed had been suffering for many hours inside the car.

After jumping off the train, I realized that we were just outside of the Zhang-mu-tou Station in Dongguan. I managed to take out the money and food stamps hidden in my shoes and wanted to buy something to eat. The money and food stamps were soaked up with sweat; after the meal, we took the train back to Guangzhou. The classmate rushed himself to the Dade Road Provincial Hospital of Traditional Chinese Medicine, being admitted into the emergency room, and the doctor asked of him if he had not eaten for several days, and that plus the extremely stressful situation that we had been through, together with the prostration, and his anus drooped for one and a half centimeters.

On another occasion, the "railway boy" provided a number of a tagged car loaded with goods bounded for Hong Kong, and somehow we couldn't pry open the window of this car with all our might, so we opened instead the vents on the roof of the car one by one to peek through and see if there were goods with English label in the cars, this kind of search is commonly known as "feeling blind and crutching"; doing so for quite a while and we identified a car in which was with the goods labeled "Parrot brand white cement, made in Shanghai, People's Republic of China", so we judged that the car with the goods were destined for Hong Kong, so we pried open the car window and hid inside among the cement bags, for more than 50 hours with only water just enough for one day; sadly, our mouths were so dry that we couldn't even swallow the biscuits, and we had to find water, otherwise we would die of thirst before we crossed the border. At about six or seven o'clock in the morning, Sanmao pushed away the white cement above his head to slip outside to look for water, and saw the notice board of Guangzhou South Railway Station, it turned out that the train had already arrived at Guangzhou Huang-sha South Station, the station and the wharf are in one, where the goods would be ready to be loaded onto a ship for export to foreign countries, and there are a few porters unloading goods in other cargo train rucks (after returning home, I heard the neighbor who was the driver of the second transport company of the city said that there would be armed police on duty in the station at eight o'clock in the morning ). Sanmao hurriedly came back and called, and the three of us climbed out were , and that the road below would be Huang-sha Road, the opposite road would then be Cong-Gui Road, through Cong-Gui Road we could get to the tenth Fu-road, Tao-Tao-Ju Tea House is near the intersection, the three of us managed to get to the restaurant , while we were keeping ourselves busy with the tea and snacks like the "hungry Ghost", the tea house gusts sharing the same table asked us what we do for living, we said that we were porters. It was that we noticed that the white cement had turned our hair into angry white hair, and us three into white-haired monsters, with the whole body being dehydrated, and the skin being toasted.

And still another time, also being unable to pry open the window the target car, had to pry open the window of the other car and hide in it, we, this time around, intended to find a way back to Chenzhou as soon as the train stopped, only to find out that as soon as the train stopped, there was a ladder leaning against the window, and we noticed that someone from outside was using a crowbar to insert to try to pry open the window , we hurriedly used a crowbar to stand between the window door and the window frame, desperately resisted, we fought for a quite a while and heard them speaking in Mandarin, presumably soldiers, and that they were told to come check and a see if the car door was broken open, and or if someone had hid inside the car, shortly after, somehow they stopped their trying Maybe when the time came for the train to stop, they gave up the effort to open the windows and the train started to move forward again . We hopped off the train at the next stop and hitchhiked back to Chen-Zhou.

With still another failed attempt, with that I was forced to give up in the middle of the journey and turned home, fortunately without being caught and imprisoned.

## Death of Yang Jae-heung

Now, as mentioned earlier, I am going to talk about the death of my neighbor Yeung Zaixinging, who was hit and almost killed instantly when he jumped out of the train-car upon arriving in Hong Kong.

In February 1980, my next-door neighbor Yang Zaixing, who we grew up together and my second brother-in-law and two others boarded a train bounded for Hong Kong in Chen-Zhou station, Hunan. After the train crossed the border, they jumped off the train near the Mong Kok railway station, Yang Zaixing and one other fellow jumped down first, by the time my second brother-in-law and another fellow wanted to jump, the train had already entered the tunnel, so they had to wait till the train passing the tunnel and stopped at the Ho Man Tin station, and they quickly got off the train, wanted to get help by knocking on the door of a house not too far from the station, only to find out when the woman who answered the door telling them that it was a police dormitory and urged them to leave quickly. They immediately left the building, took a taxi instead, arrived safely at the Amway Building, Fung Tak Road, Phoenix-new-village where I was staying, using the phone in the store next to the Amway building to call me, and I went down to pick them up and took them to the Immigration Department in Queensway the next day to get their identity cards.

After that, there was still no news of my neighbor Yang Zaixing and the other fellow for a whole month, we got very worried and there should have been some news of them even if they were arrested by the police, deported and returned to Guangzhou. I remember that the day of my second brother-in-law's arrival in Hong Kong, I once saw a news in the Oriental Daily News Paper that passengers of a northbound train had seen someone injured and lying next to the tracks at the exit of the tunnel at Mong Kok Railway Station. I decided to go to the Mong-Kok police station to inquire, and the assistant-on-duty dug out the files at that time for me to identify the body of a photo, and sure enough, I immediately recognized that it was Yang Zaixing, who was apparently crushed by the train with his hands and feet broken, and a large crack on his head, and he died three days after he arrived at the hospital. Just wanted to be 100% sure, I found and asked a few more people who also know of Yang Zaixing to go to the Mok Kok police station to help identify the photos, and they all confirmed that it was Yang Zaixing. (Yang Zaixing was sent to Hainan Island and had returned to Guangzhou to work.)

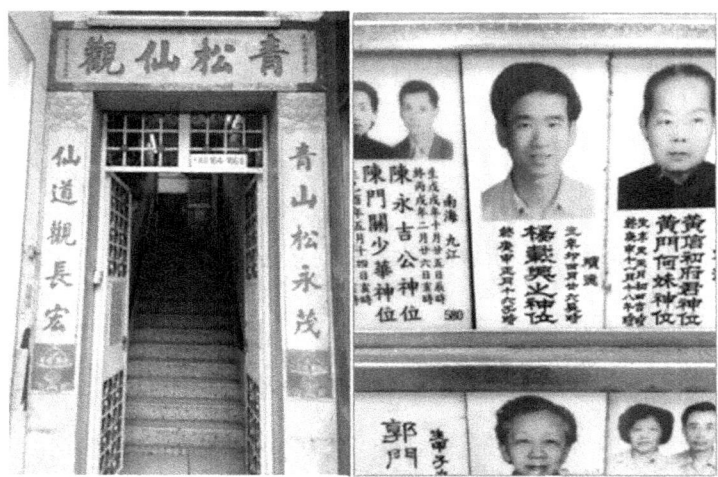

*On May 2, 2019, Wei Qiang returned to Hong Kong to participate in the memorial activities to pay tribute to the escapee victims, and went to Qing-song-guan again to pay homage to Yang Zaixingsame*

The Mong-Kok police station issued a certificate for me to go to the funeral management office to apply for Yang Zaixing's death certificate and found out that the burial place was a cemetery near the Luohu Railway Station by the Sino-British Boundary River, which was dedicated to burying stowaways (escapees crossing the border). We found that Yang Zaixing was buried in Tomb No. 80274 in the "Pi" section of the Sha-Liang Government Cemetery, and the cemetery staff claimed that by then the bodies of many escapees were sent there for burial every day. After we paid our respects, we went to the of the exit the tunnel where the fatal accident had happened, and we were able to find one of the shoes that belong to Yang Zaixing, in which it contained some renminbi and national food stamps, and a pool of blood stain on the third railroad tie. After Yang Zaixing's second elder brother in the United States learned about all the details involved, he sent a lumpsum of money and wanted me to make used the money to help set up a memorial tablet in Qing-song-guan. Seven years later, Yang Zaixing's relatives eventually picked up Yang Zaixing's remains and cremated them, and my second younger brother took the ashes back to Guangzhou to hand them over to his family. There was also the other fellow who jumped off the train-car together with Yang Zaixing, was also seriously injured and had a bone in his head repaired in a Hong Kong hospital, and was subsequently being deported back to Guangzhou after the treatment, where he lived on Da Nan Road in Guangzhou and lay in bed for the rest of his life.

## My family's history of escape

Arrived at Hong Kong two months after me, my second brother in law also riding on the same Fire Dragon, If he had jumped off the train a few seconds earlier, then it would be him who died instead of Yang Zaixing, because his delayed action, so he escaped the catastrophe, and he was lucky again to decide hurriedly out of the next stop, the Ho Man Tin Station where the train had made a temporary stop , waiting to enter the terminal station( the Hung Hom Station), where there would be plenty of police guarding, anyone getting off at Hung Hom would inevitably be arrested and deported.

In July 1982, my lucky second brother-in-law hid in the bilge of a cargo ship with me for 24 days and successfully smuggled ourselves into the United States.

In January 1980, one month after I arrived in Hong Kong, my second younger brother and his friend also riding the "Fire Dragon" arrived in Hong Kong, my eldest younger brother and Sanmao went to pick them up near the Hong Kong Chinese University, when I met them, the second brother's fellow-escapee was bleeding badly with blood-stain all over his face, with the left over hydrogen peroxide(H2O2) I did manage to clean up and band-aided his wounded forehead and cracked chin.

And the next day I took them to the Hong Kong People's Immigration department to apply for the Identity Certificate. The other two people who were traveling with the second brother were not as lucky, ending up being arrested and deported by the police and returning to the mainland.

My eldest younger brother arrived in Hong Kong in 1974, and he was the first member in my family to escape successfully.

Among the brothers and sisters, my eldest sister was the most miserable one. She graduated from junior high school in 1965, and at that time was also rather "revolutionary", she stole the household registration booklet and changed her part of the household registration all by herself first, without our parents knowing about it. she even preached everywhere around town about the Mao's principle, and that everyone should just "go to the place where the motherland needs it the most" ......, and she ended up answering the call herself and became a farmer. If one wanted to know how "revolutionary" she had become, you only need to be aware of one thing she did by then: while she had no way to get herself a copy of "the booklet of Chairman Mao's quotations", she actually borrowed a copy from someone else and hand copied the entire booklet word by word, page by page!?

It was the year 1975, "the reality" finally taught the eldest sister a cruel lesson that her so called "Royal to the political-party and homeland" had no future for her, and she became so determined in wanting to fled to freedom immediately; and even self-proclaimed that not until she reached Hong Kong, she wouldn't even go for a "Xiang-gian" (meaning a blind date in Cantonese), not to mentioned about getting married, She bought a "hard edge"(a "code word" for a border pass; in the early days, the "temporary border card" issued to the residents living in the border areas was a kind of paper certificate with a photo, stamped with a red seal at the beginning, and was later changed to the stamping with a steel seal, and it was still proven being relatively easy for the escapees to duplicate by replacing the photo;

Later, the authorities introduced a hard border control card, which was overmolded on both sides and hot-pressed around the perimeter, this kind of border pass card was then commonly known as the "hardedge", and it was obviously much more difficult to counterfeit, but as long as there is a demand, it would not be as difficult as impossible, with this "hard edge", one could simply use a razor to cut open the edge and pressed it, carefully removed the original photo, and replaced it with their own photo. Of course, the photo had to be with a similar hard-press outline of a steel seal, also with a press-outed approximate glyph of the "border certificate" by using a small screwdriver, and finally glued it with universal glue, or hot pressed the back, so a 'hard edge' is born! Naturally, one could just purchase this kind of border pass card regardless of the name and address, only with the correct gender and the age being in the right proximity.), used it the right way, with a little luck, she managed to arrive safely in Shenzhen, and the first thing she did was to clip the "hard edge" in the book and send it back to her home in Guangzhou at the post office.( this would be a typical procedure for any escapee to follow, so that 'border pass card' could be reused again if needed by someone, and or just in case that he or she failed themselves in the Border crossing, and wanted to try it again!?)

Somehow luck was never with my eldest sister when it comes to escape, in fact it's extremely bad for her to fail four times, all of which were caught when she had gotten so close to the 'goal', right at the beach side at one time, was next to the seashore at another time…… After being arrested for the first and second time, she was transferred back to Guangzhou after a few stopovers in different detention centers, and the tremendous pain inflicted on her both physically and mentally while being captive in those detention centers was inevitable. And it's worse for "repeat-offender"; The third time she was arrested, she was sent to the Guangzhou Sack Factory for forced labor, and the people in Guangzhou at that time knew that the "study class" of the Guangzhou Sack Factory was famous being dedicated to taking in thieves, gang members, prostitutes and the like.

Half a year later, the eldest sister escaped from the "study class" of the sack factory, and almost immediately went on for her 4th attempt, and the public security personnel stationed in the sack factory came to inquire about her where-about and wanted to arrest her.

This time, the 4th attempt, the eldest sister failed and was arrested again, and our family got the news of her failure early this time, because we unexpectedly received a note from her about her fate, which was written on a piece of paper. She said in the note that she was arrested this time and definitely would be sentenced to a labor camp, and the home address was written on the top of the note, and it was written on the note that whoever picked up the note please send it to this address. The eldest sister later said that she had written the note in the "checkered cell", and on the way to the detention center for the next transfer, she saw a man in the car pedaling a bicycle and following the car, she then dropped the piece of paper from the car, and saw the man actually picked up the piece of paper, and the man later put the note paper into an envelope, copy my home address as shown in the note, and sent it to our home with a postage stamp.

After receiving the note, there was no other news of her for half a year, and we didn't know where she was, my mother had been crying almost every day, at one day my mother's factory leader summoned my mother to his office and asked of my mother if she had an eldest daughter, and what would be her name and where she would be…..my mother told him everything she knew, saying that she had been missing for over half a year already; by then we assumed that they probably already had known where my eldest sister would be, but just did not wanted to let us know by then.

It was not until quite a while later that we learned that she was kept in the detention center in Shi-xing County in northern Guangdong province because of "Bao-liu" (used a false name and address), she knew that she had multiple failed escape and been arrested so many times before, this time around she would most likely be sent back to the same hard labor camp, and facing much worse treatment, so she purposely put down the false personal information, that she herself was from Shi-xing County in northern Guangdong, because there were fewer escapees in northern Guangdong, and even they were caught they would be generally released quicker, but the bad luck was with my eldest sister again, she couldn't pass the customs' check this time.

In desperation, she finally gave in and was sent back to Guangzhou, where she was detained by the Huanghua Detention Center and sentenced to two years of "re-education through labor" and was sent to a labor re-education farm in Sanshui County. I had a chance to visit the Huanghua Detention Center in Guangzhou to give some clothes to my eldest sister, and officer only accepted the clothes on her name, but I didn't get to see my eldest sister, and later when I accompanied my mother to visit her in the San-shui Labor Camp, we were allow to meet with her, but only with a heart broken feeling seeing her being totally out of shape, imagined what she had gone through!

After all, she had been imprisoned for more than three and a half years in total for her trying to flee to Hong Kong; and she had not yet been released when I escaped and arrived at Hong Kong in December 1979.

At the end of 1980, upon my eldest sister being released and wanted to try another run to Hong Kong, I was worried that even if she arrived in Hong Kong, she would not be able to obtain a Hong Kong Identity Card due the new Arrest and immediate-deportation policy being in place already by then, and that if she were to returned back to the mainland, her prison term would be much longer. I immediately went to the Ocean Terminal to send her a telegram, saying "don't come, no ID card would be issued to you", hoping that she would be deterred, but since she had gone through such an ordeal through the years and became resolute and did not hesitate to fight even harder. It wasn't until she and her partner called me from the store next to the building where we lived, and said that they just arrived in Hong Kong, and were down stair now, I immediately went downstairs for her.

I arrived in Hong Kong on Christmas Day 1979 via the fire-dragon route, and my eldest sister arrived in Hong Kong on Christmas Day 1980 via the same fire-dragon route, exactly one year after my arrival on October 23, 1980, the Hong Kong government abolished the "barricade policy", which means that all escapees who arrived in urban areas would not be granted legal residency. When the eldest sister set off, the Hong Kong government had implemented the "catch and immediately deport "Policy for escapees for over two months, and it was probably because of this that China and Britain both had relaxed their border management.

The eldest sister and a female companion got on the freight train with the help of a friend of the Hunan "Railway Boy" Jian-cai and arrived at the Hung Hom terminal in Hong Kong in the same day, the Christmas Day, and they even manage to, with a gentleman's help, arrived safely at the building where I lived by taxi.

*After a lot of hardships, the eldest sister arrived in Hong Kong on December 25, 1980, and the photo was taken on December 26, 1980.*

In the year that the eldest sister arrived in Hong Kong, because she had no Hong Kong identity-card, she hid here and there, moving around from time to time, and she was living in fear of being arrested and deported back to the mainland. I immediately knew that I had to reach out to protect this strong and hard-working eldest sister. I, myself being in Hong Kong for not much longer, and with my meager income, I would still wanted to find a way out for her, even if I have to pay for it for her way out of the 'trap' (through-out these time without the Hong Kong ID card, living in fear of being picked up and deported by the police on the street, and could only work as an illegal-worker, as a dishwasher in a restaurant and other "low-end" jobs.), and I even tried really hard to find a way for her to migrate to a foreign country, i.e., Australia and Panama, the united States of America……knowing that it might end-up being very expensive, the family value still came first!

Finally, I did find a way, an expensive way, to smuggle her to the United States, borrowed as much as I could from anyone that I knew of by then, I eventually scraped together enough money, and sent my beloved eldest sister to the container ship bounded for the United States, with a bit better luck this time around, she arrived in the United States of America safely in the in December in bilge of a container ship on December 1981, and she obtained a U.S. green card a few years later, and her life was finally liberated.

Unexpectedly, a week after my eldest sister boarded the container ship, I suffered an unwarranted disaster, and the reasons and processes were: A female friend who came to Hong Kong with my eldest sister was detained for "illegal entry", and she gave up my eldest sister to gather with her phone number to the police, The Hong Kong People's Immigration Department found out my address accordingly, so they came to arrest her, I happened to have just stuffed the eldest sister's fake ID card into the crack between the woods, and the immigration officer managed to break in, but couldn't find any things, yet it was still dangerously close since in-possession of a fake identity card alone is a crime against me. Fortunately, my eldest sister had already set off in the containership, so she took me instead to the Investigation Division of the People's Immigration Department in Li Baochun Building in Hong Kong for interrogation and wanted me to confess my eldest sister's whereabouts. The officer handcuffed me to the iron-bar of the chair, threatened me with a wooden stick, and told me that he would beat me three times a day until I confessed; I told him that it would be illegal to beat people in Hong Kong, if you dare to do it, with me being released within 72 hours, I would definitely file a complaint against you! and if I didn't go back to you to settle the accounts, I wouldn't be a real person, would my life worth more or yours would worth more!?

That officer then said, if you dare to intimidate Sir…? Even though he said this, he didn't dare to hit me at all but just tightened the handcuffs. I told the officer immediately that if he didn't loosen the handcuffs, I would, after I got out, also file a complaint about his disguised torture. It took almost twenty days for the handcuff marks on my wrists to heal. Later, because there was no evidence, I was released after almost the whole day, but my Hong Kong travel document was detained, and it was not returned to me until a month later. The reason why I was so bold to stand up to the immigration officers was that firstly my eldest sister was already on her way to the United States, and I had confidence in me with that; Second, after all, we were in Hong Kong, and I had been in Hong Kong for more than two years, and I did know a little bit about the rule of law in Hong Kong. If I were in the iron hand of the powerful "dictatorship of the proletariat" of the "motherland", it would have been a different story.

The reason why I knew to take the road of "fire dragon" and "escape" was entirely because after the first time I was arrested for escaping, I got to know of Sanmao, the "railway boy" in Guangzhou, and when I was doing hard labor in Paitan, I got to know more Hunan "railway boys", and we all were in the same boat on the escaping road, we in return were able to help when them all just arrived in Hong Kong for the first time and also because of their lack of connections and the language/communication issues, and their survival was more difficult. While my eldest sister and my second brother-in-law were able to arrive in Hong Kong smoothly were with their being instrumental, which would all be the so-called God's reward.

### Why did I choose to Escape

In 1954, my father and a friend co-founded a small factory, and in 1956 the so-called "socialist transformation of the private ownership of the means of production" movement looted the factory, unwillingly the business owner were to celebrate the movement while their solely owned businesses were simply being forced into a co-ownership with the government.

At the beginning of the movement, the capitalists (private business owners) were guaranteed to be paid with fixed interest in their capital-investment for the next 20 years, which was then the so-called national-redemption policy forced on to the capitalists (private business owners).

And things were still considered normal since my father was still considered in the management level, was still involved in the purchase of the raw material, taking business trip to Shanghai from time to time… On the eve of the Cultural Revolution, the designated communist party secretary of the factory had asked my father to leave the management position, and to create his own application to not only "voluntarily" giving up his cadre quota to others but also transferred himself to the high-temperature workshop as a production worker. The so-called fixed interest was only received for 10 years, and it was gone as soon as the Cultural Revolution came along, the monthly salary also being downgraded to 28 Yuan from 121 Yuan…… so my father often talked to us about the Communist Party's lack of credit, and because of being his own boss he was automatically classified as a capitalist, was then destined to be sent to the Keiwo Reservoir for hard-labor reform, the reservoir was infected with a bad cold during a reservoir-accident-rescue-mission, somehow it turned into chronic bronchitis, and then became a severe emphysema, the relaxed left lung pushed out the left chest into a barrel chest, compressed the heart into a cor pulmonale, often infected with high fever, alveolar perforation to form a pneumothorax, from time to time the doctor had to penetrate the hose between the anterior chest and flank bones, the other end into the glass bottle filled with half a bottle of water to deflate the lung a bit, just as the saying goes, "top the heart and lungs", pushing the hose against the lungs would be very painful, my father kept on moaning throughout the process. with such an extreme medical situation, upon demand my father would still have to go on stage to be openly criticized, being constantly insulted with…. together with illness, poverty and anxiety, my father's physical condition deteriorates rapidly, he simply couldn't even lie down normally to sleep. Trying to help out with the situation, I nailed together a wooden frame for him to sleep with.

Suffering with so much for so long, to my father, Life simply wasn't better than death, the whole situation got much worse quickly, and he finally died at the age of 62.

I remembered, before I entered the factory as a worker, my father always had headache trying to make the ends meet for the family's expenses every month, since he had been so sick I often had to go to the Guangzhou Federation of Industry and Commerce in Dadongmen to try to borrow money from them on behalf of my father, and the guard at the gate wouldn't even let me in, I could only register outside and would get 10 yuan only after trying a few times.

When I first joined the job, my monthly income was only 20 yuan, and I had to give 10 yuan to my family. There often would not be enough money left even to buy pork or clothes with the meat tickets and cloth-tickets allotted to the family, and the quilts at home are tattered like fishing nets. Meanwhile we brothers and sisters would still have to bear the name of being born in the "bourgeois family" and being looked down upon by people around us, simply living in a lower class, be a sub-human being.

I was a junior high school graduate of The GuangZhou 99th. Middle School (that is, Yonghan Middle School before the Cultural Revolution), and I stayed in school until the year 1979 due to my hepatitis. At that time, the vast majority of young students had to "go up to the mountains and go down to the countryside" to be re-educated, and those who could stay in the city were called the "lucky ones", life of which was much better than those who were driven to the countryside; so I was satisfied with my status, and was not effected by the trend of escaping by then.

It wasn't until my eldest younger brother returned to Guangzhou from Hong Kong in early 1979, that an incident directly stirred me up and made me decide to flee.

The eldest younger brother fled to Hong Kong in 1974, and by 1979, the authorities' policy began to loosen up, not considering the escapees with "treason and defecting to the enemy" but only being an express "illegal" family visits, allowing these people to come back home legally to visit their relatives. My eldest younger brother brought back a color TV set that was the envy of the neighborhood, and then watching the other escapees in the neighborhood doing the same thing and brought back large bags of Hong Kong goods. One night before my eldest younger brother returned to Hong Kong, he invited the whole family to the "Guangzhou Restaurant" at the intersection of Wenchang Road for a family reunion and had a meal that costed more than 400 yuan. I was struck all of a sudden, the whole person was like being blindfolded, with me working for nine years straight, did not smoke, and I did not drink, and I still could only accumulate some 300 Yuan with me.

I must leave here, I said to myself, and I must go to Hong Kong even if I would die doing so!

## Smuggled to the United States

When I first arrived in Hong Kong, my first job was to work as a construction-site worker in the Cheung Sha Wan MTR project, every day, I first entered a large round iron bucket that was lay down horizontally, with the added air pressure, and then opened an iron cover below at a certain time, grabbed the iron ladder handrail and climbed down a few floors, dredged the mud, nailed the formwork, poured concrete, and dismantled the formwork after the concrete was hardened. The working surface area was dozens of meters underground, the entire work space was tightly sealed in a high-pressure state (to prevent groundwater seepage), and the air would be extremely hot, and everyone would be wearing just a pair of underwear sweating throughout the work hours…… till the end of the day, we would have to reverse the process, would need to climb up the iron ladder and sit ourselves in the same large iron bucket to be decompressed gradually for three hours before you can get out onto the ground.

At that time, the salary was 190 yuan a day, while the normal work was only about 30 yuan a day.

Anyway, knowing the dangerous working conditions involved, I had decided to change course: At first, I became a hawker selling cotton underwear in the market near Wong Tai Sin, pushing a cart to sell them from one street-market to the next, and later I sold electronic watches in the women's market, and switched to selling T-shirts in Summertime, sold belts before the Spring Festival, and sold military ragged in cold weather.

Had been caught twice by the police fined by the court for "blocking the traffic", and the 'rule' was If you didn't cooperate when you were caught, you would be charged with one more offence of selling on the street with "no license", and you would be fined 90 yuan for each offence; As a rule of thumb, you should bring at least 500 yuan with you when you start your work, so that you can use it as a guarantee to bail yourself out upon being arrested, and upon pleading guilty in court and accept the fine-amount set by the judge I could then go back to the to the court counter to ask for the balance of the money,(money left over after paying the fine with your bail money of $500 yuan); and I considered myself lucky since I was charged with only one offence of "blocking the street" each of the two arrests, and was fined with 90 Hong Kong dollars each time, and I treated it as if I were paying my share of the taxes to the Hong Kong government.

*Weiqiang assembled the electronic watches at home for sale, with the watchcase, the watch straps, the watch cores, the watch faces all ordered from different factories.*

There was one occasion, while I was in court I witnessed a hawker who had been locked up for a week since he had no money to bail himself out, the judge announced in the court that because the hawker had already served his time while being locked up for a week, he would be exempted from the fine and be released on the spot.

With this kind of unlicensed hawker's "walking ghost"-like career, although I could barely keep up with the food and clothing and lodge expenses, would never be a long-term solution I desired. I set my sights on the United States and got a promise from a friend to become my guarantor. In the first half of 1980, I went to the "Caritas Centre"(a charity organization) in Hong Kong Island to apply for refugee status and migrate to the United States and was later informed to go to the U.S. Consulate to fill out an appropriate form and had my fingerprints taken, and in 1981 the U.S. Consulate notified me to go for an interview. The consulate officer told me then that the United States has abolished the seventh category of immigrants (refugees), and asked me if there were any relatives in the United States who could help me transfer to family related immigration process instead, and I said that I only had friends and no relatives in the USA, and the consulate officer then concluded, and said that it would not be possible to process the immigration status for me.

Being so disappointed, and if I still wanted to settle down in the USA, it all seem to point to only one solution for me which would be to be a 'Stowaway', curled up myself like a snake and hiding in the corner of the cabin, and many people who smuggle to Macao successfully using this method to escape themselves into Hong Kong. I hitched a ride, negotiated the price, and embarked on the road of "escaping" again. On the afternoon of June 26, 1982, my second brother-in-law and I hired a motorized wooden boat at Tai Kok Tsui Wharf for HK$200 and drove to the waters near Kwai Chung, climbing up a cargo container ship, a crew member took us to his room, and then when we were walking down to the bottom of the ship in the middle of the night, the crew member suddenly noticed that one of his colleagues standing on the deck above looking at us. The crew said that the trip had to be canceled because he couldn't get along with that colleague and was afraid of bad things that could likely happen. He used a flashlight to signal to find a nearby boat owner to send us ashore, but there was no response from any of the nearby boat owner, and the crew then asked if we dare to take a chance, and we replied yes immediately, and followed him all the way to the bottom of the ship, we went around and round again a few times, climbed into an attic against the dead end of the hull, and hid. He said to us before he left us that the next port of call for the ship would be the port of Keelung, Taiwan, and there would be customs officers coming down to check around, but as long as we could manage to passes this one, it would be almost certain that we could successfully reach the United States eventually, because no one else would come down to check when the ship stop over the next two Japanese ports. When I docked at Keelung Port, I found that somehow a plastic bag containing urine was broken, and urine flowed down the attic to the bilge, so I quickly climbed down and took off my underwear to wipe clean the urine. An hour later, customs officers came down to check around, and the flashlight shone through the outside of the place where we were hiding, but fortunately they did not climb over to check.

After the ship left Keelung Port, the crew took us to the cabin with a hatch on the top, and every night the crew cooked for us a pot of rice and brought it down, as well as some bread, bananas and apples, and took our urine and poops and threw them into the open sea on their way out. When we arrived at the two ports in Japan, the ship was to be berthed for a few more days because the freighter needed to be repaired, and it was freezing cold we had to count on the sacks and burlaps shared with us by the crews when we passed close to the Soviet Union. When we arrived in the United States, the waves were very strong, while getting closer to the outside of the Long Beach Pier in Los Angeles to wait for the next available berth, we found out that the cabin door was closed by the crew-supervisor, and end up we were kept inside there with no food or water for more than 40 hours, and yet still have to deal with the hungry, the diarrhea with which I had troubles with for the next forty some years.

On July 19, 1982, after a few days of mooring outside of the harbor waiting for the assigned berth, the crew took us ashore along the gangplank, and a Vietnamese drove us to his home, taking turns and extra effort to clean up the accumulated dirt, after all it's the first bath after 24 days of hiding in the ship, each person had a small bowl of noodles before going to the airport for the plane ride, at that time boarding the plane did not need to show any documents, however, with stomach was still quiet empty, we had to and did manage to use our hand signal/body language(that we had practiced in Hong Kong for some times) to make the stewardess understood that we were hungry, they end up giving us a lot of small packets of crunchy snacks , and then there was a normal meal with the transfer flight.

We did it again, from Hong Kong to USA!

*WeiQiang photo On May 28, 2015, revisted the Long Beach Terminal Los Angeles, USA, where I first entered the United States the early morning of July 19, 1982.*

## Thanksgiving America

When I first came to the United States, I didn't know any English, except the five letters of A, B, C, D, L, the Cultural Revolution deprived us of the opportunity to receive a normal education.

I know that I had to work and find a simple job which would require no formal education nor experience, starting from the bottom of the society… first, I worked as a dishwasher at a restaurant in Maryland, collecting dishes… then I worked as a chef's assistant at the end of the wok-ranch in a small restaurant in the countryside, working hard with no complain at all since I knew who I was, and I simply couldn't understand when I was asked to bring an ashtray over... After that, I had a chance to work in the cinema collecting tickets and learning how to use a 'box' showing movies.

After a few years, I received the legal resident identity-card, I was able to work in the casino as a card "dealer" (dealing), in order to increase my income, I helped people doing decorative work during daytime, dealing cards in the casino at nighttime, with two jobs, again, I worked hard but still with no complain, simply there would not be any "class struggling there, there would not be any "family social-classification", and there would not be any "individual social-classification" hat to capped with, as long as you keep up with your own work, having enough food and clothing would not be of any worry, and one live in peace and work happily in contentment.

*On August 16, 1982, WeiQiang, who had set foot on American soil for less than a month*

While working, I met my other half who also was a restaurant worker and got married, and we started a family; my wife was qualified to apply for low-income childbirth when she was pregnant, including prenatal check-ups, caesarean section we were only charged with USD$900.00

including two dozen eggs, two gallons of milk, and two cans of orange juice every week until delivery. To protect the health of the next generation, the government required and paid for me being the father to go through the "whole body check-up", with a TB Positive test result they even 100% covering the expenses for my TB (Tuberculosis, TB) medication together with the monthly X-ray test for six months.

My wife stay at home taking care of the baby, and one day I received a call that the child had a fever and was sent to the DC Children's Hospital, and I rushed to the hospital from the restaurant where I worked, and the hospital staff and doctors saw that I was all covered in oil-stain, and there was no medical insurance...with no sign of any discrimination at all, they reassured us that they would treat the baby the same as those with full insurance coverage. The child was hospitalized for four days, and after being discharged, most of the fees were waived, only charged us $3000.00, and I later paid off the $3000.00 in installments, and then the social workers of the hospital helped us apply for free medical care for the whole family for another half of a year. Because the government helped my family through the neediest period, I, am grateful from the bottom of my heart to the great country of the United States, and the American government is truly the government of the people.

*WeiQiang'shome/ houseintheUnitedStates*

*WeiQiang, a new "ZhiQing (知青)" in the United States, showing the harvest in the family's fruit and vegetable garden in the backyard of the house*

When I went to Hong Kong and landed myself in the United States, I was always a decent person, with no taste of any prostituting, gambling, drinking, slutting, and smoking, because it was so difficult and dangerous to fled to Hong Kong and the to the United States, I would never take anything for granted, although there were some that I knew of would not agree and I truly feel sorry for.

We, like the Chinese in general attached great importance to education, and the second generation had been soon fully integrated into the community, the society, and I smuggled to the United States in 1982 empty handed, and struggled for decades, I was able to accumulate enough to build a few houses of mine, supporting both daughters to go private colleges, with the eldest daughter graduated from New York Y U, four years later she graduated with a master's degree from Boston Tahu University, and the younger daughter also graduated with her bachelor degree from Boston U University on the same day. As I watched my both daughter receiving their diplomas from their university principals on the stage, I couldn't help but burst into tears, remembering that I had been in China, in a nominal secondary school for only a few months during the Cultural Revolution. My father was classified as a "capitalist", a pariah in a family, inferior to others, how could I not be thankful being able to witness my two daughters' university graduation today, I did want to cry, Crying happily!?

*This photo was taken wearing my eldest daughter's hat at her master's graduation ceremony, and my youngest daughter graduated from college with a bachelor's degree the same day.*

As soon as I became a naturalized citizen at the end of 1988, I applied for a visa for my mother, who then came to the United States in the second half of 1989. If she hadn't said to me by then that, "You should leave quickly now, the future of your life is important, and it wouldn't matter as much if you were present or not when he(my father) pass away!", I wouldn't be where I would be that day, my mother's great maternal love had changed my life and changed the fate of my entire family. After I came out, I remembered my mother's kindness, I had been diligent and righteous, I took care of my brothers and sisters, and my mother suffered a lot for her children, and I would always remember it for the rest of my life.

When my mother came to the U.S., didn't live in a nursing home and lived with me instead, her pension in Guangzhou was only a few tens of yuan, and a few months after she settled down, she went back to work as a cleaning lady in a casino and only stopped working after three years. In the United States, there is no responsibility to support her parents as a child, she has no income if she does not work, she applied for the government's SSI (i.e., low income or no income) benefits, at that time it's more than $600.00 US dollars per month, and the money was automatically transferred into her bank account on the 1st of each month, and there were more than $100.00 worth of food coupons to buy food every month, and free medical insurance and drug insurance. Five years after my mother came to the United States, being diagnosed pancreatic cancer, she was admitted to the hospital, because it was found to be in the advanced stage and there was no cure, the government sent electric beds and other appropriate hospital equipment to my home, and every day there were nurses who came to the door to hang nutrient solution and draw blood and performed other care, and when the situation was serious, I called an ambulance to send her to the hospital for a few days' close-monitoring, till the condition was relieved, and these happened for many times during her being treated. Because it would be a reasonable cost of $10,000 or more a day for my mom in hospitalization, she finally died in the hospital, and I was by her bedside watching her swallow her last breath in the hospital, and I was with her till the end, doing my filial piety.

A few years later, I managed to bring with me my father's ashes to the United States to be buried with my mother and for them to be reunited in Heaven.

On my mother-in-law's 79th birthday, my wife and I drove four hours to my uncle's house to celebrate her birthday. Doing the same as it were with my mom, I took my mother-in-law back to my home in New Jersey, and more than a year later, she suffered from dementia, and even forgot where the toilet was, and urinated casually, and when I opened my eyes, she would shouted, "was there anyone, was anyone here?" and we just couldn't sleep at all. After the hospital told the doctor that our husband and wife had to go to work and could not take care of her, the social workers of the hospital interviewed us and sent her directly to the nursing home in an ambulance, where she stayed for almost 10 years until she died. When my mother-in-law being a heavy smoker in her young age, her lungs had been problematic, during the time she lived with us, the oxygen concentrator was installed next to her bed, and there was a miniature oxygen cylinder that could be carried out to see a doctor, and when she was living in a nursing home, she often had lung infections and had to be transferred to the hospital for inpatient treatment. My grandmother was a housewife when she was in Shanghai, she came to the United States in her 50s and did not work, she helped her son take care of her granddaughter, and after the age of 65, she began to receive benefits until she died at the age of 90, which costed the U.S. government an unknown amount of money.

Whenever my mother and my mother-in-law were sick, and my mother-in-law were in a nursing home, all being paid by the U.S. government, and we didn't spend a penny as their children.

As mentioned earlier, my second brother-in-law and I smuggled into the United States together on the bottom of the containership, asked a lawyer to handle the immigration filing as a special technician (Chinese chefs) that the United States lacked, and after obtaining an immigrant visa, my second sister and nephew also successfully immigrated to the United States together.

My second brother and two younger sisters applied for their family under the category of citizen's brothers and sisters, and with a 10-year wait, three families of nine people all came to the United States round t the same time in July and August 2000.

My entire family lives in the United States, and I could proudly comfort my parents in the heavenly spirits.

The United States sheltered me when I was in trouble, rescued me when I was in danger, gave me food and clothing, gave me room to make progress in life, and gave me freedom from fear. The United States, with its breadth and magnanimity, has contained me, my dear mother, and my family. There is a famous saying: Where there is freedom, there is mymotherland, I love the United States, I am grateful to the United States! The United States is my homeland!

*American "farmer" Weiqiang*

# POSTSCRIPT

Since China's Cultural Revolution, the so-called movement of the educated youth to the countryside was published in December 1968 in the People's Daily, "It is necessary for educated youth to go to the countryside and receive re-education from the poor and mid-level peasants" till 1974, according to the statistics of the Hong Kong People's Immigration Department, the number of successful escapees who entered into Hong Kong and applied for residence was 79,083, and most of them were young students during this period. The mortality rate is quite high due to the treacherous and dangerous routes of the student's escape, the pursuit and merciless shooting of soldiers and para militiamen, the shark-infested seas and the vagaries of the weather in the south. Counting the people who were captured on the way escaping, there had been hundreds of thousands of young students who had joined the wave of fleeing from Guangdong province to Hong Kong and Macao.

Few of the true stories described in the book involved students from the same middle school, where there was one case with which, a total of 52 students in one class, 9 of them successfully escaped to Hong Kong, and 4-5 who failed, it's accounting for: about 25% of the one class in some school had attempted escaping to Hong Kong and Macau during that period of time.

During the Cultural Revolution, in addition to educated youths, there were also many persecuted high-level intellectuals who fled, the most famous being the musician Ma Sicong and his wife, whose flight shocked China and the world.

However, on the border between Chinese mainland and Hong Kong and Macau, this was not the largest and the most tragic wave of flights. Since the founding of the People's Republic of China in 1949, there had been few waves of exodus, together it had become one of the largest in the history of escape-in-peacetime in the world: in addition to the abovementioned wave of 1968-1974, the others occurred in 1949-1957, 1059-1962 and 1978-1980.

The first wave of exodus from 1949 to 1957 can be said to be an inevitable event of the change of dynasty after the civil war between the Kuomintang and the Communist Party, with millions of refugees flocking to Hong Kong or passing through Hong Kong to Taiwan or Western countries, including the parents of the famous writer Eileen Chang, then 32 years old, the famous historian Yu Yingshi, the literary critic Xia Zhiqing, and later Taiwan's democratically elected President Ma Yingjeou. Later, the CCP followed the example of the Soviet Union and ruled the country against the trend, and even worse, some people dreamed of becoming the leader of the Third World Alliance for their own selfish desires, disregarded the common people, donated generously to the outside world, and acted perversely at home, resulting in the absurd Great Leap Forward and the ensuing famine after the absurd Great Leap Forward and the Three Red Flags in China in the 1960s, and the people of southern China and other provinces rushed to Hong Kong like a tide to breaking through the barriers and support the families in order to have food, clothing, and freedom, and the number of people reached as many as 300,000-500,000. This wave of hungry people mainly walked directly from Wutong Mountain in Shenzhen and walked across the barbed wire fences of Lo Wu and Sha Tau Kok to the New Territories of Hong Kong. At first, the Hong Kong government was caught off guard by the influx of illegal immigrants and refused to allow them to enter the city in the New Territories, resulting in incidents that shocked China and the rest of the world in which Hong Kong people rescued their relatives. Later, in 1974, the Hong Kong government, under the pressure of world public opinion, enacted the so-called "touch-base policy" in response to public opinion. Under the new rules, illegal immigrants will be granted legal status as long as they are able to successfully reach the city of Hong Kong. This stage coincided with the take-off of Hong Kong's industry and commerce, and the "Touch-base Policy" just filled the demand for a large number of workers, providing a great impetus for Hong Kong's economic development.

The wave from 1979 to 1980 was not much lose in magnitude, with more than 300,000 people fleeing, just after the end of the 10-year Cultural Revolution, through which the Chinese at this stage had been so devastated. After the Cultural Revolution in 1978, the Chinese government implemented a policy of reform and opening up, the political environment was gradually relaxed, the economy developed rapidly, and the number of people fleeing Hong Kong dropped significantly. But even with the Hong Kong government's catch-and-deport policy, tens of thousands of Chinese were illegally smuggled into Hong Kong every year throughout the 90s.

Looking at these events of the Great Escape, each one is a great tragedy that must be recorded in history. Countless people risked their lives, crossed mountains and mountains on foot, waded through waters, suffered from hunger and cold, struggling against the angry sea, and died in the belly of fish, countless people being killed or injured. For what? Confucius said: tyrannical government is fiercer than a tiger!

The author hopes that politicians will remember these bloody historical events and learn lessons from them.

The following are the statistics of the number of illegal entrants to Hong Kong by various types of organizations from 1945 to 1997:

*1945 – 1950: 1,700,000 (Wikipedia, estimates of population change from Hong Kong, including those who came to Hong Kong through legal procedures. )*

*1049 – 1952: 750,000.00 (Hong Kong Annual Report, Phoenix.com).*

*1959 – 1963: 300,000 – 500,000 (Hong Kong Annual Report, Chat GDP).*

*1970 – 1974: 79,083 (Overseas Chinese Daily).*

*1975:        8,250 (Hong Kong Immigration Department, the same below)*

*1976:        8,054*

*1977:* 8,361
*1978:* 28,100
*1979:* 192,766
*1980:* 150,089
*1981:* 9,221
*1982:* 11,160
*1983:* 7,604
*1984:* 12,743
*1985:* 16,010
*1986:* 20,539
*1987:* 26,707
*1988:* 20,808
*1989:* 15,841
*1990:* 27,826
*1991:* 25,422
*1992:* 35,645
*1993:* 37,517
*1994:* 31,521
*1995:* 26,824
*1996:* 23,180
*1997:* 17,819

The so-called number of people illegally entering Hong Kong recorded by the Immigration Department of the Hong Kong Government including the very limited number of people who have entered Hong Kong illegally from other countries or regions.

According to China's official "Guangdong Provincial Party Committee Leading Group Office for Border Ports," from 1954 to 1980, the cumulative number of people who "fled Hong Kong" was recorded in official texts.

According to the Hong Kong Ming Pao on September 17, 1971, the day before the publication of the Hong Kong Ming Pao (i.e., the day when the escapees in the first true story "九一六 (916) "of this book arrived in Hong Kong), the number of people who were arrested for smuggling into Hong Kong on that day was 45, so roughly calculated as an average of 16,425 people per year, during this period of time, it is likely that young people from the countryside were the main body of smugglers, and the total number of people in the decade from 1968 to 1978 would have been 164,250 (if the statistics of the Hong Kong People's Immigration Department are used, Between 1974 and 1999, excluding the years 1979 and 1980, the average number of illegal immigrants per year was 19,045, slightly more than this average of 10 per cent). In 1979 and 1980, the number of illegal immigrants to Hong Kong swelled to 342,855, for a total of 507,105. This figure is only for the smugglers who successfully entered Hong Kong, and if we conservatively calculate the number of people arrested in China halfway, then the number of people involved in the escape to Hong Kong during this period (1968-1980) would be more than one million! It is difficult to estimate the number of casualties their way fleeing, but it is also in the tens of thousands, assuming a conservative calculation of 5%.

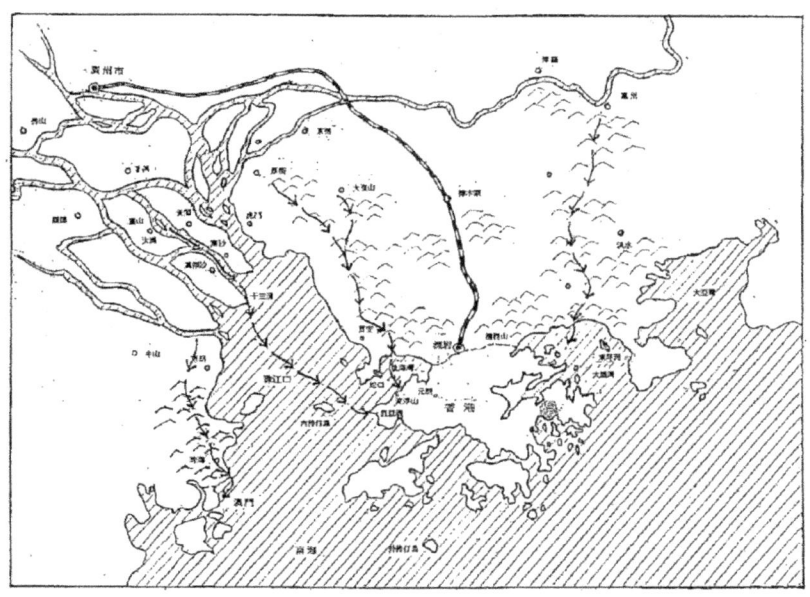

1966 – 1975 年代广东下乡青年偷渡香港的常见路线图

1）东莞 – 宝安 – 后海湾 – 香港流浮山一带
2）惠州，汕头 – 惠阳（淡水）- 宝安 – 大鹏湾 – 香港西贡一带（含东坪洲）
3）珠江口附近县市（番禺，中山，东莞等）- 九龙，香港岛
4）中山，珠海 – 澳门

*A common road map for the smuggling of young people from the countryside in Guangdong to Hong Kong in the years 1966-1975.*

# 人民日报

**毛主席语录**
一切可以到农村中去工作的这样的知识分子，应当高兴地到那里去。农村是一个广阔的天地，在那里是可以大有作为的。

## 毛主席最新指示

知识青年到农村去，接受贫下中农的再教育，很有必要。要说服城里干部和其他人，把自己初中、高中、大学毕业的子女，送到乡下去，来一个动员。各地农村的同志，应当欢迎他们去。

### 全国城乡一片欢腾庆祝毛主席最新指示发表

# 亿万军民热烈响应毛主席伟大号召
# 掀起了知识青年到农村去的新高潮

广大革命群众敲锣打鼓，集会游行，各级革委会立即制订落实措施，大批知识青年兴高采烈地奔赴农村

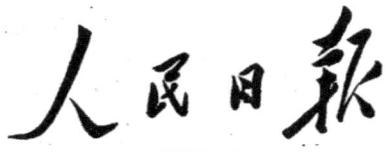

*People's Daily's political report*

*Hong Kong Ming Pao reported on 17 September 1971.*

*Hong Kong Ming Pao reported on 21 September 1971.*

*Hou Hai Bay*

*Dapeng Bay*

*Lingding Island*

*Rotten Kok Tsui, Kowloon, Hong Kong (near Lau Fau Shan)*

*Yuen Long Police Station, Hong Kong*

*Tanglang Mountain*

www.ingramcontent.com/pod-product-compliance
Lightning Source LLC
Chambersburg PA
CBHW052135070526
44585CB00017B/1837